D1554863

TALES OF THE BIG GAME HUNTERS

TALES OF THE BIG GAME HUNTERS

SELECTED AND INTRODUCED BY KENNETH KEMP

ST. MARTIN'S PRESS
NEW YORK

For Almuth, Caroline and Dominic

TALES OF THE BIG GAME HUNTERS Copyright © 1986 by The Sportsman's Press. All rights reserved. Printed in the United States of America. No part of this book may be used or reproduced in any manner whatsoever without written permission except in the case of brief quotations embodied in critical articles or reviews. For information, address St. Martin's Press, 175 Fifth Avenue, New York, N.Y. 10010.

Library of Congress Cataloging-in-Publication Data
Tales of the big game hunters / selected and introduced by Kenneth
    Kemp.
            p.   cm.
        ISBN 0-312-02989-6
            I. Big game hunting.   I. Kemp, Kenneth,   1933-
    SK33. T334   1989
    799.2′6—dc19   89-4154
                                                                CIP

First published in Great Britain by The Sportsman's Press.
First U.S. Edition
10 9 8 7 6 5 4 3 2 1

ACKNOWLEDGMENTS

The Publisher would like to thank the following for their help in providing photographs and other material used in this book:

Mr Edward H. Bryant of Vandeleur Antiquarian Books of London SW14, who generously and exhaustively searched for material and lent a number of valuable big game books.

R.E. & G.B. Way, Antiquarian Booksellers of Newmarket, Suffolk.

Elizabeth Clifford Photography, London.

Mr Tim Best of Holland & Holland, London W1, who gave advice on books published by Rowland Ward Ltd.

The British Museum (Natural History) whose excellent library of big game material was made available with courtesy and efficiency.

CONTENTS

NORTH AMERICA

RIFLES

ILLUSTRATIONS

SOURCES

Front cover illustration *from* a drawing by Stanley Berkeley, The World of Adventure (Cassell 1891)
Line drawings within the text *from* Wild Sports of the World (Ward Lock 1861) and Routledge's Picture Natural History (Routledge c.1880)

INTRODUCTION

One of the particular pleasures in compiling an anthology, lies in recalling one's own memories within the scope of the subject. I was reminded of half-forgotten nights spent as a boy, almost buried under the bed clothes (it was generally bitterly cold in English bedrooms then), devouring *The World of Adventure*, a vast three volume work crammed with incredible adventures in every part of the globe, many of them in pursuit of big game.

The shooting incidents included in this collection are mainly drawn from Africa and Asia. I make no apology for including some of the most famous names among them, Selous, Cumming, Abel Chapman, Demidoff, Sanderson, the two great elephant hunters, Neumann and Sutherland, and perhaps the greatest of them all, Sir Samuel Baker. They will be well known to devotees of this literature, but my purpose is not to wander off in pursuit of the minor, but often very interesting, works in this genre, but rather to introduce a small sample of the rich literature of big game hunting to those who are not familiar with it. I have deliberately chosen longer extracts than is usual in many anthologies, because I believe that nothing is more irritating than a book of snippets drawn from a large number of sources, never long enough to allow one to get into a piece before it ends. This means inevitably that many famous hunters have to be left out so great was the interest in big game hunting in the 19th century.

Big game hunting has, of course, always been controversial. James Greenwood writing in his splendid book for boys, *Wild Sports of the World*, circa 1861, was severely critical of Gordon Cumming for his cold-blooded attitude to the killing of game: "Why even Mr Cumming, on whom, as a rule, sentiment or anything approaching it sits about as easily as a dove on the back of a porcupine . . . found it hard to slaughter the gentle and beautiful giant (giraffe) without a pang of remorse". Such criticism did not stop Cumming's bestseller *The Lion Hunter* going into eight editions between 1850 and 1911 with many reprints from some editions. But by no means all the hunters were there to secure a rich haul of ivory, as Cumming certainly was. Some were eminent naturalists: Selous, for example, presented many of the Natural History Museum's finest exhibits; others saw it as their duty to protect local villagers from the ravages of man-eating lions and tigers (again a problem in India today, where in 1881, according to Major-General E. F. Burton, 2,757 people, not to speak of some 41,644 cattle, were killed by wild beasts).

Today, we can admire the amazing courage, skill and resourcefulness of the 19th century hunters, not only risking their lives in pursuit of dangerous game, but facing death from fever without the benefit of modern medicine. There are now signs, in a number of countries, that governments are beginning to realise that responsible and carefully controlled hunting positively aids the conservation of wild animals and that it can do much to boost the hard pressed economies of countries such as Zimbabwe, Zambia, Tanzania and Botswana, to name but a few of the countries now actively encouraging big game hunting.

I hope, therefore, that an anthology of big game writing is more timely and less controversial than it would have been even three years ago, and that it may encourage more people to seek out the big game classics, which are regrettably becoming rare and expensive in the second-hand bookshops.

London, 1986   **KENNETH KEMP**

AFRICA

An Adventure with a Lion

WILLIAM CHARLES BALDWIN

n Friday the old Masara captain paid me a visit; he had seen a lion on the path, and left a lot of Masaras to watch him. I had been working hard all day in the hot sun with an adze, making a dissel-boom for the wagon, and was tired, lame, and shaky in the arms, and did not feel at all up to the mark for rifle-shooting; but I ordered Ferus to be saddled, who was also not at all fresh, having had a tremendous burst in the morning across a flat, after a lean eland cow. Just after I caught sight of about twenty-five Masaras sitting down, all armed to the teeth with shields and assegais, my attention was attracted to a Kaffir skull, which struck me as a bad omen, and the thought entered my head, that it might be my fate to lay mine to bleach there. I did not, however, suffer this thought to unnerve me, but proceeded, and found that the lion had decamped. The Masaras followed his spoor about a couple of miles, when he broke cover. I did not see him at first, but gave chase in the direction in which the Masaras pointed, saw him, and followed for about 1,000 yards, as he had a long start, when he stood in a nasty thorn thicket. I dismounted at about sixty or seventy yards, and shot at him; I could only see his outline, and that very indistinctly, and he dropt so instantaneously, that I thought I had shot him dead. I remounted and reloaded, and took a short circle, and stood up in my stirrups to catch a sight of him. His eyes glared so savagely, and he lay crouched in so natural a position, with his ears alone erect, the points black as night, that I saw in a moment I had missed him; I was then about eighty yards from him, and was weighing the chances of getting a shot at him from behind an immense ant-heap, about fifteen yards nearer. I had just put the horse in motion with that intention, when on he came with a tremendous roar, and Ferus whipt round like a top, and away at full speed. My horse is a fast one, and has run down the gemsbok, one of the fleetest antelopes, but the way the lion ran him in was terrific. In an instant I was at my best pace, leaning forward, rowels deep into my horse's flanks, looking back over my left shoulder, over a hard flat excellent galloping ground. On came the lion, two strides to my one. I never saw anything like it, and never want to do so again; to turn in the saddle and shoot darted across my mind, when he was within three strides of me, but on second thoughts I gave a violent jerk on the near rein, and a savage dig at the same time with the off heel, armed with a desperate rowel, just in the nick of time, as the old manikin bounded by me, grazing my right shoulder with his, and all but unhorsing me, but I managed to right myself by clinging to the near stirrup-leather. He immediately slackened his speed; as soon as I could pull up, which was not all at once, as Ferus had his mettle up, I jumped off, and made a very pretty and praiseworthy shot, considering the fierce ordeal I had just passed (though I say it who ought not), breaking his hind leg at 150 yards off, just at the edge of the thicket. Fearful of losing him, as the Masaras were still flying for bare life over the velt, with their shields over their heads, and I knew nothing would prevail on them to take his spoor again, I was in the saddle, and chasing him like mad in an instant. His broken leg gave me great confidence, though he went hard on three legs; and I jumped off forty yards behind him, and gave him the second barrel, a good shot, just above the root of the tail, breaking his spine, when he lay under a bush roaring furiously, and I gave him two in the chest before he cried "enough". He was an old manikin, fat and furious, having only four huge yellow blunt fangs left. Then I had to hunt up the Masaras, who, of course, never came near, nor never would have done so, if he had taken a day and a half to eat up my carcase. The gloomy forebodings which the skull gave rise to at starting, were much nearer being fulfilled than I reckoned for; and why a man risks his life for no earthly gain, is a problem I cannot solve. I only know this, there is a secret feeling of inward satisfaction at having conquered, that is almost worth the risk to be run, though there are no applauding friends or spectators present. I wish my powers of description equalled those of a Masara; I think I never enjoyed a greater treat than to hear one of them describe this adventure. I did not understand a word he said, but his gestures and attitudes were splendid; his eyes flashed fire, he broke out into a streaming perspiration, and mimicked the lion so perfectly, as to make me feel quite cold. It would be impossible to surpass his imitation of the horse galloping, with myself spurring him, and all the other incidents of the chase. I had the satisfaction of seeing that I held the very first place in his estimation, and ever since the Masaras have paid me great attention, bringing wood and water unasked.

AFRICAN HUNTING FROM NATAL TO THE ZAMBEZI
(Richard Bentley 1863)

A Skirmish with a Column of Elephants

ABEL CHAPMAN

assing over tedious days spent fighting with fever at Nakuru – days while tropical thunderstorms raged every afternoon and I was held up a prisoner in my tent – an incident occurred that altered all our plans. There arrived direct news of elephants – news on which we could rely; the elephants, moreover, were close at hand. Within five-and-twenty miles a big herd had been seen on the Molo River to the westward, and were reported to be moving across us towards the northeast.

Now throughout that season of 1905–6 herds of elephants had been rambling here and there within our British territories, and their presence at various points had already been reported to us. Hitherto, however, all such reports had been more or less indefinite, and in every case the distance considerable. Elephants, we knew, move fifty miles in a night – our own extreme mobility being twenty; hence all seductions had hitherto been declined. But here the case was wholly altered. If the herd now reported – said to number forty – held the line of march stated, we lay almost on their flank, and, by a smart move, might cut them out.

It was a clear chance – the chance, maybe, of a lifetime – and we seized it. Though personally ill and weak, we were into the saddle and away by daybreak. Our plan of campaign was to march direct on Lake Solai, a marshy *vlei* lying some twenty-five miles to the northeast among the outliers of the Laikipia Range, and which was known to be an occasional resort of elephants – in the hope either to cut their spoor on route, or, alternatively, to find the herd at Solai itself.

After rounding the crater of Meningai, our course lay up that broad upland valley we had already traversed in 1904 and leaving the safari to pursue the direct path, we deflected with our gun-bearers into the wooded foothills of the northern slopes. Therein, during that morning, we encountered evidence of elephants on a scale the like of which we have not seen before or since. For miles this forest was absolutely devastated – wrecked: huge trees overthrown, one upon another, their limbs rent asunder; cedars and cypress, mimosas and acacias torn to shreds, the tall grass trampled flat; while, amidst the ruin, chewed branches and disgorged masses of bark and fibre everywhere littered the ground. We could plainly distinguish places where several elephants had worked collectively to overthrow some extra strong tree. This destruction had no relation to the herd of elephants we were now in search of; our men reckoned it dated a week previously, and our own judgment confirmed that view; yet we enjoyed the excitement of pushing forward through the wreck, picturing to ourselves a vast pachyderm at every forest-opening! We also struck quite fresh spoor of buffalo, though we saw nothing except waterbuck. In the belt of brushwood bordering the veld below East-African Bohor reedbuck were now numerous, though none were seen here in 1904, and W—— shot a couple. We also killed to-day a puff-adder.

This country, eighteen months previously, had been full of Masai with their cattle, sheep and donkeys. Now these savages had been "removed" into the Laikipia Reserve; their kraals were burnt and deserted, while elephant, buffalo and other game had reappeared.

At midday we halted on the Alabanyata River, intending to push on at 4 p.m.; but to our unspeakable vexation, the usual thunder-storm burst, torrential rains obliged us to encamp, and forbade all hope of further advance that night. A second shock followed. As dusk fell, we observed through the pouring rain *another* safari approaching up our valley. They presently encamped a mile or so below us. This signified nothing less than a serious crisis. After deep consultation held, we decided that, being ahead, we would maintain that position at all costs, and accordingly gave orders to mask tents, extinguish all fires, and to strike camp at 3 a.m. next morning.

February 23. – This eventful day began with a two-hours' scramble in black darkness through pathless forest and jungle, and shortly after dawn we struck the spoor of a solitary buffalo bull. This being quite fresh, W—— followed it towards the right, taking my tracker, Kenana (who alone knew the route to Solai), with him. The safari being on lower ground to the left, I rode on alone with my two gun-bearers, Mabruki and Salim, and a syce. Suddenly there recommenced that terrible tropical downpour, driving in our faces on the bleakest and most bitter gale I ever remember in Africa. It was worthy of the Hardanger Vidden at its worst, and in half-an-hour I was seized with a fresh attack of fever. Being all separate, without means of communication, aggravated the miseries of the moment; spirits fell below zero, and the whole venture, in my then state, now appeared sheer madness – suicidal. Hope was all but dead within my breast when Farra, the syce stopped and, pointing through the viewless torrent along the hillside, whispered, "Kifaru!" (rhinoceros). The excitement of that word effected wonders, renewing life and hope and pulling me together. After a short stalk I descried a vast bulky form, half hidden amid thorn-scrub on the slope above. The head was not in sight; but indeed through that driving mist and deluge all details were invisible — one could scarce see to distinguish the foresight, and the ball struck very low, behind the fore-leg. The rhino whipped round and vanished as a rabbit might, giving no chance for a second shot, but after galloping 100 yards up-hill fell over, squealing, and was dying ere we reached the spot. This was a female, with only poor horns, though those details could not before be seen. Both lungs were penetrated. These organs, in a rhino, extend low down.

An hour later, while trudging along in flood-water that surged ankle-deep down the valley-floor, we descried three men approaching from the opposite direction. They proved to be my brother, with Ali and Kenana, on their way to Solai. But we also thought we were proceeding thither! Obviously one party or the other was hopelessly astray. But for that purely fortuitous tumble-together I should inevitably have continued walking on in the wrong direction, till finally "benighted" — soaked, ill, without food or shelter; it was a narrow escape. Such are the risks one must take in wild lands.

It was nearly noon when the rocky valley we were traversing opened out into a broad basin, with a shallow reed-embowered lake in its midst, the whole encircled by stony mountains; and we saw, sheltered by a cleft in the western escarpment, our white tents established at Solai.

Thankfully we ordered lunch to be ready in half-an-hour, each meanwhile retiring to his tent for a warm bath and change. But during that half-hour the crisis arrived. Within ten minutes, an excited black head had pushed itself through the flap of my tent, exclaiming those magic words — "Tembo! tembo!" (elephants).

Then from our tent-doors we saw a memorable spectacle — across that hill-girt plain beyond, hard by the gleaming marsh, and not 800 yards away, marched a column of forty elephants.

Hastily we pulled on again the soaking raiment, and within a few minutes were away. The elephants slowly filed across the mouth of our valley; then, wheeling towards us, advanced straight up its centre. Within ten minutes we were only separated from them by the width of a marsh, 200 yards across, which, overgrown with rank green flags, ran down the centre of the strath. Both my men proved so excitable that I pulled them down and placed Ali Yama in sole charge. He was coolness itself, and made a masterly approach. We presently took cover behind a single low bush from the middle of which grew a mimosa-thorn, and some fifty yards from the green flags. A steady breeze blew from the *vlei* straight up the valley, and remained unchanged throughout the entire operation.

Upon arriving exactly opposite this point where we lay watching them, the column of elephants came to a halt, and for several minutes stood there, evidently in consultation – it hardly seems an exaggeration to say in "conversation". Then they resumed their course, holding up the valley; while we followed, keeping level with them, on our side the marsh. Presently they halted again, and, after further conversation, apparently decided that the former spot was, after all, the more favourable to effect their passage of the marsh; for, wheeling on their tracks, they marched back thither in column, and presently, with great deliberation, commenced to cross to our side. We had meanwhile, for half-an-hour, enjoyed magnificent views of the whole troop, and had made out at least two first-rate bulls, one in particular riveting my attention by the splendid ivory he carried, and which he was wont to display to perfection by jaunty tosses of his head.

The point they had selected for their passage possessed the advantage – we noticed this afterwards – of a half-dry islet midway across.

The huge animals took the treacherous bog in column of six abreast, the big bulls in the van, and their line extending 100 yards to the rear. Surely a more stirring spectacle in wild-life was never presented to human eye!

We had, of course, regained our former position, and now sat squatting behind that tiny bush within a few yards of the nearest flags. But with that wondrous scene enacting before our eyes no thought was spared to considerations either of tactics or of safety.

Obviously the changed course of the elephants, now advancing directly upon us, had wholly altered the strategical situation. Beyond a doubt we should, at this moment, have retreated to some point at which we should still retain control of operations. By continuing to hold a false position, we presently lost all freedom of action and left ourselves to be enveloped, within a few more seconds, between the masses of advancing monsters.

Lucky it was that the bulls came first. Had the prohibited sex headed the column, it is neither pleasant nor useful to speculate on what might have resulted.

So directly upon our position did the unconscious elephants advance that, upon landing, the head of their column had actually to divide so as to pass our bush, some on either side. Within a few seconds the leading bull on my side. Within a few seconds the leading bull on my side (the left) towered over our low shelter not twenty yards ahead. But this first-comer was not the real monarch of the troop. His tusks, though long, were thin and ill-formed, crossing in front. The monster tusker on which my heart was set, I knew, came second. It had been agreed that I should fire the first shot; but at that critical moment, while I waited an instant longer to get a clear sight of No. 2, my wretched gun-bearer, Mabruki, giving way to sheer "funk", fired my second gun close past my ear – deafening and, for a time, half-stupefying me. At the shot, the two great bulls on my front (the nearer being then fourteen yards off) stopped short, raising their heads and spreading their huge ears laterally as a barque sets stunsails. For six or eight pregnant seconds they stood still, looking around them with majestic deliberation, and then . . . slowly turned away.

They had not seen us, simply because we were so near. As a matter of fact, the elephants, all this time, had been looking far beyond us – over our heads.

By inspiration, during that crucial interval, we all lay motionless. Then, so soon as the elephants wheeled to retire, I placed my two barrels (.450, solid) into the big tusker at twenty-five yards, aiming rather low behind the shoulder. He staggered and stopped, receiving a third ball a trifle higher up, when he moved slowly towards the marsh. Seeing that he had enough, I placed two more balls in the ribs of the next biggest bull, then moving three-quarters off, when the two retired by themselves to the left, presently entering the reeds alone, beyond the main herd.

My brother meanwhile had devoted all attention to the other big bull, the second best in the company, which had passed on his side of the bush, following the lead of two cows. This grand elephant I now saw sink stern-first among the green flags, remaining upright, dead.

The main mass of elephants were now retiring most deliberately through the bog, on the same track by which they had advanced; but my two stricken bulls, straggling to the left, lagged in the rear of the herd. We followed on through the flags in pursuit, when a badly-hit cow elephant, bleeding at mouth and trunk, turned out on our right, blocking our advance. She stood, full broadside, in front of W——, who dropped her with a single shot in the temple. Running past her, I presently overtook my big bull standing still, stern on, in the marsh. On finding himself pursued, he turned on us with cocked ears and upraised trunk; but in that treacherous bog he was slow in coming round, giving time for a careful aim at about seventy yards. The ball struck close behind the orifice of the ear, and the champion of the troop was mine. His very death was majestic. He seemed to rise up forward, the curved trunk held high in the air; then, with slow sidelong motion, gently collapsed stern-first till he finally fell over, lying like a dark-red mountain towering over the green flags.

Hurrying forward past him – with hardly time even to glance at those glorious tusks – and running easily on a broad causeway of broken-down reeds (while the elephants plunged and struggled in bog), we soon overhauled the second wounded bull. He also, at seventy yards, turned on us with cocked ears and a shrill shriek. "Shoot," said Ali, "he's going to charge." But his end was at hand. A .450 solid knocked him backwards over – passing through the hollow top of one tusk where embedded in the skull (near the eye). He struggled to regain his feet when W—— gave him a finisher, and he fell with his face to the foe.

Four enormous elephants now lay dead – three behind us, the fourth fifty yards ahead. Of this last, however, we found it impossible to take possession, owing to the aggressive attitude and dangerous temper now displayed by the main troop, which had ranged up in solid phalanx just beyond the fallen bull. No sooner had they regained firm ground than the whole demeanour of the elephants changed. Instead of retreating passively, they now faced about in open defiance, formed in battle array, ready to take the offensive. With trunks upraised on every side, ears cocked, and a chorus of explosive grunts varied by shrieks of rage, there was no mistaking their temper; and after watching the magnificent scene for a few moments, we decided to retire, abandoning our last prize to the enemy. There were, in fact, no more good bulls among the herd; so we retreated campwards – to lunch, passing by the three huge carcasses lying like islands among the reeds.

The affair had occupied probably no more than a hundred crowded minutes – many of these as full as whole epochs of routine existence; and the above pages describe the main facts as such can be put down on paper. The sensations aroused, though they may be realised in imagination, cannot be printed so. Nor can the degree of danger be defined, since the temperament and conduct of elephants differ. No two need be alike. These, for example, retired at the crucial moment; but in my own former experience on Lake Baringo, a "lone bull" charged at once on scent alone, though otherwise unmolested; and instantly repeated the charge a second time, after being wounded. Here again, at Solai, only a few weeks before, a fatal accident had occurred.[1] Beyond all doubt we enjoyed unusual good fortune in this encountering our elephants, not only in broad daylight, a steady breeze, and open country, but also taken at disadvan-

---

[1] An Englishman, as related to us, had found and stalked a single bull elephant, unaware of the presence of six others among bush on his flank, and to whose view he had thus unwittingly exposed himself during the stalk. On his firing at the bull, one of these six at once charged; and, the repeating mechanism of his rifle jamming, the poor fellow was straightway caught and killed.

tage in treacherous bog. Still there was, following on Mabruki's insane shot "into the brown", a period of supreme danger, when for some seconds all our six lives hung in the balance. Had the elephants then seen us – when almost under their trunks – nothing could have saved us. Picking out three bulls from among forty beasts necessarily involves risk.

The day's bag thus totalled –
4 elephants,
1 rhinoceros.

Estimated dead-weight, 25 tons; actual weight of ivory brought into camp, 300 lbs; value, say, £200 sterling!

That afternoon and the following day we spent in measuring and photographing our prizes. Of the four elephants, one only admitted of accurate dimensions being taken. This, by good luck, was the biggest bull of all, which lay fully extended on his broadside – the other three having fallen either upright or in such positions in the bog, with legs bent or buried beneath them, that measurements were impossible.

The following figures serve to give some idea of the size of this giant of the modern world.

ELEPHANT BULL

	ft	in
Height in straight line (shoulder)	11	1
Length, tip trunk to tip tail	24	3
Girth at shoulder	14	10
Girth of foreleg at upper part	5	8
Girth of forefoot	4	10
Ear, horizontal width	3	8½
Ear vertical height	5	9½

It should be added that an elephant measuring 11 ft at withers will probably stand 12 ft, or possibly 13, *in front*, when aroused and with head erect, as those two stood before me to-day. Their huge ears, in addition, each spreading out near 4 ft laterally, give the elephant an apparent width of, say, 10 ft, by a height of 13 ft!

The tusks of my monster bull were a beautifully symmetrical pair, the longer measuring 7 ft 1 in, by 17½ ins in girth. They weighed 137 lbs the pair. Length exposed from gum, 4 ft 7 ins; widest distance apart in curve, 2 ft 6 ins; between tips, 2 ft 2 ins.

The longer tusk of my brother's big bull measured 6 ft 2½ ins, by 16 ins girth. This pair weighed 93 lbs, one tusk being broken at the tip; those of the third bull 44 lbs, and of the cow 28 lbs: total, 302 lbs.

With regard to the latter, neither my brother nor I had shot at an animal of the wrong sex, the bull-elephants being easily distinguished from cows, even as seen from astern, by their superior height – towering an apparent fourth over the females. This unfortunate animal had undoubtedly received her wound in the first instance from Mabruki's reckless shot. Grievous to add, she was followed by a well-grown calf, about 4 ft high. This was endeavoured to capture, but the *toto* proved altogether too big. On our approach, the determined little beastie (it must have weighed half-a-ton!) came on in most savage style, cocking his ears and screaming, till we were fain to leave him alone. We heard him calling during that night, but by morning he had gone.

Immediately the shooting was over, I discharged Mabruki on the spot, taking the rifle from him and landing him a brace, right-and-left, on his snub nose to drive the lesson home. Next time I saw him, six weeks later, he was working in a docker-gang on the wharves of Mombasa. The punishment seemed severe – the fall from gun-bearer at twenty-five rupees a month to labourer at six – and for a moment I relented; but second thoughts clinched the matter. Mabruki was totally disqualified to act as gun-bearer, and should never have been rated as such. Already, within two months, his want of nerve and self-control had twice placed us in jeopardy, and he should not have the chance of doing the same to others. Nor should East African shooting-agents "sign on" gun-bearers unless they have reasonable certainty in believing such to be safe and reliable men.

The last view we had of our elephants, they were slowly retiring northwards through the scattered trees that fringed the drier ground, and with the same majestic deliberation and coolness that they had displayed throughout the encounter; while beyond them, above the tall green flags of the *vlei*, we descried the backs of a *second* herd slowly moving towards the east. We regretted afterwards that we neglected to take any steps to ascertain which way they finally went, for heavy rains soon obliterated the trail. But in that moment of supreme triumph we were perhaps too exhilarated – in a state of mental intoxication after those deep draughts of excitement and success.

ON SAFARI
(Edward Arnold 1908)

My First Day's Elephant Hunting

R. G. GORDON CUMMING

n the 25th we trekked about five hours in a north-easterly course, through an open country, sparingly adorned with dwarfish old trees, and in the distance the long-sought mountains of Bamangwato at length loomed blue before us. We halted beside a glorious fountain, which at once made me forget all the cares and difficulties I had encountered in reaching it. The name of this fountain was Massouey, but I at once christened it "The Elephant's own Fountain", for it was on the southern borders of endless forests inhabited by that animal, at which I had at length arrived. The spring, deep and strong, was situated at the eastern extremity of an extensive open vley, in a level stratum of old red sandstone, and here and there was a thick layer of soil upon it, covered with the fresh spoor of elephants; the very rock around the water's edge being worn down by the gigantic feet which for ages had trodden there.

The soil of the surrounding country was white and yellow sand, but grass, trees, and bushes were abundant. From the borders of the fountain a hundred well-beaten elephant foot-paths led away in every direction, like the radii of a circle; the breadth of these paths was about three feet, and those leading to the north and east were the most frequented, the country in those directions being well wooded. We drew up the waggons on a hillock on the eastern side of the water; for this position commanded a good view of any game that might approach to drink. I had just cooked and commenced my breakfast when my men exclaimed, "Almagtig keek de ghroote clomp cameel"; and, raising my eyes from my sassaby stew, I beheld a magnificent sight. Up the middle of the vley stalked a troop of ten colossal giraffes, flanked by two large herds of blue wildebeests and zebras, with an advanced guard of pallahs. They were all coming to the fountain to drink, and would be within rifle-shot of the waggons before I could finish my breakfast; but I continued to swallow my food with the utmost expedition, and directed my men to catch and saddle Colesberg. In a few minutes the giraffes were slowly advancing within two hundred yards of me, stretching their graceful necks, and gazing in wonder at the waggons. Grasping my rifle, I mounted my horse and rode slowly forward until I was within one hundred yards of them, when, whisking their long tails over their backs, they made off at an easy canter. As I pressed upon them, they increased their pace; and before we had proceeded half a mile I was riding by the shoulder of a dark-chestnut old bull, whose head towered high above the rest. Letting fly at the gallop, I wounded him behind the shoulder, soon after which I broke him from the herd, and presently, going ahead of him, he came to a stand; I then gave him a second bullet, somewhere near the first. These two shots took effect, and he was now in my power, but I would not lay him low so far from camp, and, having waited until he had regained his breath, I drove him half-way back towards the waggons; here he became obstreperous, so, reloading one barrel, and pointing my rifle upwards, I shot him in the throat, when, rearing high, he fell backwards and expired. This was a magnificent specimen of the giraffe, measuring upwards of eighteen feet in height. I stood for nearly half an hour engrossed in the contemplation of his extreme beauty and gigantic proportions; and, if there had been no elephants, I could have exclaimed, like Duke Alexander of Gordon when he killed the famous old stag with seventeen tine, "Now I can die happy." But I longed for an encounter with the noble elephants, and thought no more of the giraffe than if I had killed a gemsbok or an eland.

In the afternoon I drew up my waggons among some bushes about four hundred yards to leeward of the water. In the evening I was employed in manufacturing hardened bullets for the elephants, using a composition of one of pewter to four of lead, and had just completed my work when we heard a troop of elephants splashing and trumpeting in the water; this was to me a joyful sound, and I slept little that night.

On the 26th I arose at earliest dawn, and, having fed four of my horses, proceeded with Isaac to the fountain to examine the spoor of the animals which had drunk there during the night; a number of the paths contained fresh spoor of elephants of all sizes, which had left it in different directions. We reckoned that at least thirty of these gigantic quadrupeds had visited the water during the night.

Having breakfasted, I saddled up, and proceeded to take up the spoor of the largest bull elephant, accompanied by after-riders and three of the guides to assist in spooring; I was also accompanied by my dogs. Having selected the spoor of a mighty bull, the Bechuanas went ahead, and I followed; it was extremely interesting and exciting work; the footprint of this elephant was about two feet in diameter, and was beautifully visible in the soft sand. The spoor at first led us for about three miles along one of the sandy footpaths in an easterly direction without a check; we then entered a very thick forest; the elephant had here gone a little out of the path to smash some trees and plough up the earth with his tusks, but soon returned and held along it for several miles.

We were on rather elevated ground, with a fine view of a part of the Bamangwato chain of mountains before us; the trees were well grown, but not strong enough to resist the inconceivable strength of the mighty monarchs of these regions, for half the branches were broken short, and at every hundred yards we came upon entire trees, and these the largest in the forest, uprooted clean out of the ground, or broken short across their stems; I observed several with their roots uppermost in the air. Our friend of whom we were in search had halted here, and fed for a long time upon a wide-spreading tree which he had broken within a few feet of the ground. After following the spoor some distance farther through the dense mazes of the forest, we got into ground so thickly trodden by elephants that we were baffled in our endeavours to trace it farther; and after wasting several hours in attempting by casts to take up the proper spoor, we gave it up, and with a sorrowful heart I turned my horse's head towards camp.

Having reached the waggons, I reviewed the whole day's work, and feeling much regret at my want of luck in my first day's elephant-hunting, resolved that night to watch the water, and try what could be done with elephants by night-shooting. I accordingly ordered the usual watching-hole to be constructed, and having placed my bedding in it, repaired thither shortly after sundown. I had lain here about two hours, when I heard a low rumbling noise like distant thunder, caused (as the Bechuanas affirmed) by the bowels of the elephants which were approaching the fountain. I was on my back, with my mouth open, listening attentively, and could hear them ploughing up the earth with their tusks. Presently they walked up to the water, and commenced drinking within fifty yards of me, approaching so quietly that I fancied it was the footsteps of jackals, and I was not aware of their presence until I heard the water which they had drawn up in their trunks and were pouring into their mouths, dropping into the fountain. I then peeped from my hole with a beating heart and beheld two enormous bull elephants, which looked like two great castles, standing before me; but I could not see very distinctly, for there was only starlight. Having lain on my breast some time taking aim, I let fly at one, using the Dutch rifle carrying six to the pound; the ball told loudly on his shoulder, and uttering a loud cry he stumbled through the fountain, when both made off in different directions.

All night large herds of zebras and blue wildebeests capered around me, coming sometimes within a few yards; several parties of rhinoceroses also made their appearance, and feeling a little apprehensive that lions might join the party every time that hyænas or jackals lapped the water, I looked forth, but no lions appeared. At length I fell into a sound sleep, nor did I again raise my head until the bright star of morn had shot far above the eastern horizon.

Before proceeding further with my narrative, it may here be interesting to make a few remarks on the African elephant and his habits. This wonderful animal is met with in herds of various numbers through the vast forests. The male is very much larger than the female, consequently much more difficult to kill; he is provided with two enormous tusks, which are long, tapering, and beautifully arched; their length averages from six to eight feet, and they weigh from sixty to a hundred pounds each. In the vicinity of the equator elephants attain a greater size than farther south, and I am in the possession of a pair of tusks of the African bull elephant, the larger of which measures ten feet nine inches in length, and weighs one hundred and seventy-three pounds; the females, unlike Asiatic elephants in this respect, are likewise provided with tusks. The price which the largest ivory fetches in the English market is from £28 to £40 per hundred and twelve pounds. Old bull elephants are found singly or in pairs, or consorting together in small herds, varying from six to twenty individuals; the younger bulls remain for many years in the company of their mothers, and these are met with in large herds of from twenty to a hundred individuals. The food of the elephant consists of the branches, leaves, and roots of trees, and also of a variety of bulbs, the situation of which he discovers by his exquisite sense of smell: to obtain these he turns up the ground with his tusks, and whole acres may be seen thus ploughed up. Elephants consume an immense quantity of food, and pass the greater part of the day and night in feeding. Like the whale in the ocean, the elephant on land is acquainted with, and roams over, wide and extensive tracts; he is extremely particular in always frequenting the freshest and most verdant districts of the forest, and when one district is parched and barren, he will forsake it for years and wander to great distances in quest of better pasture.

The elephant entertains an extraordinary horror of man; a child passing at a quarter of a mile to windward will put a hundred of them to flight, and when thus disturbed they go a long way before they halt; it is surprising how soon these sagacious animals are aware of the presence of a hunter in their domains. When one troop has been attacked all the other elephants frequenting the district are aware of the fact within two or three days, when they all forsake it, and migrate to distant parts, leaving the sportsman no alternative but to inspan his waggons, and remove to fresh ground: this constitutes one of the greatest difficulties a skilful elephant hunter encounters. Even in the most remote parts, which may be reckoned the head-quarters of the elephant, it is only occasionally, and with inconceivable toil and hardship, that the eye of the hunter is cheered by the sight of one. Owing to habits peculiar to himself, the elephant is more inaccessible, and much more rarely seen, than any other wild animal, excepting certain rare antelopes; they choose for their resort the most lonely and secluded depths of the forest, and generally at a very great distance from the rivers and fountains at which they drink. In dry, warm weather they visit these every night, but in cool and cloudy weather they drink only once every third or fourth day. About sundown the elephant leaves his distant midday haunt, and commences his march towards some fountain, which is probably from twelve to twenty miles distant; this he generally reaches between the hours of nine and midnight, when, having slaked his thirst and cooled his body by spouting large volumes of water over his back with his trunk, he resumes the path to his forest solitudes. I have remarked that full-grown bulls, having reached a secluded spot, lie down on their broad-sides, about the hour of midnight, and sleep for a few hours; they usually select an ant-hill, which is often from thirty to forty feet in diameter at its base, and lie around it with their backs resting against it; the mark of the under-tusk is always deeply imprinted in the ground, proving that they lie upon their sides. I never remarked that females had thus lain down, and it is only in the more secluded districts that the bulls adopt this practice; for I observed that, in districts where the elephants were liable to be disturbed, they took repose standing on their legs beneath some shady tree. Having slept they feed immensely. Spreading out from one another, and proceeding in a zigzag course, they smash and destroy the finest trees which happen to lie in their way. The number of them which a herd of bull elephants will thus destroy is utterly incredible. They are extremely capricious, and on coming to a group of five or six trees not unfrequently break down the whole of them, when, having perhaps only tasted one or two small branches, they pass on and continue their wanton work of destruction. I have repeatedly gone through forests where the trees thus broken lay so thick across one another that it was almost impossible to ride through them, and it is in situations such as these that attacking the elephant is attended with most danger. During the night they will feed in open plains and thinly-wooded districts; but as day dawns they retire to the densest covers within reach, which nine times in ten consist of impracticable wait-a-bit thorns, and here they remain drawn up in a compact herd during the heat of the day. In remote districts, however, and in cool weather, I have known herds to continue pasturing throughout the whole day.

The appearance of the wild elephant is inconceivably majestic and imposing; his gigantic height and colossal bulk, so greatly surpassing all other quadrupeds, combined with his sagacious disposition and peculiar habits, impart to him an interest in the eyes of the hunter which no other animal can call forth. His pace when undisturbed is a bold, free, sweeping step; and from the spongy formation of his foot, his tread is extremely light and inaudible, and all his movements are attended with singular gentleness and grace; this, however, only applies to the elephant when roaming undisturbed in his jungle, for when roused by the hunter, he proves a most dangerous enemy, and far more difficult to conquer than any other beast of the chase.

On the 27th, as day dawned, I left my shooting-hole, and proceeded to inspect the spoor of the wounded elephant; after following it for some distance I came to an abrupt hillock, which I ascended, fancying that from the summit a good view of the surrounding country might be obtained. In this I was not disappointed, and looking east, beheld to my inexpressible gratification a troop of nine or ten elephants quietly browsing within a quarter of a mile of me. I allowed myself only one glance, and then rushed down to warn my followers to be silent; a council-of-war was hastily held, the result of which was my ordering Isaac to ride hard to camp, and return as quickly as possible with Kleinboy, my dogs, the large Dutch rifle, and a fresh horse. After this I once more ascended the hillock to feast my eyes upon the enchanting sight before me; and, drawing out my glass, narrowly watched the motions of the herd; this consisted entirely of females, several of which were followed by small calves.

Presently, while reconnoitring the surrounding country, I discovered a second herd of five bull elephants, quietly feeding about a mile to the northward, while the cows were towards a rocky ridge that stretched away from the base of the hillock on which I stood. Burning with impatience to commence the attack, I resolved to try the stalking-system with these, and hunt the troop of bulls with dogs and horses. Having thus decided, I directed the guides to watch the elephants from the summit of the hillock, and the ground and wind favouring me, I soon gained the rocky ridge. They were now within a hundred yards, and with a beating heart I resolved to enjoy the pleasure of watching their movements as they came slowly towards me, breaking the branches from the trees with their trunks, and eating the leaves and tender shoots. At length two of the troop walked gently past, and the finest which I had selected was feeding with two others on a thorny tree about sixty yards from me.

My hand was now as steady as the rock on which it rested, so, taking a deliberate aim, I let fly at her head a little behind the eye; she got it hard and sharp, just where I aimed, but it did not seem to affect her much. Uttering a loud cry, however, she wheeled about, when I gave her the second ball, close behind the shoulder, upon which they all made a strange rumbling noise and set off in a line at a brisk ambling pace, their huge fan-like ears flapping in the ratio of their speed. I did not wait to reload, but ran back to the hillock, and on gaining its summit the guides pointed out the herd standing in a grove of shady trees, the wounded one being some distance behind with another elephant, doubtless its particular friend, who was endeavouring to assist it; these elephants had probably never before heard the report of a gun; and, having neither seen nor smelt me, were unconscious of the presence of man, and did not seem inclined to go any farther. My servants now came up, but I waited some time, that the dogs and horses might recover their wind. We then rode towards the elephants, and had advanced within two hundred yards of them, when, the ground being open, they observed us, and made off in an easterly direction; the wounded one dropped astern, and next moment was surrounded by the dogs, which, barking angrily, engrossed her attention.

Having placed myself between her and the retreating troop, I dismounted within forty yards of her, in open ground; and Colesberg, being extremely frightened, gave me much trouble, jerking my arm when I tried to fire. At length I let fly; but, on endeavouring to regain the saddle, my horse would not allow me to mount; and when I tried to lead him, and run for it, he backed towards the wounded elephant. At this moment I heard another close behind me; and looking about beheld the "friend", with uplifted trunk, charging down upon me at top speed, trumpeting shrilly and following an old deaf pointer named Schwart, that trotted along before the enraged animal. I felt certain she would have either me or the horse, nevertheless I determined not to relinquish my steed, and held on by the bridle. My men, who of course kept at a safe distance, stood aghast with their mouths open, and for a few seconds my position certainly was not an enviable one; fortunately, however, the dogs took off the attention of the elephants, and just as they were upon me, I managed to spring into the saddle, expecting every second to feel one of their trunks lay hold of my body. Kleinboy and Isaac, pale and almost speechless with fright, now handed me my two-grooved rifle, when I returned to the charge, and sent another brace of bullets into the wounded elephant, but Colesberg was extremely unsteady, and destroyed the correctness of my aim.

The friend now seemed resolved to do some mischief, and charged furiously, pursuing me several hundred yards; I therefore deemed it proper to give her a gentle hint to act less officiously, and having loaded, and approached within thirty yards, gave it her sharp, right and left, behind the shoulder, upon which she at once made off with drooping trunk, and evidently with a mortal wound. I never recur to this my first day's elephant shooting without regretting my folly in contenting myself with securing only one elephant; the first was dying, and could not leave the ground; the second was also mortally wounded, and I had only to follow and finish her; but I, foolishly amusing myself with the first, which kept walking backwards, and standing by every tree she passed, allowed her to escape. Two more shots settled her: on receiving these she tossed her trunk up and down two or three times, and, falling on her broadside against a thorny tree, which yielded like grass before her enormous weight, uttered a deep hoarse cry, and expired. This was a very handsome old cow elephant, and, as I have before remarked, was decidedly the best in the troop; she was in excellent condition, and carried a pair of long and perfect tusks. I was in high spirits at my success, and felt so satisfied with having killed one, that, although it was still early in the day, and my horses were fresh, I allowed the troop of five bulls to remain unmolested, trusting to fall in with them next day. So little did I then know of the habits of elephants, or the rules to be adopted in hunting them!

Having knee-haltered our horses, we set to work with our knives and assegais to prepare the skull for the hatchet, in order to take out the tusks, nearly half the length of which, I may mention, is embedded in bone sockets in the fore part of the skull; to remove the tusks of a cow elephant requires barely one-fifth of the labour requisite to cut out those of a bull, and by the time the sun went down we had only managed by our combined efforts to detach one of the tusks, with which we triumphantly returned to camp, having left the guides in charge of the carcass, near which they volunteered to take up their quarters for the night. On reaching the waggons I found Johannus and Carollus in a happy state of indifference to all passing events; they were both very drunk, having broken into both wine-cask and spirit-case.

On the 28th I rose at an early hour, and, burning with anxiety to look forth once more from the summit of the hillock which the day before brought me such luck, I made a hasty breakfast, and rode thither with after-riders and my dogs; but, alas! I had allowed the golden opportunity to slip. I sought in vain; and although I often ascended my favourite hillock in that and the succeeding year, my eyes were destined never to hail a troop of elephants from it again.

We were now within two days' march of the kraal of Sicomy, king of the extensive territory of Bamangwato; this great chief was reported to be in possession of large quantities of ivory, and as I had brought a number of muskets and other articles for barter, I was anxious to push on and conclude my trading before resuming elephant hunting; more especially since it was not improbable that, having once led the way, other adventurers might follow in my track, and perhaps spoil my market. Taking this into consideration, I marched on the morning of the 30th upon the kraal of Sicomy, and held for the Bamangwato mountains, the summits of which we could see peering above the intervening forest in an easterly direction. On our march we passed near to the carcass of the elephant which I had slain three days before; the number of vultures congregated here was truly wonderful – my guides had baked a part of the trunk and two of the feet, and these they now brought to the waggons. It was always to me a source of great pleasure to reflect that, while enriching myself in following my favourite pursuit of elephant hunting, I was frequently feeding and making happy the starving families of hundreds of the Bechuana and Bakalahari tribes, who invariably followed my waggons, and assisted me in hunting, in numbers varying from fifty to two hundred. These men were often accompanied by their wives and families, and when an elephant or other large animal was slain, all hands repaired to the spot, when every inch of flesh was reduced to biltongue, viz. cut into long strips, hung in festoons upon poles, and dried in the sun: sometimes even the entrails were not left for the vultures and hyænas, the very bones being chopped to pieces with their hatchets to obtain the marrow, with which they enriched their soup.

THE LION HUNTER OF SOUTH AFRICA
(John Murray 1850)

Among the Gorillas

PAUL B. DU CHAILLU

y determination to go farther into the interior has aroused the jealousy of the Ashiras. All the chiefs came in to Olenda and expressed their disapproval of my project. They do not wish their trade interfered with, and are fearful, if a white man once reaches the far East beyond them, those people will not be content to trade with the Ashira longer. I stated my objects, and that I did not go as trader, but as traveller, and to collect new animals. At last Olenda said, "This white man must go where he wishes. He has been sent to me by my friend Quengueza. He must do what he pleases."

Then the rascally chiefs asked me what I would give them as presents if I was permitted to go. To this I put on a show of anger, and asked if I was not their guest, their stranger, and why they were so mean as to beg me for my goods? They seemed much ashamed. Of course I gave them some trifles afterwards for good will.

There was a show of reason for their fears. Among my train were several men from Goumbi, slaves of influential men of that town, who had been sent with me with trade articles, such as the Ashira most want, in order to bring back to Goumbi ivory and the bongo cloth (grass-cloth), which is the staple export of the Ashiras. Of course it was feared that not only I, but also these fellows, would confuse and break up the Ashira monopoly of trade with the farther interior. It is curious to see how greatly slaves are trusted in this country. The owners of these fellows had no security for their return, nor for the goods they intrusted to them; for I, of course, would not become responsible for them. But they were sure to return. They, who were originally themselves from an interior tribe, have come to feel greatly attached to Goumbi, and look down with contempt on the Ashira, whom they call "men of the woods".

Dec. 4th. Food has been collected and cooked for my trip. I am to give the Ashira men six fathoms of cloth each to go with me to the Apingi country and wait for me there. Olenda gave me a numerous band, including three of his sons to accompany me, Minsho, Iguy, and Aiaguy, the latter a very common name here.

It rains nearly every day, and every few days we have tremendous storms of wind and rain. All the rivers are swollen, and the prairie looks very green and beautiful.

We set out on Dec. 6th. Early in the morning Olenda called us around him, and after telling his sons to take good care of me, the venerable old man proceeded formally to bless us, wishing us good success. It was a touching scene. At the close he took a sugarcane, bit a piece of the pith, and spat a little of the juice in the hand of each one of the party, at the same time blowing on the hand. Then he said solemnly, "Let all have good speed with you, and let it be as smooth (pleasant) as the breath I blow on your hand." Then Minsho received the cane, which he is to bring back.

I found that the prairie was much more swampy to the eastward, towards the foot of the hills, than I had supposed. We had to walk through much mud, and often to wade through considerable pools and swamps of standing water, produced by the constant heavy rains. In one of these swamps we had to wade up to our middles in muddy water, and some of the party slipped down on the roots with which the bottom is covered.

The forest beyond the line of the prairie is also inhabited. We passed over a dozen villages, the people of which flocked out to see the "white spirit". They were all Ashira.

Towards noon we approached the Ovigui River, a mountain-torrent, which was to be crossed by a rude and very dangerous bridge. This bridge I had dreaded all day, and when at last I saw it I was by no means reassured. The stream was about thirty yards wide, and rushed through the forest overflowing its banks. The waters were very swift, and I saw that even a good swimmer would be helpless here, and would soon be dashed to pieces against the fallen trees which jutted out in every direction.

Now I swim but very little, and the bridge was a complicated, shaky structure.

It appears that the Ovigui had its bed, till some years ago, not here, but some hundreds of yards on the other side. This is a trick that some of the mountain-streams of Africa have. Now in the new bed stood certain trees which native ingenuity saw could be used as the piers for a bridge. In this place two trees, standing each about seven or eight yards from one side, were chosen. Other trees opposite on the banks were so cut as to fall into these. Thus were formed two portions of the bridge, and these, though sufficiently rude, were not seriously bad for a traveller. It now remained to unite the still open space in the centre, between the two "piers", and here came the tug.

Unable to transport heavy pieces of timber, they had thrown across this chasm a long, slender, bending limb, which sagged down in the middle until, when it bore a man's weight, its centre was three feet below the surface of the rushing tide. Of course no one could walk on this without assistance, so a couple of strong vines had been strung across for balustrades; but as these vines were of necessity so slack as to be parallel with the bamboo, they were of the very slightest assistance.

My heart failed me as I stood looking at this breakneck concern. To add to the pleasurable excitement of the scene, Minsho told me that this was a much better crossing than some others they had lower down, but admitted that even here some half-dozen of their people had been drowned within a year.

I watched the party crossing with great interest. One man slipped when midway, but luckily recovered himself. He dropped only a box of mine containing two pairs of shoes. Another, who was carrying a gun, so narrowly escaped falling as to drop that, which was also swept off and lost. Meantime I wondered if I should follow in the wake of my shoes and gun.

At last all were across but Minsho. I had stripped to my shirt and trousers, and set out on my trial, followed by Minsho, who had a vague idea that if I slipped he *might* catch me. It was an unpleasant suspense in every way; and as I crossed the centre part, and felt the current beating against my legs and almost seeming to have a hold on me, with purpose to drag me away, I vowed I would never try such navigation again. However, I managed to hold on to the vine and drag myself up, very weak and pale with excitement, but outwardly necessarily calm, as it would not do to let these natives see me make a difficulty of anything they could do.

Again we plunged into the primeval forests of ebony, bar-wood, India-rubber vines, and other strange woods. After about two miles of travel we came to a curious little *strip* of prairie, which was five or six miles long, but only a few hundred yards wide. This they called *Odjiolo*, but they could not tell me its origin. It was not inhabited.

A few miles farther on the path led over a curious steep mount called Mount Ocoucou. We had to climb the almost perpendicular sides, and I had to grasp branches or vines as I ascended the face of this high hill. Having surmounted that and three others, with intervening plains and valleys, all covered with dense forests, we at last found ourselves on the banks of another little purling mountain-brook which skirted the base of our last hill, the Aloumy. Here we lit fires, built shelters, and camped for the night. This day we made but twenty miles, fifteen of which were due east.

Dec. 7th. As we advance the country becomes more rugged and mountainous. On every side brooks and rills and small streams are wending their way down to the Ovigui, or towards the Apingi river, and very frequently we have to march along the bed of a purling brook, the only way which the broken and rocky country affords us. This day was exceedingly trying for our feet. We picked our way through a forest dense and gloomy, every step obstructed by rocks and broken ground. This is evidently the favourite haunt of gorilla. Several times during the day we heard his roar in the distance. We heard also the cry of a nshiego mbouvé at a little distance, and started in pursuit, but the animal made its escape, having probably heard us. At the foot of a tree we found some leafy branches gathered, while in another tree was a shelter completed. No doubt a pair had been at work together. The negroes here told me also that these apes work in pairs, both collecting branches, and the male building the shelter when the material is brought together, while the female carries it up to him.

Judging from his cry, one of the gorillas we heard in the afternoon seemed to be so near that I was tempted to hunt him up. He proved farther off than any of us thought. We wandered nearly three-quarters of an hour through the forest before we reached him. His almost incessant roars, which seemed to denote that he was enraged at something, gave us a good clue to his whereabouts.

I find that I do not get accustomed to the roar of the gorilla. Notwithstanding the numbers I have hunted and shot, it is still an awful sound to me. The long reverberations, coming from his potenteous chest; the vindictive bark with which each roar is begun; the hollow monotone of the first explosion, all are awe-inspiring, and proclaim this beast the monarch of these forests.

When the animal became aware of our approach he at once came towards us, uttering a succession of the short bark-like yells which denote his rage, and which have a peculiarly horrible effect. They remind one only of the inarticulate ravings of a maniac.

Balancing his huge heavy body with his arms the animal came towards us, every few moments stopping to beat his breast, and throwing his head back to utter his tremendous roar. His fierce gloomy eyes glared upon us; the short hair was rapidly agitated, and the wrinkled face seemed contorted with rage. It was like a very devil, and I do not wonder at the superstitious terror with which the natives regard it.

His manner of approach gave me once more an opportunity to see with how much difficulty he supports himself in the erect posture. His short and slender legs are not able firmly to sustain the vast body. They totter beneath the weight, and the walk is a sort of waddle, in which the long arms are used, in a clumsy way, to balance the body and keep up the ill-sustained equilibrium. Twice he sat down to roar, evidently not trusting himself to this exertion while standing.

My gun was fresh loaded, and could be depended upon, so I stood in advance. I waited, as the negro rule is, till the huge beast was within six yards of me; then, as he once more stopped to roar, delivered my fire, and brought him down on his face dead.

It proved to be a male, full grown, but young. His huge canine tusks, his claw-like hands, the immense development of muscle on his arms and breast, his whole appearance, in fact, proclaimed a giant strength.

EXPLORATIONS AND ADVENTURES IN EQUATORIAL AFRICA
(John Murray 1861)

Elephant Hunting in the Cashan Mountains

CAPTAIN W. C. HARRIS

efore daybreak the following morning, it was discovered that the oxen having been alarmed by Lions, had made their escape from the pond. A party was despatched in pursuit of them, and we proceeded into the hills to look for Buffaloes. The thunderstorm having purified the atmosphere, had rendered the weather delightfully cool, and a deep wooded defile which had not been approached by the conflagration of the day before, was filled with game that had fled before the flames. A rhinoceros was killed almost immediately, and before we had reloaded, a noble herd of near one hundred and fifty Buffaloes was perceived on a slope overhanging a sedgy stream. Having crept within five and twenty yards, we despatched two Bulls before the alarm was spread. Crashing through the forest, they overturned decayed trees in their route, and swept along the brow of the opposite hill in fearful confusion, squeezed together in a compact phalanx, and raising an incredible cloud of dust to mark their course. We mounted our horses, and after sticking some time in the treacherous mud of the rivulet, gained the opposite bank and brought two more to bay, which were despatched after several charges. Our savage friends, still torpid from their yesterday's feast, had not made their appearance; we therefore despatched Claas, after breakfast was over, to bring in some marrow bones, in the act of collecting which delicacies, he was put to flight by a Lion that jumped out of a bush close to him, and did not leave him time to think of his gun. After some hours, however, he mustered courage to proceed with a large party to recover it.

Early in the afternoon the Hottentots returned with the oxen, and we proceeded without loss of time to the Eastward, following the course of the mountains through very high grass, and passing between two conical hills of singular appearance which stood like sentinels on either hand; after crossing six inconsiderable streams, we with some difficulty gained the vicinity of a remarkably abrupt opening in the range, which through a telescope appeared to afford a practicable road to the Northward. Both our waggons stuck fast in the Sant river, and were with difficulty extricated by the united efforts of the teams. The heat was intense, not a breath stirred, and heavy black clouds fast collecting bade us prepare for a deluge. We therefore formed the camp in a sheltered and elevated position, under the lee of a high stone enclosure, which only required the entrance to be closed with bushes to make a secure pound for the cattle. Scarcely were these arrangements completed, when a stream of liquid fire ran along the ground, and a deafening thunder clap, exploding close above us, was instantly followed by a torrent of rain, which "came dancing to the earth", not in drops, but in continuous streams, and with indescribable violence, during the greater part of the night; the thunder now receding and rumbling less and less distinctly, but more incessantly among the distant mountains – now pealing in echoes over the nearer hills, and now returning to burst with redoubled violence above our heads.

> "Far along
> From peak to peak, the rattling crags among,
> Leapt the wild thunder, not from one lone cloud,
> But every mountain soon had found a tongue."

The horses and oxen were presently standing knee deep in water; our followers remained sitting all night in the baggage waggon which leaked considerably, but our own, being better covered, fortunately resisted the pitiless storm. Sleep was however out of the question, the earth actually threatening to give way under us, and the lightning being so painfully vivid that we were glad to hide our heads under the pillow.

Those only who have witnessed the setting in of the South West monsoon in India, are capable of fully understanding the awful tempest I have attempted to describe. About an hour before dawn its fury began to abate, and at sunrise it was perfectly fine, but the rivers were quite impassable. I proceeded with some of the Hottentots to reconnoitre the pass, but found that it was impassable for waggons, being nothing more than a narrow channel flanked by perpendicular crags, between which the Sant river rushes on its way to join the Lingkling, making a number of very abrupt windings through a most impracticable country, intersected by a succession of rocky ac-clivities. From the highest peak we saw several herds of Buffaloes, and whilst descending, came upon the tracks of a huge Elephant that had passed about an hour before. This being the largest foot print we had seen, I had the curiosity to measure it, in order to ascertain the animal's height – twice the circumference of an Elephant's foot being, it is notorious, the exact height at the shoulder. It yielded a product of about twelve feet, which notwithstanding the traditions that have been handed down, I believe to be the maximum height attained by the African Elephant. We followed the trail across the Sant river, which had now considerably subsided – and finding that it proceeded Eastward along the mountain chain, returned to our encampment for horses and ammunition.

Leaving the waggons to proceed to a spot agreed upon, we again took the field about ten o'clock, and pursued the track indefatigably for eight miles, over a country presenting every variety of feature. At one time we crossed bare stony ridges, at another threaded the intricacies of shady but dilapidated forests; now struggled through high fields of waving grass, and again emerged into open downs. At length we arrived amongst extensive groups of grassy hillocks, covered with loose stones, interspersed with streams, and occasional patches of forest in which the recent ravages of Elephants were surprising. Here to our inexpressible gratification we descried a large herd of those long sought animals, lazily browsing at the head of a distant valley, our attention having been first directed to it, by the strong and not to be mistaken effluvia with which the wind was impregnated. Never having before seen the noble Elephant in his native jungles, we gazed on the sight before us with intense, and indescribable interest. Our feelings on the occasion even extended to our followers. As for Andries he became so agitated that he could scarcely articulate. With open eyes and quivering lips he at length stuttered forth "*Dar stand de Oliphant*". Mohanycom and 'Lingap were immediately despatched to drive the herd back into the valley, up which we rode slowly and without noise, against the wind; and arriving within one hundred and fifty yards unperceived, we made our horses fast, and took up a commanding position in an old stone kraal. The shouting of the savages, who now appeared on the height rattling their shields, caused the huge animals to move unsuspiciously towards us, and even within ten yards of our ambush. The group consisted of nine, all females with large tusks. We selected the finest, and with perfect deliberation fired a volley of five balls into her. She stumbled, but recovering herself, uttered a shrill note of lamentation, when the whole party threw their trunks above their heads, and instantly clambered up the adjacent hill with incredible celerity, their huge fan-like ears, flapping in the ratio of their speed. We instantly mounted our horses, and the sharp loose stones not suiting the feet of the wounded lady, soon closed with her. Streaming with blood, and infuriated with rage, she turned upon us with uplifted trunk, and it was not until after repeated discharges, that a ball took effect in her brain, and threw her lifeless on the earth, which resounded with the fall.

Turning our attention from the exciting scene I have described, we found that a second valley had opened upon us, surrounded by bare stony hills, and traversed by a thinly wooded ravine. Here a grand and magnificent panorama was before us, which beggars all description. The whole face of the landscape was actually covered with wild Elephants. There could not have been fewer than three hundred within the scope of our vision. Every height and green knoll was dotted over with groups of them, whilst the bottom of the glen exhibited a dense and sable living mass — their colossal forms being at one moment partially concealed by the trees which they were disfiguring with giant strength; and at others seen majestically emerging into the open glades, bearing in their trunks the branches of trees with which they indolently protected themselves from the flies. The back ground was filled by a limited peep of the blue mountainous range, which here assumed a remarkably precipitous character, and completed a picture at once soul-stirring and sublime!

Our approach being still against the wind was unobserved, and created little alarm, until the herd that we had left behind, suddenly showed itself, recklessly thundering down the side of the hill to join the main body, and passing so close to us, that we could not refrain from firing a broad side into one of them, which however bravely withstood it. We secured our horses on the summit of a stony ridge, and then stationing ourselves at an opportune place on a ledge overlooking the wooded defile, sent Andries to manœuvre so that as many of the Elephants as possible should pass before us in order of review, that we might ascertain by a close inspection, whether there was not a male amongst them. Filing sluggishly along, they occasionally halted beneath an umbrageous tree within fifteen yards of us, lazily fanning themselves with their ample ears, blowing away the flies with their trunks, and uttering the feeble and peculiar cry so familiar to Indians. They all proved to be ladies, and most of them mothers, followed by their little old fashioned calves each trudging close to the heels of her dam and mimicking all her actions. Thus situated we might have killed any number we pleased, their heads being frequently turned towards us, in such a position, and so close, that a single ball in the brain would have sufficed for each; but whilst we were yet hesitating, a bullet suddenly whizzed past Richardson's ear and put the whole herd to immediate flight. We had barely time to recede behind a tree, before a party of about twenty with several little ones in their wake were upon us, striding at their utmost speed, and trumpeting loudly with uplifted heads. I rested my rifle against the tree, and firing behind the shoulder of the leader, she dropped instantly. Another large detachment appearing close behind us at the same moment we were compelled to retreat, dodging from tree to tree, stumbling amongst sharp stones, and ever coming upon fresh parties of the enemy. This scene of ludicrous confusion did not long continue – and soon approaching the prostrate lady, we put an end to her struggles by a shot in the forehead. Andries now came up in high good humour at his achievements, and in the most bravado manner discharged his piece into the dead carcase, under the pretence that the animal was shamming. His object evidently was to confound the shots – for thrusting his middle finger into the orifice made by my two ounce ball, he with the most modest assurance declared himself the author of the deed, being pleased altogether to overlook the fact of the mortal shot having entered the Elephant on the side opposite to that on which he was stationed, and that his own ball, whether designedly or not, had all but expended my worthy and esteemed fellow traveller.

On our way to the camp, of the exact position of which we were uncertain in consequence of the late inundation, we passed three other large herds of Elephants. One of these standing directly in the route, we attacked it and pursued the fugitives about a mile over loose stones. Much has been said of the attachment of Elephants to their young, but neither on this, nor on any subsequent occasion, did we perceive them evince the smallest concern for their safety. On the contrary they left them to shift for themselves, and Mohanycom and 'Lingap, who were behind us, assegaied one, the tail of which they brought in. We slew another old female as we ascended the brow of an eminence, and at the same moment perceived our waggons within a few hundred yards of the spot. The whole herd dashed through the camp causing indescribable consternation amongst cattle and followers, but fortunately no accident occurred, and after the fatiguing day's work we had undergone, we were not sorry to find ourselves at home.

Watery clouds hung about the sun as he set heavily behind the mountains. Loud peals of crashing thunder rent the air, and ere it was dark, we had a repetition of yesterday's storm, the river roaring past us with frightful fury. Troops of Elephants flying from the scene of slaughter, passed close to our waggons during the darkness, their wild voices echoing amongst the mountains, and sounding like trumpets above the tempest. It was impossible to keep the fires burning; and the oxen and sheep were alarmed to such a degree, that they broke from the kraal, and sought safety in the wilderness. Tired as I was, the excitement I had undergone banished sleep from my eyes. I ruminated on the spirit-stirring events of the day, and burned with impatience to renew them. Heedless of the withering blast that howled without, I felt that my most sanguine expectations had been realised, and that we had already been amply repaid for the difficulties, privations and dangers, that we had encountered in our toilsome journey towards this fairy land of sport.

NARRATIVE OF AN EXPEDITION INTO SOUTHERN AFRICA
DURING YEARS 1836–1837
(American Mission Press, Bombay 1838)

Waiting for the Lions

F. VAUGHAN KIRBY

t is absolutely necessary to make yourself comfortable *before* the lions arrive, as that is the moment when excitement is apt to make you feel *uncomfortable*. Having sat in a *scherm* one night for three lions, which winded me and decamped, I tried a tree next night, and, just as they came, endeavoured to shift myself from a cramped position, when the stage gave way and I fell to the ground, nearly 12 ft. The attendant who was with me succeeded in holding on to a branch. The lions growled ominously, but in the silence that followed they cleared out. The best plan, after all, for night-watching is to place the bait in a shallow creek and make a shelter of branches on the bank, 20 ft from the bait, below wind – the bait must have been previously dragged in such a way that lions coming along the drag will be seen, at any rate a few moments before they reach the carcase. If you are dealing with their own kill, you will note the direction of their departing spoor, and build your *scherm* accordingly, remembering that they are nearly sure to return *along the same track*; or a shooting hole can be made, covered in with logs and thorn branches. It should be 5 ½ ft long, 4 ft wide, and 3 ft to 4 ft deep, and a hole must be left to shoot through. I have nearly been hooked out of one of these by a lion, owing to the hole being too narrow to admit of my turning, and partly to my somnolent condition, so I do not very strongly recommend the plan. Moonlight should be chosen for night-watching, otherwise it is very difficult to make out a lion even when only six or eight paces distant. Blue-lights are often useful; in my previous work I have dealt exhaustively with this subject. It does not pay to have a boy with you; they *will* sleep, and *inevitably snore*. When the lions come, *be quite ready*, but *do not fire hurriedly*. I prefer to let them feed for an hour. It is most interesting to watch them by moonlight. But when you *do* fire, *aim low*; one is very apt to *overshoot at night*. Do not leave the *scherm* if one is shot, for the others, if there was a party, are quite likely to return. Always be prepared against the rush of a wounded beast. I have been through that experience also, and it is just a little too exciting; for that reason I never fire at a lion facing me, at night, except of course in self-defence.

I will now relate an adventure I had with lions in May 1894, near Majekan's kraal in the Sabi Poort, on my way down to Delagoa Bay. The night we reached this camp some lions roared freely after midnight, about 2 miles away, and as they continued their moaning grunts after daylight, always apparently in the same spot, I thought they might possibly have a kill in that direction, so I set out with a couple of boys to hunt them up. An hour's walk, during which the lions seldom ceased grunting, brought us near the spot, and we found the fresh spoor of a male lion which had been chasing a hyæna, and, close by, his returning spoor, which we followed through a stony spruit and up a slight incline towards a thick grove of trees and some dense scrub-bush on the ridge. I now distinctly heard the growl of a lion in that direction, and, from some spot nearer, the worrying, snarling sound of a creature eating at a carcase. Within 30 yds of the trees lay a dead hyæna, and I walked towards it, keenly alert, trying to make out amongst the trees the creature that was eating; but I was all the time overlooking it, for it lay in a patch of grass just beyond the hyæna – a fine young lion cub, about six months old. I pulled up instantly, expecting each moment to see the lioness, but heard her give a deep purring call to her cub from the top of the ridge, and the little beast instantly scampered off as fast as its enormously distended belly would permit, while I ran to try and intercept it. On the ridge the cub turned to the left, while the lioness was growling on the right. The low scrub was very thick, but as I ran on I saw four or five great yellow objects trotting along in front of me. One of these almost immediately pulled up, and turned, facing me, growling furiously. Though close, it was a difficult shot through the thick scrub, but thinking it was the mother of the cub, and that she was about to charge, I fired at once, tumbling her on to her head, roaring tremendously. Unfortunately my rifle was single-barrelled, and as my boy was lagging behind with the double-12, I lost the chance of giving her another shot, as she picked herself up and made off after the others. I ran in pursuit, and reached the bank of a wide creek in time to see a fine old male lion entering the bush on the other side: it was a snapshot, but by the way he growled I thought I hit him somewhere. Before following them, I went back to try and secure the cub, but found that it had rejoined its mother (which evidently was not the lioness I wounded) and gone off in another direction. The lions had killed three impalas and dragged the remains into the grove of trees, and the hyæna, an old dog, had probably been killed for trying to annex a feed. His right hind-leg was broken and nearly torn from the body, and there were fang-wounds in the head. We followed the blood-spoor for over two miles, always in the direction of camp, the lion and three lionesses[1] keeping together, but eventually lost it in a dense thorn-jungle close to camp; and, as we were all hungry, I resolved to go to the tent and get something to eat, and tackle them again afterwards. I found a brother sportsman awaiting my arrival, Mr C. E. Parsons, a gentleman who had been shooting through Portuguese Territory, and he at once consented to accompany me back to the spot, and help hunt up the wounded lions. However, we met with no better luck than before, so I suggested our separating, and each making a long forward cast, he with one boy to the right, I with another to the left. This plan was so far successful, that, while crawling on hands and knees through some dense bush, on the bank of a deep, dry river-bed, I found, first a single blood-spot, then, 20 ft beyond, a broad smear of it on some long dry grass at the edge of the bank. I at once whispered to my boy to go and fetch Mr Parsons, and when he had crept away, I clambered down the bank – a drop of over 8 ft. As I was in the act of doing so, a loud growl saluted me from a spot under the bank, which here overhung considerably, the scour of the water round the bend in flood-time having washed it out. As I gained my feet and turned quickly, I saw a lion standing under the bank, watching me, looking very grand but very fierce, with crest defiantly erect, and a savage gleam in his eyes; while a few yards beyond him a lioness lay on the sand, whisking her tail about and also watching me intently, but in silence. I mentally thanked my stars that I had my double-12 rifle, as, almost immediately I found footing, the lion advanced a few steps, growling hoarsely (he was then eleven measured paces from me), holding his head low and twitching his tail from side to side, while his eyes were fixed on mine with a look of concentrated rage. It does not do to hesitate at such a moment, and as he jerked his tail up (a lion often does this, and *always* charges after doing so), I knelt down, got a quick sight on his chest, and fired. He reared up on his hind-legs, roaring loudly and clawing at the air, then fell back dead. It all happened then in a moment. Through the smoke I saw the lioness spring to her feet and rush towards me. Escape was impossible – a huge tree-trunk lay across the river-bed behind me, the banks were unscalable at a moment's notice – and with desperate coolness I fired my remaining barrel as she came on, uttering hoarse coughing grunts and flashing fire from her eyes. I missed her clean, and as the bullet struck the sand up under her belly and I saw that I had failed to stop her, I took a step

[1] The spoors of adults of each sex are easily distinguishable, one from the other, those of the fore-foot of the lion being disproportionately larger than those of the hind-foot, whereas those of the fore and hind-feet of the lioness are nearly equal size.

backwards in the futile hope of getting another cartridge into my rifle, and fell, scarcely two lengths in front of the furious beasts. Had she been wounded nothing could have saved me from a mauling, or worse; but, whether because she was unhurt, or because she saw my companion appear at that moment on the bank above, I cannot say, at all events she swerved to one side, sprang lightly on to the fallen tree, where Mr Parsons missed a shot at her, and thence on to the bank, where a second shot told loudly and received an answering growl. She now got away into some thorn-bush, where we followed her, after I had taken my single rifle from the boy (the double-12 was useless, the breech-action being choked with sand), and shot her without further incident. My companion, who was elated at thus securing his first lion, said he saw the charge, and saw her swerve as he reached the bank; his second shot had hit her high and far back in the flank, partly paralysing her hindquarters. My lion was a splendid old male. My first shot at him was nearly a miss, the bullet having passed through the fleshy part of the hind leg, inside, grazed the belly, and entered the brisket obliquely; the 12-bore bullet had passed through his heart and completely raked him.[1]

Regarding rifles for lion-shooting, I should think a good double Lee-Metford would prove very efficient, but have no experience of them for this work. I have shot lions with several kinds of weapons, but unhesitatingly give the preference to the .461 Metford; it never fails to stop a lion if held straight, for a lion is a very easily killed beast, if hit in the right place, and is nothing like as tough as the antelopes. I have used various charges, No. 1 Gibbs 75/540, No. 1 Gibbs Express 90/360, and No. 2 Gibbs Express 90/570, and although I have shot more lions with the 90/360, I consider the No. 2 the most efficient; either, however, are admirable. All rifles for use against lions and other dangerous game should be *double*. As lion-shooting is so often done in the half-light of morning and evening, the standing back-sight should be roughed and undercut; this does away with all shimmering in the open V, while for moonlight, or the faintest daylight, enamel-fronted sights, made to slip over the foresight, are very effective. A few words of caution. Avoid a head-shot at a lion if possible, unless, when he is looking at you, you can catch him half-way between the nose and the eyes; otherwise the bullet will surely glance. Behind the shoulder, aiming for lungs or heart, is the very best shot for a lion, and if moving across in front of you, always wait, if possible, till the beast has passed you,

---

[1] We never found the lioness I first hit, though I am confident she lay dead not far off.

for if you fire as he advances, and fail to drop him, his first rush is likely to be in your direction.

GREAT AND SMALL GAME OF AFRICA
(Rowland Ward 1899)

Ndorobo Elephant Hunting

ARTHUR H. NEUMANN

n getting back to my camp there, I was warmly welcomed by my Ndorobo friends, who told me (of course) that there had been no end of elephants in the neighbourhood during my absence, and (which was more to the point) that some still frequented the extensive jungle between there and the Seya River. I was very sorry, though, to hear of the death, while I was away, of one of the Ndorobo elephant-hunters whom I had got to know well. He came by it in this wise. He had gone out after some elephants; and, getting near them, had prepared for action by fixing a dart into the handle of his harpoon. I should explain though, first, that, when after elephants, an Ndorobo hunter carries a wooden harpoon handle (fairly heavy) and a large quiver containing a number of darts with iron heads as sharp as razors, the shafts of which fit into the handle. The darts are smeared with the deadly poison they obtain from a particular wood which grows in the mountains, and each is carefully wrapped up in a thin strip of skin prepared for the purpose. On getting near the game he takes out two of these darts, removes the skin wrapping, and, fixing one with the greatest nicety into the handle, carries it in his right hand while the spare one he takes in his left. He then enters the bush perfectly naked, having divested himself of his skin cape, belt with hunting-knife[1] attached, and anything else he may have about him, which he leaves together with his quiver. Creeping stealthily up, through the thicket, to within a few paces of the nearest elephant (or the one most favourably situated of those next him as he approaches up wind), he delivers his blow with all his strength, and instantly dives through the bush to avoid a possible charge. The elephants having stampeded, he picks up his harpoon handle, inserts his spare dart, and follows up. The most deadly spot to aim at with this weapon is the part of the stomach where lie the small intestines, about the flank. In the present case my friend had gone in as described; but not being able to get up to within striking

[1] A kind of long, heavy, spatula-shaped dagger, called a "simé", carried in a sheath.

distance of his game at once, had sat down to chew tobacco, putting his weapons down beside him. In taking them up again as he rose, one of the excessively sharp points scratched his leg, with the result that he was unable to leave the spot and died right away.

Perhaps I cannot do better than quote the account of my first success, after this long spell of bad luck, from my diary as entered at the time. I had moved from my standing camp to a temporary one near to the part of the bush where the elephants were reported to be then. "Ndorobo elephant-hunter came early and said a herd of elephants was in the bush. I went with him soon after sunrise towards the foot of the range, where dense bush extends with hardly any break for miles. Before long we came on lots of quite fresh spoor; but, before following in the direction the elephants had taken, we worked round to leeward, and then struck in. My guide kept frequently taking up dust from the ground and letting it trickle out of his fingers to test the air-currents, though for my own part I prefer to be 'still plucking the grass to try where sits the wind', dry grass crumbled in the hand being more sensitive to the slightest breath. We soon heard the elephants making their curious sounds, and again came on warm spoor, which we followed carefully. After following only a very short way, the solemn intestinal rumblings were heard, which so often give warning that the game is close ahead though still hidden by the thick bush. I stole on (having left my surplus followers), till the Ndorobo gave place to me to pass him. The bush, though a dense thorny scrub, is cut up by the elephants' paths into a check pattern. Rounding a corner I came in view of three elephants only a few yards away standing in a little bare space. The nearest (a large one) had its stern to me, and seemed to be amusing itself by picking up dust to throw over its back. Two others stood opposite, sideways on; one a small one with little ivory, the other a large fellow but with only moderate tusks. The last was my mark. He appeared to see me and turned his head a little towards me, somewhat interfering with the perfection of the shot afforded. I did not like to wait more than a few seconds, though, lest the chance should be lost, so let him have a bullet in the temple in what seemed to me the right spot. He fell to the shot, but rose at once, staggering and dizzy. I was ready for him, and gave him the other barrel (the others had fled). He did not fall again, but staggered about, very dazed and groggy. I kept close by his side, and when he tried to move away gave him a couple more shots in the region of the heart. He once got my wind (I having incautiously gone on the wrong side of him) and made a short spurt, I after him, losing my hat and getting arms, face, and clothes torn by the thorns. I was so close all the time I could have put the muzzle of my rifle against him easily by moving a pace or two more; and no doubt that was why he could not see me, as I was behind his line of sight, or he would have gone for me. But he could not go far and soon pulled up again, seemingly at his last gasp. He seemed once to try to come through a thick clump of scrub for me; but his strength appeared to fail, and he subsided backwards into a quaint sitting posture, his hind legs thrust forward on each side of his huge belly, his forelegs straddled out in front, while his head was kept quite straight upright by one tusk being against a small tree which was between it and his trunk. One would not have known that he was dead, only that now the curious rumbling noises he had been making all the time had ceased. He was a big bull, but his tusks were small (about 40 lbs apiece)."

I was pleased to have, as it were, broken the spell and at last killed an elephant again. Contrary to my usual custom I did not follow the rest of the herd again that day, as I was suffering from a touch of fever, and, having got the sun on my head (very powerful in the scrub) when I lost my hat, felt somewhat exhausted. My Ndorobo hunter was anxious to go and fetch his family to commence cutting up the meat. The whole community of Ndorobos now shifted their quarters and went and camped near the carcase, so that they might be near their work; and for several days I could not get any of them to go out hunting with me, so much taken up were they with feasting and drying for future use strips of meat and even pieces of the skin. For when pushed by hunger, as very frequently happens, they are glad to fall back upon old bits of elephant or rhinoceros hide, which they cook and eat. It is a curious sight to see a party of these people, men, women, and children, swarming around, upon, and inside the carcase of an elephant, like ants with a big beetle, fairly wallowing in gore and thoroughly enjoying themselves.

I was not myself averse to a couple of days' spell, having fever on me; for though I am so thoroughly salted, from many bygone encounters with this enemy of African travellers during long years of wandering in unhealthy regions, as to be so far fever-proof that I am never laid up or incapacitated for any needful exertion, I still feel the attacks to the extent of their affecting my comfort and buoyancy, and upsetting the nerves, thus interfering with one's shooting. But I soon got tired of taking it easy, though I amused myself with my little .250 rook rifle (a much handier weapon in Africa than a shot-gun) by shooting pigeons which congregated in the trees every afternoon to drink at the pool where we got our water. These made a pleasant variety to one's bill of fare too, either in a stew with elephant's heart, which I dignified by the name of "pigeon pie", or roasted on a stick; in the latter way, with a piece of elephant's fat skewered over them, they are excellent. Butterflies, the search for which is a great resource at odd times as well as on the march, were at this time almost absent here. So on the third day I went out with only my gunbearers, the Ndorobo being still immovable. I took a round in a direction I thought it likely the elephants might have retired in, and climbed a high koppie to get a view over the country. Sitting on the top with my glasses, I was able to get a glimpse of two or three elephants some miles away in a valley close under the hills, as they passed through a small open space at its mouth. However, my luck did not bear me out in spite of this good beginning; for the wind was most perverse, and though I eventually did get a glimpse of one's head, as it was almost a front view the chance was a poor one, and my shot had perhaps better not have been fired, as it did no good and I failed to get up to the elephants again. My experience is that a shot in the head, though it may not touch the brain, will almost always stun a cow, thus giving one time for another shot as she rises; but a big bull is not so easily felled, his massive skull resisting the force of the blow better, nor is his brain so easily reached. In this dense scrub, however, one had to make the most of such glimpses as one could get, though, as I became more at home in it, I found it possible to manœuvre close up to the elephants and get better shots than I dared attempt before.

The following day I was off before sunrise. My hunter had not yet turned up again, so I first went to seek him at his new camp. I found another Ndorobo clan (also friends of mine) had just come to make their encampment close by, in order to be handy for future feasts should I have further successes in hunting. Not finding my man, I took a couple of young volunteers along with me. We struck right through the bush to a point at the foot of the hills beyond where I had found the day before, in order that we might cut the spoor should the herd have trekked. We found no track, however, and walked back along the base of the hills towards the valley above mentioned. On getting near it, we came upon plenty of quite fresh spoor where the elephants had been feeding that morning. Having brought it up to the little swampy spring where they had drunk, I sat down to have a bit of a spell, as it was by this time noon, and eat a snack by way of lunch. I never carry anything that could be called a meal, but something just to spoil one's appetite; something sweet I find the best for the purpose, such as a few raisins or a bit of chocolate with a few fragments of biscuit, washed down with a drink of water.

Meanwhile I sent out my natives to find out which way the elephants had gone from there. I knew by this time they would be taking their mid-day siesta and must be standing somewhere in the bush not far off; and, sure enough, by the time I had finished my little repast, my scouts came running back to say they heard the elephants in the scrub quite near. I cautiously made off in the direction, the wind being right and, fortunately, steadier to-day, though gusty with lulls. My Ndorobo climbed a tree and saw a little bunch, and, having pointed out to me where they were, stayed behind and I crept on alone. With cat-like steps I advanced, caught a glimpse of one through the bush, and approached without making a sound or being seen to within ten yards of the nearest one, a large cow, of which I then suddenly, for the first time, came in full view, facing me. She also saw me, but apparently could not make out what I was, though she looked attentively and suspiciously at me. I always wear clothes of a reddish-brown colour – often using a decoction of mimosa bark to stain them if too light – thus resembling the colour of many tree trunks; and when standing motionless (the wind being favourable) I think an elephant takes one, so disguised, for a dry stump. I waited anxiously for her to give me a chance, at the same time noticing that two or three others, which I could see indistinctly behind her, seemed all smaller; so that, though my *vis-à-vis'* tusks were not large, I decided she must be my victim. She once or twice offered to approach me, and once actually came, head up, ears stretched out, to within five or six yards at most. I stood firm, having inwardly sworn not to spoil this chance by hurried or nervous shooting, and ready, should she come right on, to give her a shot in the chest and jump aside, though my object in waiting was the hope of getting a chance for a temple-shot, knowing that if I succeeded in that, dropping her dead on the spot (as can only be done by a shot in the brain), the others might probably stand and give me a chance with my second barrel. She, however, hesitated, her courage seeming to fail her at the last moment, or she was not sure what I was; anyway she backed away again and I ventured, in spite of crackling twigs, to go a step or two nearer.

The breeze there had been as I came up to them had died entirely away, and there was a dead calm, with a suspicion of eddies the wrong way. The elephants felt for scent with their trunks, and suddenly turned and ran the other way. I was after them instantly; and, as my cow was the last and they only got slowly through the jungle at first, in a few strides I was within a few yards of her stern, meaning to give her a shot in that quarter and try at least to cripple her. But before I could do so she suddenly rounded on me with a scream, having clearly heard me following and meaning to charge. But before she was well round I had put a bullet in her temple, which felled her, to my great relief and joy. As she struggled on the ground I gave her the other barrel in her head again, and then, as she still thumped her head about, screaming loudly, I shot her in the chest, the bullet penetrating her heart and finishing her. Following the others, which seemed to have lost their leader and ran about backwards and forwards, standing at short intervals, I sighted them two or three times, but could not get a shot. They were all small females with thin tusks, but I did not then know there were any more near, so was bound to try and score all I could. Shortly after, I got sight of two of them standing, and, the breeze being just then favourable, I got up, waited till one turned her head right, and dropped her. Going on again, Juma (one of my men) spotted another from a tree I had sent him up. I got close up and found there were three or four standing together, larger than the others, and which had evidently not been disturbed. Opposite me again was a cow, similar to the first I had shot, with a calf by her. The calf saw me, but I heeded it not nor its mother, having caught sight of a much larger tusk than she possessed behind a thick clump of scrub to the right, only a few yards from where I stood. Determined to try for this fellow at all hazards, I moved round this clump of wattles. As I came in view he swung round preparatory to decamping. But I was too quick for him, and as his head went round from me I plugged him right in the ear, dropping him dead on the spot. He was a small bull, very short in stature, but with nice teeth.

I now went back to the small elephant to get some water, and foolishly stayed some time while more was fetched for the men. This delay, I think, certainly cost me at least another elephant. When I did follow up again, leaving Juma to get out the fat, etc., on coming over a rise we saw the whole herd (perhaps thirty strong, but apparently all cows) going up the other side of a little valley in front of us, some 300 or 400 yds ahead. I doubled after them – an open glade here allowing it, – but, on topping the next rise, they were already disappearing over another, getting away from us at a run. Two were, however, behind, and had not yet crossed the gully, so I ran down to try to cut them off; but they put on a spurt and I only managed to get a stern shot at one. Being above her the bullet caught her in the back (as it afterwards turned out), and told loudly; but they went off, and we had to give up the chase, as it was getting late. This cow was, however, found a few days after by some Ndorobos, and I got the ivory all right.

On starting back for camp I sent one of my young Ndorobo companions to call the two headmen of their clans, and on reaching camp, about sundown, they met me. There being heaps of meat in the wind they made no delay or excuses. I am bound to say, though, that these people are far more reliable, as a rule, than most Central African savages. On giving them leave to take possession of the elephants (apportioning each tribe its share, to prevent any quarrelling), I told them they must bring me some honey. This they promised to do as soon as they had eaten the elephants. They fulfilled their promise loyally later on, bringing me a liberal supply of the most beautifully clear, luscious honey. I find that honey is almost a necessity in the "bara". It is the only sweet thing one gets, for sugar one cannot carry sufficient of to last; and when living on nothing but the simplest and coarsest food with meat, one has a craving for something sweet and does not feel satisfied or strong without it. The Ndorobos depend largely on it, especially for their children. It is a wonderful country for flowers, and seldom dries up near the Lorogi owing to the frequent mountain showers; and bees in consequence thrive and accumulate great stores. I found a kind of wild fruit or bean (something like acorns), which the natives eat, very good when thoroughly boiled and eaten with honey, and it was a great stand-by while I was in that part. My poor old Ndorobo follower whom I called "Papa" had cut his hand while cutting up the elephant shot previously, and the meat, being somewhat high, had poisoned his blood and quite spoilt the old chap's pleasure during these times of plenty, and he eventually lost half the wounded finger.

These were great times with the Ndorobos of the whole country-side. They all camped in the vicinity and in a few days got quite sleek and fat, so that I could hardly recognise my recently starved-looking neighbours. As, however, they had overrun the elephants' favourite haunts, there seemed no chance of more luck for me thereabouts for a time; so I determined to move a little farther off again. I was sorry to leave my pleasant camp at El Bogoi, with its pure little stream of water and shady tree with a canopy of creepers under which I could sit and rest in the cool. I was pretty hard worked there though, for game had to be sought a considerable distance away to keep up the supply of meat, as my men had not yet overcome the stupid Swahili prejudice against eating elephant meat, though they did eventually when they got nothing else. I was much inclined to move up on to the Lorogi range, where there are extensive forests of the kind called by the Ndorobos "Subugo" (a name applied to all similar high, damp forest tracts), and several times told my native friends I wanted them to guide me there. They did not refuse, but always tried to dissuade me and evidently disliked the idea, their principal objections being the cold and wet. One headman and particular friend of mine expressed the hardship he would think it to have to go there, by asking – "If I had a donkey" (he did not add "what wouldn't go") "would I take him to the Subugo?" So, as during the whole of my stay in the district the mountains were almost continually enveloped in cloud, I concluded their advice was good; for not only would the climate be extremely unpleasant, but the elephants only frequent these cool, swampy forests, when, through drought, water is very scarce elsewhere. Moreover, I had already made one mistake, against their advice, in going to Nyiro mountain. I therefore only went across the Leseya (or Seya) River (one day's march); and I did but little good there, only once finding any elephants, on which occasion I came across four cows, three of which I killed. While there I was very nearly caught in one of the fall-traps we frequently came across in that part (the El Bogoi Ndorobos never set them). I was walking along a path, with my eyes on a spoor which led in that direction, when suddenly my forehead came in contact with a cord stretched across it, and, looking up, I saw the murderous harpoon in its heavy shaft hanging right above my head. Luckily the owners do not set them "tickle", lest the wind should set them off, and I had not pressed the string hard enough to release the impending javelin.

The little river Seya, which drains the Lorogi range, afforded clear proof of the quantity of rain that was falling on the tops, being very full all the time. It is curious that none of the water from all the country north of the Jambeni hills finds its way to the sea, but is poured into swamps or lakes, with no outlet. The Seya runs into such a swamp, near the Matthews range, called El Gereh.

I had a fair amount of success during the whole of this month; but it would be tedious were I to recount all the details of every day's hunt. I will, however, add the particulars of the killing of one or two of my big bulls; for I was lucky enough to get several fine old fellows with heavy tusks. I was back again in the neighbourhood of El Bogoi, the two headmen of that district (my particular friends) having come after me to report that another large herd had appeared; and as I had had but indifferent success where I had gone after leaving there, I was ready to go with them at once. The first day I was unsuccessful, getting only an indifferent chance and failing to bag the elephant I shot at, though, oddly enough, I killed the same one on a subsequent occasion.

I was having my early breakfast the morning after this disappointing day, when three Ndorobo lads came to say one of them had heard elephants quite near. I got ready at once and went with them; and we had only gone a comparatively short way from my temporary camp (which was then right under the mountain, in a little open valley, the wide expanse of scrub stretching away in all directions below) when we heard the elephants. The breeze being happily favourable for once, I got up close without much difficulty, and made out two or three enormous bulls standing together. One faced me, another, whose tusks (from the glimpse I got) seemed as good, stood broadside on. By great good luck I could see the vulnerable part of his ribs, just behind his shoulder, through a little opening among the leaves, etc., and was able to get a shot by kneeling. Following, as they disappeared instantly after I fired, there was just a colour of blood (a very spot or two only); and, though I felt positive my aim had been true, I began to fear another failure. But, just after, he was heard ahead, and a little way on we came up to him standing in a little bare place. I gave him two more shots and he toppled over. Rushing up, we cut off his tail, and I had just brushed past his hind legs and pointed out my first shot (right over the heart), when he got on to his legs again and we cleared out of his way sharp. Getting the "cripple-stopper", I gave him a couple more shots, but they were unnecessary; for, though so huge a beast takes some time to die from a tiny pellet of a bullet, he could not move away from where he stood, and, after swaying and tottering some time, he fell over again with a great crash, fairly bounding up again on to his stern, like a ship going down with its bows in the air; sitting up, as it were, for a moment, his huge head and tusks aloft, before collapsing to rise no more. A truly gigantic beast! What a little pop-gun my rifle appeared to such monsters. The skin of his back was like the bark of some great tree: all hard, scaly lumps, as is that of a big old crocodile. I measured him as accurately as I could and copy the entry as follows:– "He measured fully 10 ft 8 or 9 in high at shoulder by tape; 14 ft long from root of trunk to root of tail; circumference of fore foot 5 ft; his body 5 feet 6 in deep, from ground to highest part of side as he lay."[1] His tusks were massive but not very long (they weighed between 70 and 80 lbs apiece), – a well-earned reward for much hard work. I followed the others (five or six monsters) and got near them once more, but the wind again baulked me, and I had to be satisfied for that day.

The following day I did not hunt, but went early to get the tusks of the bull out and carried to camp. I often here left them for some days, when they would come out quite easily without chopping; but, as I intended leaving soon, I chopped these out at once. Though it was still quite early, the Ndorobos had already cut up the whole of the upper half of the huge mass. They were swarming all around; the bush was full of them and covered with meat cut into strips or piled in junks. They had made fires all about; and eating and work were going on everywhere. The next day's hunt is the last of which I shall, at present, give a description; for any one who may have had sufficient endurance to follow my prowlings in the bush so far, must by this time have had enough of elephant-hunting for a while.

I was off again, then, at dawn as usual, with two Ndorobo youths as well as, of course, my usual attendants. The latter are three: "Squareface", my principal gun-bearer, who carries the double .577 Juma, the second ditto, carrying the "cripple-stopper", and "Smiler"

---

[1] This was immediately after death and before he had become distended by the gases generated in the stomach.

(properly Ismail or Ishmael), with an axe and sundry other trifles. The last I always leave some distance behind when approaching game, as well as any surplus natives, and when going right up to my shot, the others wait too until I fire. On the way towards the Bogoi valley we found fresh spoor, and the rolls of chewed fibre the elephants are always spitting out when on the feed. That is to say, such is their habit in this part of the country, where their chief food is the plant called "mkongi" by the Swahili. Being, unfortunately, no botanist, I do not know what it really is; but I call it vegetable bayonets. It is just like a bunch of green bayonets springing out of the ground, with points as sharp as real ones and capable of giving most painful wounds to any one who unwarily runs against one slanting towards him. The bush is full of this plant, and the elephants chew it and reject the fibre; consequently the ground in their haunts is often strewn with it, more or less dry according to the time that has elapsed since its juice was partaken of. When it is green and moist, and smells quite sweet, it is freshly chewed; after a little exposure it gets sour. The fibre of this plant is very strong, and makes excellent cord or rope. I have often thought that it might be turned to profitable account in places where it grows in great profusion near enough to the coast, as, for instance, on the Sabaki River.

On reaching the edge of the broad, nearly level valley, we ascended a little prominence to get a view over it. A good deal of this scrub is not very high, so that if one can get on to a rise, or even sometimes into a tall tree (though such are not many in this kind of cover), and look down upon the jungle, it is often possible to see the tops of elephants' heads and backs, which the owners make more conspicuous by throwing dust from the red ground over them. Sometimes, even though the animals themselves may be invisible, a little cloud of red dust may every now and then be seen, like a puff of smoke, issuing from the bush. In the present instance we were inspired with hope by making out the raddled heads and slowly flapping enormous ears of two big bulls in the jungle across by the valley. Worming our way down through the dense thicket, we crossed the little stream and followed up a little dry gully on the other side, near which, farther up, one of the elephants (they were some distance apart) was standing. I got up to him beautifully, without his knowing of my approach, as he stood fanning himself with his windmill sails, as is their wont when resting. I got a nice shot at his side at close quarters; but, owing to only a bit of him being visible and the necessity of making the best of such chances as it is possible to get in such thick cover, I was not able to put the bullet quite so close up behind the shoulder as it should be for an ideal shot. For an elephant's stomach seems to me to come farther forward towards his chest cavity than does that of most animals; so that, if the shot is a trifle too far back, not only the heart but the lungs may be easily missed. However, I felt sure this was not so far aft as to allow the latter organs to escape. The grunt he gave also sounded confirmatory of my belief, and this was borne out by a little frothy blood on his retreating spoor. Feeling that he was sure to succumb soon to this wound, and being anxious to go after the second bull (both were huge beasts), I did not follow the spoor of the wounded one beyond a few steps, but, leaving him to be sought for afterwards, turned my attention to his mate. I may add that I did recover him all right, though not that day. He was found dead by my Ndorobo friends not far from my camp, straight towards which he had, curiously enough, made. He had only one tusk. Single tusks are commonly reported to be usually very large; but this was no heavier than an ordinary large bull's tooth (weighing 75 lbs). I examined the skull, and found he never had a second, as there was no socket on the other side.

But to come back to my day's hunt. My Ndorobo lads were very lukewarm and disinclined to go on, their hearts being with the meat at their kraals; and, finding the other bull had moved on, it was not without some persuasion that I got them to go on, though I was determined to follow, whether or no. However, they came, and I was glad of it, as they were useful, knowing the country intimately and being somewhat better spoorers and much quicker of hearing (an important qualification) than my own men. On catching the faintest sound of an elephant blowing, or a slight rustling of branches, they will at once fix the exact place whence the sound, very likely inaudible to other ears, proceeds. The second bull had gone over the rise bordering the valley on the north, and, on reaching the top, we turned off a little to the right of the spoor to ascend a small koppie. The bush was here too tall and leafy to allow of anything being seen; but, after listening a little while, my Ndorobo companions heard him. Being too near the wind, we made back and came cautiously up it, after a circuit to the left, instead of following the spoor again. Having arrived near the spot where he had been heard, we waited again for another sign, and so long was it without his making a sound, that we almost came to the conclusion he must have winded us when on the koppie and gone on; but I persisted in proceeding with the greatest care until we should again cut his spoor, and before we had advanced many steps farther we all heard him blow distinctly quite close ahead. Motioning my attendants to remain there, I picked my steps gingerly on, intensely on the look-out, but could not see him until I got within a very short distance, when a little open track in the bush showed me his huge hind-quarters towards me. This being the only opening to leeward, I came up behind him, and stood within a distance I had time to deliberately calculate to be no more than five paces from his tail. To the right I dared not go, on account of the wind; to the left the jungle was dense. There was nothing for it but to wait.

Now there is a curious contrast in the aspect at close quarters presented respectively by the two ends of an elephant, apart from the obvious difference in the moral effect on the hunter according to which extremity is towards him. When viewed from the rear there is a comically clownish, baggy-breeched, knock-kneed look about his drooping hinder parts; while a front view of his majestic head, armed with gleaming tusks and furnished with a far-reaching supple trunk, and set off by the grotesque great ears, outstretched as if to catch any suspicious sound – all raised aloft on colossal fore quarters, so that the top of his massive forehead may be not less than 11 ft from the ground – is as singularly impressive and awe-inspiring. I had now an opportunity of observing these two effects. The wind died away as I waited, hoping he would move of his own accord so as to give me a chance to shoot. I silently plucked a bit of grass; the fragments floated down with a tendency very near his direction. Sure enough just after he got a whiff; for he suddenly moved forward three or four yards across a little bare space ahead of him, wheeled round and stood facing diagonally half towards me, his head up, trunk raised and ears out, all on the alert, the opposite of his previous sleepy attitude. I knew he would be off now, so instantly aimed at his chest, in front of his left shoulder, which was towards me, and pulled both triggers together. I had made up my mind to try this the next chance I got at one of these huge bulls, after failing to stop the one that morning. The gun gave me a smart kick in the face, but the elephant went off with very suggestive grunts and I felt I had given him a good shot. Following his track, we found a good deal of blood spattered about, and a very short way on one of my Ndorobo lads (who had come up with my gun-bearers after the shot) started to run for it, a sure sign he had caught sight of our elephant.

Advancing cautiously, I found him (the elephant) standing in a fairly open bit of straight path. His position being just what it had been (as regards me) when I first fired at him, I gave him another similar shot, though only one barrel this time. He did not move, except to slue a little more directly facing me. I was considering whether to give him the left barrel in his eye, his head being a little inclined to one side, and for that purpose took another step forward, when – this movement of mine having no doubt enabled him to make me out – he suddenly rushed at me. As there were not more than ten yards between us and he came straight for me at a quick run, there was no time for hesitation. There was luckily a little opening to my right; into this I slipped, crouching to be less readily noticed. "Squareface" was just behind me, and the elephant charged past me after him like a locomotive. He followed my example and dodged to one side into the bush, leaving Juma, who was clad in raiment "by way of being" white, in full view just in front of the enraged beast. (I never had to complain of my gun-carriers decamping in moments of emergency, as one so often hears travellers say their men do; on the contrary, I had oftener to reprove them for persisting in sticking close behind me, when I wanted to go on alone.) Juma, it afterwards turned out, foolishly ran straight along the path we had approached by, the bull within a few yards of him; but instantly the latter passed my retreat, I, having an eye over my shoulder and being only two or three yards off, had swung round and given him my left barrel in his ribs before he had got many yards beyond me. This, it would seem, changed his mind, or else his powers were becoming exhausted, for he turned back and retreated to a little farther than where he had stood before.

My men now came back to me, and I made Juma climb a little tree. He saw the bull, only some thirty yards off, standing in the jungle. I felt I must do something, but did not think myself bound to advance hurriedly upon him again in his present frame of mind, being sure he was dying. So I climbed the tree, in spite of thorns; but these were straight, and, being so much accustomed to the villainous hooked kind, one gets to despise such as comparatively harmless. Getting near its slender top, I could see the elephant staggering; and, while I looked, his hind legs gave; he backed into the curious sitting posture they often fall into when about to collapse; his head went up, and, throwing his trunk into the air, as it were in sign of defeat, he went over with a crash, and, after a few struggles, lay still. Going cautiously up, I found him dead. Another massive beast, hardly so colossal as the last, but with rather heavier ivory (84 lbs and 70 lbs). His back was not so rough as that of the other, and he was fatter; perhaps a somewhat younger animal. My three bullet-holes formed a triangle on his chest; two went through the heart.

ELEPHANT HUNTING IN EAST EQUATORIAL AFRICA
(Rowland Ward 1898)

Hunting Trip in the Mashuna Country

F. C. SELOUS

arly in May 1878, I again reached the Matabele country, but being in a very weak state of health, the result of long-continued semi-starvation, and the over-fatigue occasioned by having been obliged to walk day after day whilst suffering from repeated attacks of fever, it was not until August that I felt sufficiently strong to start upon another hunting trip; but towards the end of that month, having obtained permission of Lobengula to hunt during the remainder of the season in the Mashuna country, I at once prepared myself for the journey, intending to join, and if possible hunt in company with, my friends Messrs Clarkson, Cross, and Wood, who had left Gubulawayo in the preceding June.

On the 20th of August, in company with Mr Goulden (Mr Clarkson's partner), I made a start from the mission station of Inyati, taking the old hunting-road leading to the Northern gold-fields.

It was not until after crossing the Sangwe, Shangáni, and Vungo rivers – this latter was not many years ago infested by lions – that we found any game at all. On the morning of the 30th, however, shortly after crossing the last-named stream, I shot a tsessebe antelope – one of three – and trekking on again crossed the Gwelo, and reached the Gwenia just before sundown. Here we found the waggons of the well-known old Dutch hunter, Jan Viljoen. He, together with all the males of his party, consisting of one son and his two sons-in-law, was away hunting. So far, Mrs Viljoen informed us, they had met with very few elephants. Reports had come in, however, she told us, that the Englishmen (d – d Englishmen she would doubtless have called them had she been speaking to one of her own nationality) had been shooting well on the other side of Umfule. How I anathematised the illness which alone had prevented my being with them and sharing in their sport! The very day after old Viljoen and his party came here, five lions attacked and killed two pack donkeys belonging to him, which, through the carelessness of the herd, had been left out at night. The next morning the old man and his sons tackled the marauders, and amongst them killed a lioness, the others making good their escape into some reeds and long grass.

The following day we remained where we were to give our oxen a rest, so I took a ride up the river in the early morning, and shot two out of a small herd of sable antelopes.

Two days later, on September 2nd, and shortly before reaching the river Se-whoi-whoi, I came across a solitary old sable antelope bull, with a fine pair of horns, of which I wished to possess myself; but fortune willed it otherwise, for after making two bad shots, I eventually lost him amongst some stony hills and thick underwood. On my way back to the waggons I gave chase to some zebras, and shot two of them. Just before sunset next evening we reached the river Bembees, where we found a young Dutch hunter encamped with his wife and family. As yet he had shot nothing – I mean no elephants; but his Hottentot servant had bagged a fine cock ostrich, and the day after our arrival he shot another, also in good plumage. Between the Se-whoi-whoi and the Bembees I saw a great deal of eland spoor, some only a day old, but could not come across the animals themselves nor any spoor fresh enough to follow.

Between Bembees and Sebakwe, Goulden and I rode out to look for game, and meeting with a small herd of koodoo cows, he shot one. On our way back to the waggons we saw a fine cock ostrich, but as my horse was slow, and I was armed with a ten-bore rifle, I did not go after him. My friend, however, being mounted on a very fast pony, gave chase, and, in the ardour of pursuit, came foul of a thick thorn bush, which dragged him from the saddle and mauled him pretty generally, his face presenting the appearance of a man's who has just had a domestic squabble, or a severe encounter with a wild cat.

In the afternoon we trekked on to the Sebakwe river, which is only about eight miles distant from the Bembees, and into which it empties itself a few miles below the drift. At daylight on September 5, we crossed the Sebakwe, and after a four hours' trek reached a gully with some water-holes in it. In the evening, after inspanning, I rode on ahead of the waggons, and shot a tsessebe antelope.

Early next morning we reached the river "Umniati". The drift was very steep on both sides, but we managed to get through without much difficulty. Here I shot a water-buck. I also saw a herd of sable antelopes, and the fresh spoor of a white rhinoceros, beside that of a single elephant cow, not more than a day old. In the little rocky hills which here border the river, klipspringers are very plentiful.

The Umniati is one of the finest rivers that run northwards into the Zambesi from the watershed of the Mashuna country, and in many parts its large deep pools abound in hippopotami. In the hope of getting a shot at one, I walked several miles along the bank, crossing the river "Umgesi", which runs into it about two miles below the drift, but though I saw a great deal of spoor, some of it seemingly very fresh, I did not see any of the animals themselves. In the evening we trekked on again to the Umgesi, also a fine running stream of beautifully clear water. On the way Goulden shot a waterbuck ewe.

September 7th. – Reached "Gwazān", a little river, with some fine pools of water, into one of which my waggon capsized. Luckily, it being lightly laden and the ground soft, no material damage was done, so that after off-loading, we soon righted and pulled it on to firm ground again. During the morning's trek we had crossed elephant cow spoor of yesterday and the day before, and in the evening I rode out and saw more, only a day or two old. They seemed to pass backwards and forwards about here, between the "fly"-infested country to the north-west, and the hills on the southern side of the road, and had I not been anxious to push on and join my friends, I would have remained for a week or so where I was, and hunted well through the hills in the direction of "Intaba Insimbi" (the mountain of iron).

The following day we remained at Gwazān to give the oxen a rest, so Goulden and I rode out to look for elephant spoor, but saw none. Whilst returning to the waggons we came across a small herd of roan antelopes, one of which I shot. In the evening, seeing a herd of sable antelopes feeding down a valley not more than a mile from the waggons, we again saddled up and rode after them. I soon shot the best cow amongst them – her horns measured two feet eight inches along the curve – and then tried to bag the one bull that was with the herd – a fine old fellow, carrying a beautiful pair of horns. I gave him two good shots, and I could see the blood running from his nostrils; but he nevertheless managed to climb a steep, rocky hill, covered with thick underwood, and disappeared on the farther side. Up here I was obliged to lead my horse, and when I reached the top, of course the wounded antelope was out of sight. As the sun was down it was too late to follow his spoor, so I was forced to leave him. At dawn of day the next morning, I went back with my Kafirs to get the meat of the sable antelope cow, which we found untouched by either lions or hyænas. On my way back to the waggons I came across another solitary bull, and shot him. His horns, though very prettily curved, were small.

Just before sundown, as the waggons were trekking, a small herd of elands, whose spoor Goulden and I were following with the horses, winded us, and ran close past the waggons; one of them, a young bull, my driver knocked over.

The following morning, September 10, we crossed the river

Zweswe, and arrived after sundown at an encampment of Griqua hunters – the Neros – who have for many years earned a precarious subsistence in the interior by hunting elephants. That very day they had shot some close to their camp. It appeared that two of their Kafirs having gone out early to hunt, had come upon a large herd, which, when fired upon, ran straight to the Griqua encampment – out of the frying-pan into the fire, in fact. All hands then turned out, and between them – three Griquas and several Kafirs – they killed eight, all cows. This happened about midday, when we were at Zweswe drift, only seven or eight miles away. Had we only known what was going to take place, we might with the greatest ease have inspanned that morning, and come in for a share in the sport.

We heard from the Griquas that our friends had their permanent encampment on the river Umfule, only two waggon-treks from here. They said, too, that they had already shot a lot of elephants, nearly all fine bulls, and that on Sunday last, September 8, Messrs Clarkson and Wood rode right on to a large herd, and shot eight of them, all good bulls. Also that Mr Wood's foreman – that is, the man given him by the king as head man over his Kafirs – had been killed by an elephant a few days before.

We were now certainly getting amongst the elephants once more, and I hoped before long to renew my acquaintance with them.

As it was a bright moonlight night, we inspanned again about 10 p.m., and trekked on half-way to Umfule, and a couple of hours' ride the next morning brought us to our friends' encampment. They were all away, however, having left the previous day for the scene of the slaughter of the eight elephant bulls shot on Sunday last, as they intended to form another camp there and hunt from it, more to the north and east, in the direction of the river Hanyane.

Upon receipt of this news I determined to follow their waggon spoor, as I felt sure I should be able to overtake them before sundown; so, leaving directions with Goulden, who stayed behind, to send my waggon after me as soon as it arrived, I saddled up without delay. That morning, I forgot to mention, my dog caught a grys steinbuck, which, as far as I could judge, appeared to me to be identical with the grys steinbuck of the Cape Colony.

About midday, as I was riding quietly along the road, I espied a solitary old sable antelope bull, lying in the shade of a machabel tree, with a very fine pair of horns; so, dismounting, I stalked up to and shot him, and then taking the skin of his head and neck to preserve at the waggons, placed the skull and horns in a tree on the roadside, where my waggon-driver, I thought, could not fail to see them. He was a very old bull, and when in his prime must have had a magnificent pair of horns, for even as it was, though very much worn down, they measured three feet seven inches along the curve.

Late in the afternoon, while jogging quietly along, and just after crossing a little rivulet, I heard a shout, and saw three white men – at least three men wearing clothes and broad-brimmed felt hats – and several Kafirs, sitting on an ant-heap. Riding up to them, I found that, as I had already surmised, they were my old friends, Messrs Clarkson, Cross, and Wood, and right glad was I to meet them once again. Our hearty greetings over, I learned that the eight elephant bulls they had shot four days previously lay just beyond the next rise, and that the waggon was outspanned a little farther on, on the banks of a small stream, a tributary of the Umfule. My friends had just returned from an unsuccessful chase after a lion, which the Kafirs had seen feeding on one of the dead elephants. They had sighted him – a fine male; but he was too wary, and managed to make his escape in the long grass without offering a chance of a shot. Early the same day, too, Cross had severely wounded a fine leopard, which he first saw walking over the prostrate carcass of one of the elephants; but it too crept away in the grass, and, as the dogs would not take the spoor, he lost it.

We then walked back to the waggons, taking a look at the huge, and now swollen and stinking carcasses of the elephants. They were all fine bulls, and their sixteen tusks weighed from 30 to 55 lbs each.

That evening, over the camp fire, the forty odd elephants shot by my friends, since I had last seen them in the Matabele country, were killed over again. They had had nearly all their sport to the east of the river Umfule, near some Mashuna kraals, called "Matja-ung-ombe" (the hill of cattle). The chief of these kraals, "Situngweesa", is considered a very powerful "Umlimo", or god, by the Amandebele; and, unlike most other Mashuna chiefs, who are the victims of continual depredation, he is not only left in the quiet enjoyment of his own, but often receives presents of cattle, young girls, etc., from Lobengula. It is very probable, however, that his majesty – to use one of his own phrases – is only fattening this false priest, and that one day he will pounce down upon and massacre him and all his people, and take his cattle and the ivory, of which, it is said, he has a considerable store. This is only surmise; but even thus did "Umziligazi", his father, put to death, at one fell swoop, a whole bevy of Makalaka gods, to whom, up till that day, he had always shown great favour.

However, whatever may be the private thoughts and intentions of their chief, the great mass of his people believe implicitly in the power of this Mashuna god, and my friends found it expedient to pay the old fellow a visit, to obtain his gracious permission to go and "kill the elephants nicely", for, until they did this, their boys would only hunt in a listless, half-hearted sort of way, constantly saying, "What is the use of your hunting elephants in Situngweesa's country without first getting his permission to do so?" But when, by the help of presents, the old fellow's good word was obtained, and Wood's head Kafir had been given a long reed, with which, when they were on the spoor, he was to bring the elephants back on their tracks, by first pointing the way they had gone with the enchanted reed, and then drawing it towards him, they at once seemed changed beings and hunted with the greatest alacrity; and as, before my friends paid a visit to the seer, they had upon two or three occasions followed elephants without coming up with them, and were afterwards very successful, their belief in Situngweesa's power, and the efficacy of the enchanted reed, became more confirmed than ever.

It was whilst they were hunting at "Matja-ung-ombe" that Wood's head Kafir, a man named "Quabeet", from the town of "Inxoichin", was killed by an elephant. I give the story of this mishap as I heard it from Clarkson's own lips.

"Early in September, Messrs Cross and Wood having taken the waggon to some neighbouring kraals to buy corn, I rode out by myself, and crossing fresh elephant spoor, followed it, and at length came up with the animals themselves – nine bulls, one of them an enormous beast without tusks. As soon as I fired upon them the tuskless bull turned out and went off alone, and I thought I had done with him. The elephant I had first fired at only ran a short distance, and fell dead. Quabeet and another Kafir of Wood's, who carried a gun, wounded and pursued another bull, which also turned from the rest as soon as he was shot. This I noticed as I galloped after the herd. I had just killed my second elephant, and had lost sight of the others, when my gun-carrier, "Amehlo", came running up, pointing with his hand, and crying out, "Sir, sir! there goes another elephant un-wounded!" I did not see him at first, but after galloping through the forest for a short distance in the direction in which the boy pointed, I caught sight of him. As I did so, I heard an elephant trumpeting terrifically away to my left, and thought to myself that one of the Kafirs was being chased pretty smartly; however, I did not like to leave the elephant I was near, though had I known what was in reality taking place, I should most assuredly have done so. Well, I killed this third elephant, and then rode back to the one I had first shot, where I found all the Kafirs, with the exception of Quabeet. I then asked whom the elephant which had screamed so fearfully had been chasing, and the Kafir who had been with Quabeet said, "Oh, he was chasing me!" and began to relate what an escape he had had. I then asked him where he had last seen Quabeet, and he said that when he left him he was still running after the elephant they had first wounded, and that he himself had given up the pursuit because he had trodden on a sharp stump of wood and hurt his foot. We then returned to camp, and Quabeet not making his appearance at dark, we thought he must have missed his way, and would turn up the following day. Early next morning we returned to the elephants, and after chopping out the tusks, retraced our steps to camp, which we reached late in the afternoon. Quabeet was not there; the sun set, and night again shrouded the surrounding forest in darkness, and he was still absent. I now felt sure that some accident had happened to him, and only guessed too truly that the awful and long-continued screaming I had heard whilst I was engaged with my third elephant had been his death-knell. The boys, too, cross-questioned the Kafir who had been with Quabeet, and convicted him of lying. I now determined that on the morrow I would take the spoor of the tuskless bull, for to him I could not help attributing the catastrophe which I felt sure had happened, and as he had turned out by himself when I fired the first shot, I knew I should have no difficulty in doing so.

"At break of day I left camp, and riding straight to where I had shot the first elephant, took up the spoor of the tuskless bull, and had followed it for maybe two miles when I came to a place where he had stood under a tree amongst some dense underwood. From this place he had spun suddenly round, as the spoor showed, and made a rush through the bush, breaking and smashing everything before him. Fifty yards farther on we found Quabeet's gun, a little beyond this a few odds and ends of skin that he had worn round his waist, and then what remained of the poor fellow himself. He had been torn in three pieces; the chest, with head and arms attached, which had been wrenched from the trunk just below the breast-bone, lying in one place, one leg and thigh that had been torn off at the pelvis in another, and the remainder in a third. The right arm had been broken in two places and the hand crushed; one of the thighs was also broken, but otherwise the fragments had not been trampled on." There is little doubt that the infuriated elephant must have pressed the unfortunate man down with his foot or knee, and then twisting his trunk round his body wrenched him asunder. This feat gives one an idea of the awful strength of these huge beasts, and how powerless the strongest of men – even one of "Ouida's" heroes – would be, when once in their clutches.

By examining the spoor Clarkson found that when this elephant charged, Quabeet was following another – doubtless the one he had first wounded – and thinks that in all probability the poor fellow never saw the brute until it was close upon him; and this, I think, must have been the case, as it is astonishing how difficult it is to see an elephant when he is standing still amongst high and thick bush, especially if one's attention is engaged with something else.

Poor Quabeet! I knew him well, and a real good fellow he was. A Zulu by blood, he was born just before Umziligazi left Natal on his flight northwards, and was still quite a boy when he came to the Matabele country. In the rebellion of 1870, when the kraals of "Zwang Indaba" and "Induba" fought for Kuruman against the present king Lobengula, he took part with the rebels, and received several assegai wounds during the fierce hand-to-hand combat that ended in the defeat of his party. *Requiescat in pace.*

The day after I rejoined my friends we all rode out to look for elephant spoor, directing our course towards the "Hill of the Stump-tailed Bull", a large round mount which stands by itself, close to the junction of the Umbila and Umfule rivers, and forms a conspicuous landmark. On the summit of this hill, Wood told us, the veteran hunter Mr Hartley and his party shot, some years ago, an elephant bull with a stump tail, whence its rather curious name. At that time, he said, there was no tsetse fly on this side of the hill. We, however, caught some of these execrable insects upon our horses when still several miles distant from it, and had to make a hasty retreat in consequence. As we had been keeping a sharp look-out, we caught these flies – six altogether – as soon as ever they settled upon, and before they had time to stick our horses.

On our way back to the waggons we shot an eland bull and a wild pig, the latter in very good condition, and I may here say that in the opinion of most hunters there are few things more palatable than the flesh of a fat wild pig; his head baked to a turn forms a dish that an epicure would not despise. Upon reaching camp I found that my waggon had already arrived, having come on by moonlight.

My driver had, however, managed to miss the sable antelope's head that I had placed in a tree by the roadside, and it was owing to this circumstance that we killed a few elephants the following day, for, having sent two boys back at daydawn to get the horns, they returned running, soon afterwards, shouting out something whilst still a good way off. At first we thought there were lions after the horses, and seizing our rifles ran down to meet them; but it turned out that as they were following the waggon spoor they had seen a small troop of elephants, and so had hastened back to tell us. Of course we at once saddled up, and riding to where the boys had seen them took their spoor, and before long came up with the animals themselves, a small worthless lot of cows. Of these we shot the six largest.

The next day Messrs Wood and Cross rode back to the camp at

Umfule upon business, whilst Clarkson and I myself took a ride to the eastward, but saw no fresh elephant spoor.

September 16th – Messrs Wood and Cross having returned the previous evening, we determined, since we were getting no more fresh spoor, to inspan the waggons and trek over to the river Umbila. This we did, and reached the river by midday, where we were occupied during the afternoon in making a fresh camp. About here we saw a great deal of fresh rhinoceros spoor, principally that of the white species.

That evening we determined to leave the waggons the next morning, and take a round on horseback for ten days or so towards the north-east, as Wood, who had hunted this country years before, thought we should in all probability find elephants in the thick groves of mahobo-hobo (a tree bearing a very nice fruit, and only found, so far as I am aware, in the Mashuna country) which lie between the Umsengaisi and Hanyane rivers. Our preparations were soon made, and by an hour after daylight, on September 17, we were on the march, taking with us corn for the horses, and provisions for ourselves to last a fortnight.

We had scarcely forded the Umbila river when we crossed the fresh spoor of five or six elephant bulls, which we at once followed. It was about midday, and we were fast gaining upon them, when they took a turn and made straight for the "fly". As we had been all the morning upon the edge of the infested district, we now kept a sharp look-out, and it was not long before a "fly" was caught upon Clarkson's horse, which we killed, and then again took up the spoor, as Wood said the "fly" was not very numerous about here; and as we expected soon to come up with the elephants, we thought we might venture to follow them a little farther, keeping, of course, a sharp look-out all the time on our horses. It was shortly after this that the elephants we were following led us to the spoor of another large troop, also fresh. For some time the spoors were mixed, then that of the bulls turned to the left and again made for the "fly". Upon seeing this we resolved to leave the bulls – though we would far rather have shot them – and take the spoor of the troop, as it was leading us in a direction that would soon take us beyond the limit of the "fly". Shortly after making this turn we rode on to a black rhinoceros, the first animal we had seen that day. He honoured us with a hard stare, and then wheeling round trotted off, and disappeared in the bushes.

About 1 p.m. we off-saddled our horses for the first time that day, and had scarcely done so when three heavy shots, fired almost simultaneously, fell in the direction the spoor was taking, and at no great distance. Making sure it was some of Wood's Kafir hunters firing at the elephants we were following, we saddled up again, and cantered along the spoor, but, from the direction it took, soon found that the shots we had heard could not have been fired at the elephants. We now stuck to the spoor without a halt till about an hour and a half before sundown, when, fearing that it would get dark before we came up with them, we took our guns and galloped on, for the spoor was now becoming fresher every instant, and as the elephants were feeding nicely, easy to follow, by the machabel leaves alone, that lay scattered along the track.

I may here say that I was this day mounted on an old horse in very poor condition, which I had bought from Wood, my own having gone lame two days before, and that all our horses had been the livelong day under the saddle, and like ourselves had had no water. Well, we had cantered along the spoor for some distance, when we at last descried two elephants, stragglers from the main body, and then the herd itself. They were moving in a dense mass up a gentle incline on the farther side of a dry watercourse, and as the whole country about here is very sparsely wooded, we had a magnificent view of them. There must have been at least sixty or seventy, great and small, and a grand sight it was, and one not easily to be forgotten, to see so many of these huge beasts moving slowly and majestically onwards. However, as there was now but an hour of sunlight left, we could spare but little time for admiration, and so rode towards them, on murderous thoughts intent. We crossed the dry gully, and passed within a hundred and fifty yards of the two we had first seen, but they never appeared to take any notice of us. Just as we neared the herd, one of the biggest bulls turned broadside to us, and commenced plucking some leaves from a bush, offering a splendid shot, of which Clarkson was just going to take advantage, when he saw us, and wheeling round, ran off. As he did so, I noticed that he had a stump tail. The whole herd was now in motion. At first they ran in a compact body and at a surprising pace, raising a dense cloud of dust, and in the confusion one of them, half-grown, was knocked down, and must have been trampled on and half stunned, for he did not get on his legs until the herd had passed, and then at first ran back, away from his companions; but before long, finding out his mistake, wheeled about, and soon caught up to them again. We now galloped along, even with, and about one hundred yards to the side of the foremost of them, shouting and hallooing, and thus drove them round in a large circle, our object being to tire them before we commenced firing. Though I had killed many elephants, yet having always before this season hunted on foot in regions infested by the tsetse fly, I had had no experience with them on horseback, so, having been told by my friends on no account to dismount, but to shoot from the horse's back, as, in case of a charge, I should have no time to remount, I endeavoured at first to comply with their instructions; however, my horse, worse luck to him, would not stand, but as soon as I dropped the reins, always walked or trotted forwards, thus making it impossible to get a shot. Seeing that if this continued, I should never shoot an elephant at all, I determined to dismount; so, cantering up alongside of the foremost, I jumped off, and gave a young bull a bullet behind the shoulder as he came broadside past me. He only ran about a hundred yards, and then fell dead. After this I quickly killed two more with five shots – a fine cow and another young bull. The fourth I tackled, a bull with tusks scaling about five-and-thirty pounds, cost me six bullets, and gave me a smart chase, for my horse was now dead beat. I only got away at all by the skin of my teeth, as, although the infuriated animal whilst charging trumpeted all the time like a railway engine, I could not get my tired horse out of a canter until he was close upon me, and I firmly believe that had he not been so badly wounded he would have caught me. I know the shrill screaming sounded unpleasantly near.

Just as this bull fell, Wood and Cross came round with what remained of the troop, and I met and turned them back again. The poor animals were now completely knocked up, throwing water over their heated bodies as they walked slowly along, swerving first one way and then the other, as the cruel bullets struck them. A good many had turned out, and made their escape in twos and threes, and as we had been picking out all the best, there were now not many left worth shooting. My friends had fired away almost all their cartridges, but I had still thirteen left; for, owing to my horse refusing to stand, I had not commenced firing as soon as they. As the elephants were now only walking, and sometimes stood all huddled up together in a mass, offering splendid standing shots, I felt sure of killing three or four more with my remaining cartridges, and should doubtless have done so had it not been for an accident that befell me, which happened in this wise. – Having picked out a good cow for my fifth victim, I gave her a shot behind the shoulder, on which she turned from the herd and walked slowly away by herself. As I cantered up behind her, she wheeled round, and stood facing me, with her ears spread, and her head raised. My horse was now so tired that he stood well, so, reining in, I gave her a shot from his back between the neck and the shoulder, which I believe just stopped her from charging. On receiving this wound she backed a few paces, gave her ears a flap against her sides, and then stood facing me again. I had just taken out the empty cartridge and was about to put a fresh one in, when, seeing that she looked very vicious, and as I was not thirty yards from her, I caught the bridle, and turned the horse's head away, so as to be ready for a fair start in case of a charge. I was still holding my rifle with the breech open, when I saw that she was coming. Digging the spurs into my horse's ribs, I did my best to get him away, but he was so thoroughly done that, instead of springing forwards, which was what the emergency required, he only started at a walk, and was just breaking into a canter, when the elephant was upon us. I heard two short sharp screams above my head, and had just time to think it was all over with me, when, horse and all, I was dashed to the ground. For a few seconds I was half stunned by the violence of the shock, and the first thing I became aware of, was a very strong smell of elephant. At the same instant I felt that I was still unhurt, and that, though in an unpleasant predicament, I had still a chance for life. I was, however, pressed down on the ground in such a way that I could not extricate my head. At last with a violent effort I wrenched myself loose, and threw my body over sideways, so that I rested on my hands. As I did so I saw the hind legs of the elephant standing like two pillars before me, and at once grasped the situation. She was on her knees, with her head and tusks in the ground, and I had been pressed down under her chest, but luckily behind her forelegs. Dragging myself from under her, I regained my feet and made a hasty retreat, having had rather more than enough of elephants for the time being. I retained, however, sufficient presence of mind to run slowly, watching her movements over my shoulder, and directing mine accordingly. Almost immediately I had made my escape, she got up, and stood looking for me with her ears up and head raised, turning first to one side and then to the other, but never wheeling quite round. As she made these turns, I ran obliquely to the right or left, as the case might be always endeavouring to keep her stern towards me. At length I gained the shelter of a small bush, and breathed freely once more.

All this time I never saw my horse, which must have been lying amongst the grass where he had been thrown to the ground. I thought he was dead, or perhaps, to speak more truly, I was so much engrossed with my own affairs that I did not think about him at all. I stood now just on the highest ground of a gentle rise, which sloped gradually down to an open glade, in which, from where I was, I could see two dead elephants. Just then I saw a Kafir coming across the opening, and went down to meet him, leaving my elephant still standing on the spot where she had knocked me down. Being unarmed, for my gun had been dashed from my hand when I fell, I dared not go near her to look for it. Upon meeting the Kafir (Cross's gun-bearer) I hastily told him what had happened. The elephant was not now visible, being just beyond the crest of the rise, about two hundred yards distant, but I only stopped to take some cartridges from my trousers' pockets and put them in my belt, and then, accompanied by the boy, returned to the scene of the accident to look for my rifle and see what had become of my horse. On topping the rise, we saw him standing without the saddle, but the elephant had walked away, and was no longer visible. Going up to my horse, I found that he had received an ugly wound in the buttock from behind, from which the blood was streaming down his leg: otherwise, barring a few abrasions, he was unhurt. Whilst the boy was searching for my rifle, I looked round for the elephant, which I knew had only just moved away, and seeing a cow standing amongst some bushes not two hundred yards from me, made sure it was the one that had so nearly made an example of me. The Kafir now came up with my rifle and saddle, the girth of which was broken. The rifle having been open at the breech when it fell to the ground was full of sand, so that it was not until I had taken the lever out, using the point of the Kafir's assegai for a screwdriver, that I managed to get it to work. I then approached the elephant, which all this time had been standing where I first saw her, and cautiously advancing to within fifty yards of her, took a careful aim, and gave her a shot behind the shoulder, which brought her to the ground with a crash. Pushing in another cartridge, I ran up and gave her a shot in the back of the head to make sure of her.

The sun had been down some time, indeed it was fast becoming dusk, so I shouted to attract the attention of my friends, whose shots I had not heard for some time past. I immediately heard an answering halloo, and soon met Clarkson, and walked back with him to a large ant-heap, where my comrades had off-saddled. I now found that my eye was bruised, and all the skin rubbed off my right breast, and I felt very stiff in the neck and down the back. I was smeared all over with blood, too, off the elephant's chest, on the back and on the left breast. This was all that was the matter with me, and a most wonderfully lucky escape I think it was. The elephant must have rushed against the horse from behind like a battering ram, throwing me head-foremost to the ground, and the impetus of her rush must have carried her a little too far, for had I been in front of her knees, instead of behind them, nothing could have saved me. I think, too, that she was very severely wounded, and that this desperate charge must have so exhausted her that she let me escape more easily than she would otherwise have done: perhaps this, too, accounts for her not further molesting the horse.

It was now almost dark; neither our horses nor ourselves had had a drink all day, and we did not know where we should find water, so we resolved to make for the Umsengaisi river, from which Wood did not think we were far distant; it was not, however, until we had had a weary tramp of two hours or so in the dark that we at length reached it. Just where we struck it, the river was dry; but after following down its course for about a mile, we found a rather muddy water-hole, which was nevertheless most acceptable under the circumstances. Having neither food nor blankets with us, we built a large fire, and proceed to make ourselves as comfortable as we could.

Early the following morning we went to count and examine the dead elephants. I led my horse with me, after having washed his wounds well with cold water, intending to send him back to the waggons at the Umbila river as soon as my boys came up, for of all our Kafirs that had started with us the preceding morning, my friends' three gun-carriers were the only ones that had kept up with us, which was nothing to their discredit, as they were all carrying loads. The elephant's tusk had entered my horse's buttock near the anus, running obliquely into the rectum; I had it syringed out morning and evening with strong carbolic lotion, and although for some time the poor beast seemed in a very precarious condition, in two months from then the wound had quite healed up, and he had entirely recovered from its effects. When we reached the dead elephants we found our Kafirs already there, and so made breakfast on the spot, and then proceeded to count the slain. We found altogether twenty-one dead elephants, two of them having but one tusk each. We afterwards picked up another which had gone away and died near the Umsengaisi, so that twenty-two in all had fallen to our rifles. I then sent two Kafirs to the waggons with my wounded horse, telling them to bring the one I had left there lame, back with them as quickly as possible. The Mashunas now commenced to arrive in large parties, eager for the meat, which we gave them on condition that they should chop out all the tusks, and carry them to the waggons at the Umbila river. The following day by noon all the tusks were out, and every elephant cut up. There had been no big bulls amongst this herd, but there were three whose tusks weighed from 35 lbs to 45 lbs each, and the forty teeth together must have scaled about 700 lbs. The last elephant which I had shot under the impression that it was the one which had caught me and struck my horse, turned out to be a cow that Cross had wounded just above the eye; seeing her so near the horse and so near to where I had left my elephant only a minute or so before, I naturally made the mistake.

Thus the elephant that had so signally discomfited me had gone off, though only to die, I am afraid, at no great distance, for the two shots I gave her were both good ones, which she could not long survive. I would have followed her spoor, as I should much have liked to possess myself of her tusks as a memento of the day's hunt; but as we had driven the elephants all round about in every direction, it was impossible to pick out the tracks of any particular one.

The following morning my boys returned from the waggons,

bringing with them my other horse. His lameness had been caused by a stump of wood sticking into the quick of the off hind hoof, and the place being not yet quite healed up, I extemporised a shoe, made from the outside skin of an elephant's ear, lacing it up to a piece of soft leather fastened loosely round the fetlock. This shoe put on wet overnight used to dry hard to the shape of the foot by morning, but I had to renew it every other day, as the horse's weight soon wore it through.

On the 20th we again found fresh spoor, in a thick grove of mahobo-hobo trees, and followed it a long way, but the elephants eventually got our wind, having doubled back parallel to their track, and when we found this out they had already got a long start, and although we galloped after them, we could not hold the spoor well, and at last lost it altogether.

The following day we got fresh spoor once more, and again lost it in much the same way. The elephants in this country are too clever by half; for instance, these last, as soon as they scented us, instead of running in a body, as any decent, sober-minded elephants would have done, in which case we might have galloped on their spoor, scattered in all directions, in ones, and twos, and threes. In trying to follow them we got separated, and Wood and I, after hallooing in vain for our friends, made for our camp on the Umsengaisi, thinking they would do the same.

We were riding along an old footpath, through a patch of leafless bush, when I saw some large black objects that I at first thought were buffaloes, but very soon made out to be elephants. We were about eighty yards from them when the foremost saw us, and was breaking into a run when Wood pulled in his horse, and with a bullet from his eight-to-the-pound rifle bowled her over in her tracks. He afterwards shot another, and I also killed two. There were only eight of them – a tuskless cow, and seven others not full grown. Elephants are, however, now so scarce, that one cannot afford to leave even smallish ones alone. Directly Wood fired, they all scattered, and as the bush was rather thick, we could not drive them together again. Just as the last fell dead, Messrs Clarkson and Cross came galloping up, and our Kafirs followed soon after, all having heard and been guided by our shots. Finding water in a valley close to the dead beasts, and having our blankets and other traps with us, we camped on the spot, and spent the following day, Sunday, in idleness, whilst our Kafirs were engaged in chopping out the tusks.

A HUNTER'S WANDERINGS IN AFRICA
(Macmillan 1881)

Elephant Hunting in German East Africa

JAMES SUTHERLAND

ome years ago, I was hunting in that wild tract of country that lies between the Lehombero and Luwegu Rivers in German East Africa, and had pitched my camp quite close to Jumbe Iperie's village, a mere cluster of huts buried in the heart of the pori. One day, when I was taking a rest after a particularly arduous period of work, some natives of the village appeared before my tent and piteously begged me to come and kill an elephant that had for years been raiding their shambas or gardens. Nor was theft the only crime they imputed to him; he had, they said, killed several of the villagers, including three native hunters, and all attempts to destroy him or drive him away from the district had proved utterly fruitless. Indeed, so well known was he to them that they had given him the name of Kom-Kom, or, the Mighty One. With that love of mystery to which the native mind is prone, they had come to the conclusion that Kom-Kom was the reincarnation of one of their famous chiefs, who in the days gone by had been murdered by the Wangoni. Now his restless spirit had taken up its abode in the form of an elephant and was avenging the wrongs he had suffered during his existence in human shape. Furthermore, they told me that during the day Kom-Kom roamed where man seldom trespassed, deep in the heart of the Lerongie jungle and, at night, came forth to plunder their crops and instil terror into their hearts. Even the women were afraid to go and draw water from the stream that flowed near their huts, and so greatly had the reputation of Kom-Kom grown that the inhabitants of Nagoromenia's Kraal, which lay some thirty miles from Iperie's village, lived in perpetual dread of him.

Apart from the question of doing a public service, I was in quest of ivory, and it was immaterial to me whether that ivory was Kom-Kom's or not, so, informing the native messengers that I should make an effort to rid them of the inconsiderate spirit of their former chief, I dismissed them.

Next day, as soon as it was light, we set out for Nagoromenia's

Kraal. As we tramped through the bush, our clothes, soaked with the heavy dew that distils on the long grass and vegetation during the cool of an African night, clung uncomfortably to our limbs, and it was with a feeling akin to joy that we greeted the sunrise with its cheering warmth.

In the forenoon, we came across the spoor of a herd of elephants and after an exciting chase managed to bag two of them, but the natives of Iperie's village, some of whom had accompanied me, were emphatic in their declaration that neither of these animals was Kom-Kom. Lunch came as a welcome relief to the toil of the chase, and, having rested awhile, we set out for the Lerongie jungle to see if we could come in touch with the Mighty One. Passing through Nagoromenia's Kraal on our way, we reached Iperie's village and there learned that Kom-Kom had visited the natives' matama gardens on the previous night and had committed havoc among the crops. The owners of the shambas were in great distress over the loss, so we decided to pass the night in their village in the hope that the elusive marauder would revisit this convenient feeding ground under cover of darkness and leave us a fresh spoor by which to track him down on the morrow. The night, however, passed uneventfully; not a sound came from the shambas to indicate the presence of a feeding elephant, and, as the natives explained, next day, he had probably dreamt that we were in search of him and had wisely decided not to make our acquaintance.

Next morning, at break of day, we started out in quest of Kom-Kom and towards eight o'clock had the good fortune to find his tracks of the previous night. A thrill of excitement ran through our party at the discovery, and it was with an additional stock of eagerness and energy that we began to follow his spoor. By noon, we had considerably lessened the distance which separated us from our quarry; his droppings were comparatively fresh and the condition of the leaves of a nquangwa tree that he had smashed to browse upon clearly indicated that he had only preceded us by a very brief space of time. Consequently, we continued our pursuit with redoubled caution, and were making our way in almost breathless silence when the sudden, sharp snap of a breaking tree warned us that he could not be more than fifty yards ahead. Yet the bush formed so dense a curtain of foliage about us that it was impossible to catch the slightest glimpse of him, and knowing the risks incurred under such conditions I bade my tracker, Simba, who had been carefully spooring in front of me, fall behind. (This order I always give when in close proximity to our quarry.) Having taken his place, I was warily advancing, rifle in hand, when, all at once, there came to our ears the sound of an elephant crashing and smashing headlong through the bush. There was no mistaking what had occurred: Kom-Kom, having got a sniff of our tainted air, had instantly made off at a tremendous pace. We followed in hot pursuit and what a dance he led us, through the long jungle grass under the rays of a broiling sun! On all sides the upupu, or itching buffalo bean, twined among the tall grass and every accidental contact with the latter sent the dark green velvety hairs that clothe the bean-pods in showers upon our bare arms, legs, necks, and faces. As there is no method of alleviating the insufferable itching produced by these hairs, except by rubbing the affected parts with wood ashes, an impossible procedure at such a critical juncture, we had simply to endure the irritation in silence and trudge stubbornly on, buoyed up with the knowledge that we were after Kom-Kom, the Mighty One. At length, having thoroughly tired us, he entered a dense patch of entangled vegetation and began to double and redouble on his tracks, using every wile to throw us off the spoor that frequent hunting at the hands of native ivory collectors had taught him. When an elephant begins to double and redouble on his tracks, he assuredly means mischief, and feeling that Kom-Kom would prove no exception to this rule, we moved forward with the greatest circumspection. Confident that we were close upon him, we stopped for a few moments and listened with strained ears for any noise that might indicate his whereabouts, but no sound broke the peaceful stillness of the jungle, save the gentle rustle of the breeze among the dense foliage. There now occurred an incident which would have proved a ludicrous anti-climax to the tenseness of the moment, had not the situation been so fraught with danger as to preclude any element of humour. Simba, in spite of a supreme effort to restrain himself, gave vent to a loud sneeze! At once, there was a shrill angry scream and Kom-Kom made a wild, impetuous rush at us from our rear. My trackers sprang nimbly out of his way, and I had barely time to turn, raise my rifle, and fire both barrels into his fast approaching face!

Fortunately for me, the smashing impact of the bullets sent him swerving aside, and for a few moments he came to a standstill, as if dazed, not more than fifteen yards away. Seeing that I had no time to reload my rifle, Simba, with the precision and coolness that are the result of good nerves and long training, instantly handed me my 10.75 mm, but it was well-nigh impossible for me to place a decisive shot, for, from where we stood, the only portion of Kom-Kom visible was his uplifted trunk, ceaselessly moving to and fro above the dense vegetation, apparently sniffing for our scent. Luckily, the Mighty One was to windward of us, and, as if uncertain of our whereabouts, turned and advanced slowly in our direction. Even now, I was quite unable to see him clearly, so judging the probable location of his forehead, I fired once more, but the bullet, instead of stopping or turning him, only served to rouse his anger, and, trumpeting shrilly, he dashed furiously in our direction. Hastily driving another cartridge out of the magazine into the breech, I fired full in his face, but as he came thundering on with lowered head, the bullet crashed into his skull several inches above the right eye. An instant afterwards he was upon us and I was hurled violently to the ground, slightly to the left, and half buried under a mass of broken branches and torn vegetation. It was a miracle that I wasn't trampled! The impetus of Kom-Kom's attack carried him about seven yards beyond where I lay, and at that distance he came to a standstill and began sniffing the air for a whiff of my scent, while I, concealed beneath the heap of débris, could clearly see every movement he made. At once, I groped about me for my rifle and discovered, to my intense joy, that it lay undamaged by my side. Eagerly grabbing it, I cautiously opened the bolt to eject the shell and jerked the last cartridge into the breech. At this juncture, Simba and Ntawasie, who had dodged into the bush seeing the elephant almost upon me, and imagining that I must be in a sore predicament, pluckily began yelling in the hope of distracting the animal's attention. The ruse was successful: like a flash, Kom-Kom turned and crashed in their direction. Seizing my opportunity, I quickly raised my rifle and sent the remaining bullet into the vicinity of his lungs, and though not fatal, the shot had a salutary effect, for Kom-Kom immediately gave up the pursuit of my men and tore madly through the bush for some seventy yards to the left. My next move was so extricate myself and regain my feet. Ugh! how sore I felt! When I had fallen, a thick branch had struck me on the right side of my head, severely cutting me under the eye and scrubbing the skin off one side of my nose, while my left elbow, laid bare to the bone, was bleeding profusely and giving me considerable pain. These little mishaps, however, are incidental to the game of hunting and detract little from its joys, so rejoining my two men and exchanging my light for my heavy rifle, I at once decided to resume the pursuit of Kom-Kom. As the sun was now low in the heavens and the swiftly closing equatorial night not far distant, I began to view the situation with some uneasiness, for if I failed to bag Kom-Kom before dark, he might clear and his spoor get inextricably mixed up with those of other elephants. Such a contingency might end in our losing him altogether and prove a disheartening conclusion to a most arduous hunt.

The scantiness of the blood-spoor accentuated my fears on this score, for had the second bullet, which had entered his skull above the right eye, merely passed through the upper portion of his forehead without touching his brain, days would probably elapse ere he succumbed to the effects of his wounds.

As we were now to windward of him, a change of tactics was imperative, so instead of following his spoor we decided to make a detour. Here the bush presented a formidable obstacle to our progress, twigs and grass and creepers forming such a bewildering network of growth that we were obliged to crawl on hands and knees, taking care to sever the interlacing stems and branches silently with our knives lest we should give our quarry any warning sound of our advance. Scratched by thorns and cramped by this uncomfortable method of progression, we at length managed to approach within twelve yards of Kom-Kom. Though still unable to see him, we could hear the occasional flapping of his enormous ears, and feeling that any attempt at a closer approach would apprise him of our presence, we decided to remain perfectly still for a while and await developments. A few minutes afterwards, we heard the snapping of twigs and branches as he pushed his way for another fifty yards through the thicket, and hurrying to the spot which he had just vacated, we began most cautiously to follow the path which his bulky body had cleared through the matted jungle. Quietly as we had advanced, he must have heard some faint rustle of our movements (unless some treacherous eddy of air had borne him our scent), for, all at once, he turned, came back several yards on his tracks, and stood intensely still. Hoping to get a shot at him at an angle, we stole some distrance towards the right, moving the branches aside as gently as possible and taking infinite care not to break any dry twigs underfoot. At this point, the intervening bush was considerably sparser and enabled us to obtain a fairly good view of Kom-Kom who, we found, was standing absolutely motionless, with ears outstretched, intently looking back on the path which he had just made. There was something magnificent and statuesque about his whole pose as he waited there ready to give battle should his pursuers come into view. Finding that I could get an unobstructed view of his head from where I stood, I raised my rifle, and carefully judging the angle to his brain, pressed the trigger. The bullet smashed into his skull close to his ear-hole and brought him down with a stupendous crash, his head and tusks being entangled in the tough ropes of the creepers. Kom-Kom the Mighty One was no more! I raised the cry: Socolai! Socolai! (It is finished! It is finished!) and instantly my trackers repeated the exultant yell. It rang deep and sonorous through the silence of the forest and far away it was faintly echoed by my men and some villagers who were following us up: Socolai! Socolai!

Rolled up in our blankets, we passed the night in the forest not far from where Kom-Kom lay dead. From my rough couch, I could see our camp fires throwing mysterious shadows into the luxuriant tropical foliage; through the leaves above my head, shone here and there a bright star. But the beauties of nature appeal but little to a tired man and, ere long, in spite of the discomfort of a cut face and torn elbow, I had slipped into sound slumber.

Early next morning, villagers of both sexes and all ages arrived *en masse* on the scene, and their joy knew no bounds when their eyesight convinced them that Kom-Kom, the source of so many of their troubles, was actually dead. To celebrate the occasion, they brought my men quantities of food, honey, and pombe, or native beer, and runners were hastily despatched to the surrounding villages bearing the glad tidings: "Kom-Kom is dead! Kom-Kom is dead!"

Alas! a most vexatious fly was to get into the ointment! This particular insect appeared during the morning, in the shape of a sinister-faced old medicine-man, whose superior mind at once discovered that the opinion of the vulgar herd on the subject of Kom-Kom's death had been hopelessly at fault. He announced that he was greatly displeased that I had killed the Mighty One, and declared that, instead of being a matter for rejoicing, it was a serious misfortune, for although Kom-Kom had killed a few villagers and helped himself to the produce of their gardens, this was an insignificant matter in comparison with the infinite good luck he had showered upon them in the shape of food and happy children, and success on their journeys into the forest in quest of beeswax, honey, and rubber. As for Kom-Kom's peccadilloes, well, a certain amount of moral latitude must always be granted to the spirit of a great chieftain! Finding that his audience were not going to allow themselves to be scared from the prospect of a royal feast on elephant meat by any vague mumbo-jumbo concerning the spirit of a departed chieftain, his astute mind took a delightfully ingenious turn. He all at once discovered that he could make a medicine which would set Kom-Kom's spirit to rest on the score of a hearty consumption of its erstwhile earthly home. Some hours afterwards, my boy Tumbo, whom I had brought home with me on this occasion, informed me that the old fellow had begged for a little salt (a scarce commodity in these regions), wherewith to flavour the concoction which was to prove a soothing syrup to Kom-Kom's wounded feelings. Rather curious as to the nature of this elixir, I strolled over to where he was busily engaged in some mysterious operation over a fire. To my surprise, I found that the old humbug, having made the medicine, was now toasting a newly-killed puff-adder on a spit. When he had thoroughly cooked this delicacy, he devoured it and washed it down with copious draughts of an evil-looking brew, which, my boy told me, he had prepared by boiling the bark of the mlæravana tree in water and seasoning the mixture with an addition of monkey-nut oil.

Next, he anointed himself all over with Kom-Kom's coagulated blood, and while the villagers stood gravely around, solemnly invoked the Mighty One not to be a bad elephant again. Either from a profound working acquaintance with the behaviour of spirits, or by message promptly received from the other world, he must have learned that the desired end had been achieved, for, immediately on the conclusion of this ceremony, he made a solid meal on Kom-Kom's toasted heart and energetically assisted his three wives to appropriate as much of the meat as they possibly could, after the manner of the most ordinary of mortals.

For such an exceptionally large elephant, Kom-Kom's tusks were comparatively small, only scaling 65 and 67 lbs respectively. There is no doubt that he had acquired his cunning at the expense of native elephant hunters, for he bore in evidence of the fact the scars of many old wounds inflicted by their bullets, seventeen of which missiles the natives found when cutting up his tough old carcase. He was also endowed with a characteristic which I have seen in no other elephant in all my hunting career; almost all the hairs of his tail were perfectly white. Occasionally, elephants' tails have a few white hairs, but even these cases are extremely rare. I have still in my possession Kom-Kom's singular extremity, and shall always keep it as a memento of a thoroughly enjoyable day's sport.

THE ADVENTURES OF AN ELEPHANT HUNTER
(MACMILLAN 1912)

ASIA

A Monster Crocodile

SIR SAMUEL BAKER

remember an accident having occurred at Madampi, on the west coast of Ceylon, about seven years ago, the day before I passed through the village. A number of women were employed in cutting rushes for mat-making, and were about mid-deep in the water. The horny tail of a large crocodile was suddenly seen above the water among the group of women, and in another instant one of them was seized by the thigh and dragged towards the deeper part of the stream. In vain the terrified creature shrieked for assistance; the horror-stricken group had rushed to the shore, and a crowd of spectators on the bank offered no aid beyond their cries. It was some distance before the water deepened, and the unfortunate woman was dragged for many yards, sometimes beneath the water, sometimes above the surface, rending the air with her screams, until at length the deep water hid her from their view. She was never again seen.

Some of these reptiles grow to a very large size, attaining the length of twenty feet, and eight feet in girth, but the common size is fourteen feet. They move slowly upon land, but are wonderfully fast and active in the water. They usually lie in wait for their prey under some hollow bank in a deep pool, and when the unsuspecting deer or even buffalo stoops his head to drink, he is suddenly seized by the nose and dragged beneath the water. Here he is speedily drowned and consumed at leisure.

The two lower and front teeth of a crocodile project through the upper jaw, and their white points attract immediate notice as they protrude through the brown scales on the upper lip. When the mouth is closed, the jaws are thus absolutely locked together.

It is a common opinion that the scales on the back of a crocodile will turn a ball; this is a vulgar error. The scales are very tough and hard, but a ball from a common fowling-piece will pass right through the body. I have even seen a hunting-knife driven at one blow deep into the hardest part of the back; and this was a crocodile of a large size, about fourteen feet long, that I shot at a place called Bolgoddé, twenty-two miles from Colombo.

A man had been setting nets for fish, and was in the act of swimming to the shore, when he was seized and drowned by a crocodile. The next morning two buffaloes were dragged into the water close to the spot, and it was supposed that these murders were committed by the same crocodile. I was at Colombo at the time, and, hearing of the accident, I rode off to Bolgoddé to try my hand at catching him.

Bolgoddé is a very large lake of many miles in circumference, abounding with crocodiles, widgeon, teal, and ducks.

On arrival that evening, the moodeliar (headman) pointed out the spot where the man had been destroyed, and where the buffaloes had been dragged in by the crocodile. One buffalo had been entirely devoured, but the other had merely lost his head, and his carcass was floating in a horrible state of decomposition near the bank. It was nearly dark, so I engaged a small canoe to be in readiness by break of day.

Just as the light streaked the horizon I stepped into the canoe. This required some caution, as it was the smallest thing that can be conceived to support two persons. It consisted of the hollow trunk of a tree, six feet in length and about one foot in diameter. A small outrigger prevented it from upsetting, but it was not an inch from the surface of the water when I took my narrow seat, and the native in the stern paddled carefully towards the carcass of the buffalo.

Upon approaching within a hundred yards of the floating carcass, I counted five forms within a few yards of the flesh. These objects were not above nine inches square, and appeared like detached pieces of rough bark. I knew them to be the foreheads of different crocodiles, and presently one moved towards the half-consumed buffalo. His long head and shoulders projected from the water as he attempted to fix his fore-claws into the putrid flesh; this, however, rolled over towards him, and prevented him from getting a hold; but the gaping jaws nevertheless made a wide breach in the buffalo's flank. I was now within thirty yards of them, and, being observed, they all dived immediately to the bottom.

The carcass was lying within a few yards of the bank, where the water was extremely deep and clear. Several large trees grew close to the edge and formed a good hiding-place; I therefore landed, and, sending the canoe to a distance, I watched the water.

I had not been five minutes in this position before I saw in the water at my feet, in a deep hole close to the bank, the immense form of a crocodile as he was slowly rising from his hiding-place to the surface. He appeared to be about eighteen feet long, and he projected his horny head from the surface, bubbled, and then floated with only his forehead and large eyes above the water. He was a horrible-looking monster, and from his size I hoped he was the villain that had committed the late depredations. He was within three yards of me; and, although I stood upon the bank, his great round eyes gazed at me without a symptom of fear. The next moment I put a two-ounce ball exactly between them, and killed him stone dead. He gave a convulsive slap with his tail, which made the water foam, and, turning upon his back, he gradually sank, till at length I could only distinguish the long line of his white belly twenty feet below me.

Not having any apparatus for bringing him to the surface, I again took to the canoe, as a light breeze that had sprung up was gradually moving the carcass of the buffalo away. This I slowly followed, until it at length rested in a wide belt of rushes which grew upon the shallows near the shore. I pushed the canoe into the rushes within four yards of the carcass, keeping to windward to avoid the sickening smell.

I had not been long in this position before the body suddenly rolled over as though attacked by something underneath the water, and the next moment the tall reeds brushed against the sides of the canoe, being violently agitated in a long line, evidently by a crocodile at the bottom.

The native in the stern grew as pale as a black can turn with fright, and instantly began to paddle the canoe away. This, however, I soon replaced in its former position, and then took his paddle away to prevent further accidents. There sat the captain of the fragile vessel in the most abject state of terror. We were close to the shore, and the water was not more than three feet deep, and yet he dared not jump out of the canoe, as the rushes were again brushing against its sides, being moved by the hidden beast at the bottom. There was no help for him, so, after vainly imploring me to shove the canoe into deep water, he at length sat still.

In a few minutes the body of the buffalo again moved, and the head and shoulders of a crocodile appeared above water and took a bite of some pounds of flesh. I could not get a shot at the head from his peculiar position, but I put a ball through his shoulders, and immediately shoved the canoe astern. Had I not done this, we should most likely have been upset, as the wounded brute began to lash out with his tail in all directions, till he at length retired to the bottom among the rushes. Here I could easily track him, as he slowly moved along, by the movement of the reeds. Giving the native the paddle, I now by threats induced him to keep the canoe over the very spot where the rushes were moving, and we slowly followed on the track, while I kept watch in the bow of the canoe with a rifle.

Suddenly the movement in the rushes ceased, and the canoe stopped accordingly. I leaned slightly over the side to look into the water, when up came a large air-bubble, and directly afterwards an apparition in the shape of some fifteen pounds of putrid flesh. The stench was frightful, but I knew my friend must be very bad down below to disgorge so sweet a morsel. I therefore took the paddle and poked for him; the water being shallow, I felt him immediately. Again the rushes moved; I felt the paddle twist as his scaly back glided under it, and a pair of gaping jaws appeared above the water, wide open and within two feet of the canoe. The next moment his head appeared, and the two-ounce ball shattered his brain. He sank to the bottom, the rushes moved slightly and were then still.

I now put the canoe ashore, and cutting a strong stick, with a crook at one end, I again put out to the spot and dragged for him. He was quite dead; and catching him under the fore-leg, I soon brought him gently to the surface of the water. I now made fast a line to his fore-leg, and we towed him slowly to the village, the canoe being level with the water's edge.

His weight in the water was a mere trifle, but on arrival at the village on the banks of the lake, the villagers turned out with great glee, and fastened ropes to different parts of his body to drag him out. This operation employed about twenty men. The beast was about fourteen feet long; and he was no sooner on shore than the natives cut him to pieces with axes, and threw the sections into the lake to be devoured by his own species. This was a savage kind of revenge, which appeared to afford them great satisfaction.

Taking a large canoe, I paddled along the shores of the lake with a shot-gun, and made a good bag of ducks and teal, and returned to breakfast. The fatness and flavour of the wild ducks in Ceylon are quite equal to the best in England.

There is one thing necessary to the enjoyment of sport in Ceylon, and without which no amount of game can afford thorough pleasure; this is personal comfort. Unlike a temperate climate, where mere attendance becomes a luxury, the pursuit of game in a tropical country is attended with immense fatigue and exhaustion. The intense heat of the sun, the dense and suffocating exhalations from swampy districts, the constant and irritating attacks from insects, all form drawbacks to sport that can only be lessened by excellent servants and by the most perfect arrrangements for shelter and supplies. I have tried all methods of travelling, and I generally manage to combine good sport with every comfort and convenience.

A good tent, perfectly waterproof, and of so light a construction as to travel with only two bearers, is absolutely indispensable. My tent is on the principle of an umbrella, fifteen feet in diameter, and will house three persons comfortably. A circular table fits in two halves round the tent-pole; three folding chairs have ample space; three beds can be arranged round the tent walls; the boxes of clothes, etc., stow under the beds; and a dressing-table and gun-rack complete the furniture.

Next in importance to the tent is a good canteen. Mine is made of japanned block tin, and contains in close-fitting compartments an entire dinner and breakfast service for three persons, including everything that can be required in an ordinary establishment. This is slung upon a bamboo, carried by two coolies.

Clothes must always be packed in tin boxes, or the whole case will most likely be devoured by white ants.

Cooking utensils must be carried in abundance, together with a lantern, axe, bill-hook, tinder-box, matches, candles, oil, tea, coffee, sugar, biscuits, wine, brandy, sauces, etc., a few hams, some tins of preserved meats and soups, and a few bottles of curacao, a glass of which, in the early dawn, after a cup of hot coffee and a biscuit, is a fine preparation for a day's work.

I once tried the rough system of travelling, and started off with nothing but my guns, clothes, a box of biscuits, and a few bottles of brandy – no bed, no pillow, no tent nor chairs or table, but, as my distressed servant said, "no nothing". This was many years ago, when the excitement of wild sports was sufficient to laugh at discomfort. I literally depended upon my gun for food, and my cooking utensils consisted of one saucepan and a gridiron, a "stew" and a "fry" being all that I looked forward to in the way of gourmandism. Sleeping on the bare ground in native huts, dining cross-legged upon mother earth, with a large leaf as a substitute for a plate, a cocoa-nut shell for a glass, my hunting-knife comprising all my cutlery, I thus passed through a large district of wild country, accompanied by B., and I never had more exciting sport.

It was on this occasion that I had a memorable hunt in the neighbourhood of Narlandè, within thirty miles of Kandy. It was our first day's stage, and, upon our arrival, at about 2 p.m., we left our guns at the post-holder's hut, while we proceeded to the river to bathe.

We were hardly dressed before a native came running to tell us that several elephants were devouring his crop of korrakan – a grain something like clover-seed, upon which the people in this part almost entirely subsist.

Without a moment's delay we sent for the guns. The post-holder was a good tracker, and a few minutes of sharp walking through a path bordered on either side by dense thorny bush brought us to a chéna jungle ground, or cultivated field. The different watch-houses erected in the large trees were full of people, who were shrieking and yelling at the top of their voices, having just succeeded in scaring the elephants into the jungle.

The whole of the country in this neighbourhood has, in successive ages, been cleared and cultivated: the forest has been felled. The poverty of the soil yields only one crop, and the lately cleared field is again restored to nature. Dense thorny jungle immediately springs up, which a man cannot penetrate without being torn to pieces by the briars. This is called chéna jungle, and is always the favourite resort of elephants and all wild animals, the impervious character of the bush forming a secure retreat.

From these haunts the elephants commit nocturnal descents upon the crops of the natives. The korrakan is a sweet grass, growing about two feet high, and so partial are the elephants to this food that they will invade the isolated field even during the daytime. Driven out by shouts and by shots fired by the natives from their secure watch-houses, they will retreat to their cover, but in a few minutes they reappear from another part of the jungle and again commence their depredations.

The havoc committed by a large herd of elephants can well be imagined.

In this instance there were only three elephants – a large bull, with a mother and her young one, or what we call a "poonchy". On entering the korrakan field we distinctly heard them breaking the boughs at no great distance. We waited for some time to see if they would return to the field; but they apparently were aware of some impending danger, as they did not move from their strong position. This was a cunning family of elephants, as they had retreated "down wind", and the jungle being so thick that we could with difficulty follow even upon their track, made it very doubtful whether we should kill them.

We cautiously entered. It was one mass of thorns, and we were shortly compelled to crawl upon our hands and knees. This was arduous work, as we had great difficulty in carrying the guns so as to avoid the slightest noise. I was leading the way, and could distinctly hear the rustling of the leaves as the elephants moved their ears. We were now within a few feet of them, but not an inch of their bodies could be seen, so effectually were they hidden by the thick jungle. Suddenly we heard the prolonged wh-r-r, wh-r-r-r-r, as one of the elephants winded us: the shrill trumpet sounded in another direction, and the crash through the jungle took place which nothing but an elephant can produce. In such dense jungle, where the elephants are invisible, this crash is most exciting if close at hand, as in the present instance. It is at the first burst impossible to tell whether the elephant is coming at you or rushing away. In either case it is extremely dangerous, as these chéna jungles are almost devoid of trees; thus there is no cover of sufficient strength to protect a man should he attempt to jump on one side, and he may even be run over by accident.

A few moments assured us of their retreat, and we instantly followed upon their track, running at full speed along the lane which they had crushed in their headlong flight. This was no easy matter; the jungle itself was certainly broken down, but innumerable hooked thorns, hanging from rope-like creepers, which had been torn down by the rush of the elephants, caught us upon every side. In a few minutes our clothes were in rags, and we were bleeding from countless scratches, but we continued the chase as fast as we could run upon the track. The prickly cactus which abounds in these jungles, and grows to the height of twenty feet, in some places checked us for a few moments, being crushed into a heap by the horny-footed beasts before us. These obstacles overcome, we again pushed on at a rapid pace, occasionally listening for a sound of the retreating game.

We now observed that the herd had separated; the bull had gone off in one direction, and the female with her half-grown poonchy in another. Following the latter, we again pushed on at a quick run, as the elephants had evidently gone off at a great pace and were far in advance. For about half an hour we had continued the pursuit at the same speed, when we suddenly heard the warning wh-r-r-r as the elephants winded us at a distance of 200 yds, and the crash instantly following this sound told us too plainly that the game was fearfully on the alert, and gave us little hopes of overtaking them, as they were travelling directly down wind.

Speed was our only chance, and again we rushed forward in hot pursuit through the tangled briars, which yielded to our weight, although we were almost stripped of clothes. Another half hour passed, and we had heard no further signs of the game. We stopped to breathe, and we listened attentively for the slightest sound. A sudden crash in the jungle at a great distance assured us that we were once more discovered. The chase seemed hopeless; the heat was most oppressive; and we had been running for the last hour at a killing pace through a most distressing country. Once more, however, we started off, determined to keep up the pursuit as long as daylight would permit. It was now 5 p.m., and we had one hour left before darkness would set in. The wind had entirely ceased, leaving a perfect calm; the air was thick and heavy, and the heat was thus rendered doubly fatiguing. We noticed, however, that the track of the elephants had doubled back instead of continuing in the direct line that we had followed so long. This gave us hope, as the elephants no longer had the advantage of the wind, and we pushed on as fast as we could go.

It was about half an hour before dusk, and our patience and hopes were alike exhausted, when we suddenly once more heard the wh-r-r-r of the elephants winding us within a hundred yards. It was our last chance, and with redoubled speed we rushed after them.

Suddenly we broke from the high jungle in which we had been for the last two hours, and found ourselves in a chéna jungle of two years' growth, about five feet high, but so thick and thorny that it resembled one vast blackthorn hedge, through which no man could move except in the track of the retreating elephants.

To my delight, on entering this low jungle, I saw the female at about forty yards' distance, making off at a great pace. I had a light double-barrelled gun in my hand, and, in the hopes of checking her pace, I fired a flying shot at her ear. She had been hunted so long that she was well inclined to fight, and she immediately slackened her speed so much that in a few instants I was at her tail, so close that I could have slapped her. Still she ploughed her way through the thick thorns, and not being able to pass her owing to the barrier of jungle, I could only follow close at her heels and take my chance of a shot. At length, losing all patience, I fired my remaining barrel under her tail, giving it an upward direction in the hope of disabling her spine.

A cloud of smoke hung over me for a second, and, throwing my empty gun on one side, I put my hand behind me for a spare rifle. I felt the welcome barrel pushed into my hand at the same moment that I saw the infuriated head of the elephant with ears cocked charging through the smoke! It was the work of an instant. I had just time to cock the two-ounce rifle and take a steady aim. The next moment we were in a cloud of smoke, but as I fired, I felt certain of her. The smoke cleared from the thick bushes, and she lay dead at *six feet* from the spot where I stood. The ball was in the centre of her forehead, and B., who had fired over my shoulder so instantaneously with me that I was not aware of it, had placed his ball within three inches of mine. Had she been missed, I should have fired my last shot.

This had been a glorious hunt; many miles had been gone over, but by great luck, when the wind dropped and the elephant altered her course, she had been making a circuit for the very field of korrakan at which we had first found her. We were thus not more than three miles from our resting-place, and the trackers who know every inch of the country, soon brought us to the main road.

The poonchy and the bull elephant, having both separated from the female, escaped.

One great cause of danger in shooting in thick jungles is the obscurity occasioned by the smoke of the first barrel; this cannot escape from the surrounding bushes for some time, and effectually prevents a certain aim with the remaining barrel. In wet weather this is much increased.

For my own part I dislike shooting in thick jungles, and I very seldom do so. It is extremely dangerous, and is like shooting in the dark; you never see the game until you can almost touch it, and the labour and pain of following up elephants through thorny jungle is beyond description.

On our return to the post-holder's hut we dined and prepared for sleep. It was a calm night, and not a sound disturbed the stillness of the air. The tired coolies and servants were fast asleep, the lamp burnt dimly, being scantily fed with oil, and we were in the act of lying down to rest when a frightful scream made us spring to our feet. There was something so unearthly in the yell that we could hardly believe it human. The next moment a figure bounded into the little room that we occupied. It was a black, stark naked. His tongue, half bitten through, protruded from his mouth; his bloodshot eyes, with a ghastly stare, were straining from their sockets, and he stood gazing at us with his arms extended wide apart. Another horrible scream burst from him, and he fell flat upon his back.

The post-holder and a whole crowd of awakened coolies now assembled, and they all at once declared that the man had a devil. The fact is, he had a fit of epilepsy, and his convulsions were terrible. Without moving a limb he flapped here and there like a salmon when just landed. I had nothing with me that would relieve him, and I therefore left him to the hands of the post-holder, who prided himself upon his skill in exorcising devils. All his incantations produced no effect, and the unfortunate patient suddenly sprang to his feet and rushed madly into the thorny jungle. In this we heard him crashing through like a wild beast, and I do not know to this day whether he was ever heard of afterwards.

THE RIFLE AND HOUND IN CEYLON
(Longman 1898)

Where is the Tiger?

SIR SAMUEL BAKER

ccording to my own experience, there can be no comparison in the sport of hunting up a tiger upon a good elephant in open country, and the more general plan of driving forest with guns placed in position before a line of beaters. By the former method the hunter is always in action, and in the constant hope of meeting with his game, while the latter method requires much patience, and too frequently results in disappointment. Nevertheless, to kill tigers, every method must be adopted according to the conditions of different localities.

Under all circumstances, if possible, a dependable elephant should be present, as many unforeseen cases may arrive when the hunter would be helpless in the absence of such an animal; but, as we have already seen, the danger is extreme should the elephant be untrustworthy, as a runaway beast may be an amusement upon grass-land, but fatal to the rider in thick forest.

The only really dependable elephant that I have ever ridden was a tusker belonging to the Commissariat at Jubbulpur in 1880; this fine male was named Moolah Bux. He was rather savage, but he became my great friend through the intervention of sugar-canes and the sweet medium of jaggery (native sugar) and chupatties, with which I fed him personally whenever he was brought before me for the day's work; I also gave him some *bonne-bouche* upon dismounting at the return to camp.

Although Moolah Bux was the best elephant I have myself experienced, he was not absolutely perfect, as he would not remain without any movement when a tiger charged directly face to face; upon such occasions he would stand manfully to meet the enemy, but he would swing his huge head in a pugnacious spirit preparatory to receiving the tiger upon his tusks.

The first time that I witnessed the high character of this elephant was connected with a regrettable incident which caused the death of one man and the mutilation of two others, who would probably have been killed had not Moolah Bux been present. The description of this day's experience will explain the necessity of a staunch shikar elephant when tiger-shooting, as the position may be one that would render it impossible to approach on foot when a wounded and furious tiger is in dense jungle, perhaps with some unfortunate beater in its clutches.

I was shooting in the Central Provinces, accompanied by my lamented friend the late Mr Berry, who was at that time Assistant-Commissioner at Jubbulpur.

We were shooting in the neighbourhood of Moorwarra, keeping a line as nearly as possible parallel with the railway, limiting our distance to 20 miles in order to obtain supplies. This arrangement enabled us to receive 30 lbs of ice daily from Allahabad, as a coolie was despatched from the station immediately upon arrival of the train, the address of our camp being daily communicated to the stationmaster. It was the hot season in the end of April, when a good supply of ice is beyond price; the soda-water was supplied from Jubbulpur, and with good tents, kuskos tatties, and cool drinks, the heat was bearable. It was this heat that had brought the tigers within range, as all water-springs and brooks were dried up, the tanks had evaporated, and the only water procurable was limited to the deep holes in the bends of streams that were of considerable importance in the cooler seasons of the year. The native headmen had received orders from the Deputy-Commissioner to send immediate information should any tigers be reported in their respective districts; they had also received special instructions to tie up buffaloes for bait should the tracks of tigers be discovered. The latter order was a mistake, as the buffaloes should not have been tied up until our arrival at the locality; upon several occasions the animals were killed and eaten some days before we were able to arrive upon the scene.

This was proved to be the case upon our arrival at Bijôré, about nine miles from the town of Moorwarra, where the zealous official had exhibited too eager a spirit for our sport. Two buffaloes had been tied up about half a mile apart, near the dry bed of a river, where in an abrupt bend the current had scooped out a deep hole in which a little water still remained. Both buffaloes had been killed, and upon our arrival early in the morning nothing could be discovered except a few scattered bones and the parched and withered portions of tough hide.

There were tracks of tigers upon the sand near the drinking-place, also marks of cheetul and wild pigs, therefore we determined to drive the neighbouring jungle without delay.

The neighbourhood was lovely, a succession of jungles and open grass-glades, all of which had been burnt clean, and exceedingly fine grass, beautifully green, was just appearing upon the dark brown surface scorched by the recent fire.

There were great numbers of the ornamental mhowa trees, which from their massive growth resembled somewhat the horse-chestnut trees of England. These had dropped their luscious wax-like blossoms, which from their intense sweetness form a strong attraction to bears and other animals of the forests; they also form a valuable harvest for the natives, who not only eat them, but by fermentation and distillation they produce a potent spirit, which is the favourite intoxicating liquor of the country.

If game had been plentiful this would have been a charming hunting-ground, but, like most portions of the Central Provinces, the animals have been thinned by native pot-hunters to an extent that will entail extermination, unless the game shall be specially protected by the Government. When the dry season is far advanced, the animal can only procure drinking water at certain pools in obscure places among the hills; these are well known to the native sportsman, although concealed from the European. On moonlight nights a patient watch is kept by the vigilant Indian hunter, who squats upon a mucharn among the boughs within 10 yds of the water-hole, and from this point of vantage he shoots every animal in succession, as the thirst-driven beasts are forced to the fatal post.

Nothing is more disappointing than a country which is in appearance an attractive locality for wild animals, but in reality devoid of game. I make a point of declining all belief in the statements of natives until I have thoroughly examined the ground, and made a special search for tracks in the dry beds of streams and around the drinking-places. Even should footprints be discovered in such spots, they must be carefully investigated, as the same animals visit the water-hole nightly, and in the absence of rain, the tracks remain, and become numerous from repetition; thus an inexperienced person may be deceived into the belief that game is plentiful, when, in fact, the country contains merely a few individuals of a species. It must also be remembered that during the dry season both deer, nilgyhe, and many other animals travel long distances in search of water, and return before daylight to their secluded places of retreat.

This was the position of Bijôré at the period of our visit; the most lovely jungles contained very little game. Although our baits had been devoured some days ago, I could not help thinking that the tiger might still be lurking in the locality, as it had been undisturbed, and there was little or no water in the neighbourhood excepting one or two drinking-places in the beds of nullahs.

We had 164 beaters, therefore we could command an extensive

line, as the jungles, having been recently burnt, were perfectly open, and an animal could have been seen at a distance of 100 yds.

Having made all the necessary arrangements, the beat commenced. It was extraordinary that such attractive ground contained so little game. The surface was a delicate green from the young shoots of new grass, and notwithstanding the enticing food there were no creatures to consume the pasturage.

Hours passed away in intense heat and disappointment; the most likely jungles were beaten with extreme care, but nothing was disturbed beyond an occasional peacock or a scared hare. The heat was intense, and the people having worked from 6 a.m. began to exhibit signs of weariness, as nothing is so tiring as bad luck. Although the country was extremely pretty it was very monotonous, as each jungle was similar in appearance, and I had no idea how far we were from camp; to my surprise, I was informed that we had been working almost in a circle, and that our tents were not more than a mile and a half distant in a direct line. We came to the conclusion that we should beat our way towards home, carefully driving every jungle in that direction.

During the last drive I had distinctly heard the bark of a sambur deer about half a mile in my rear, which would be between me and the direction we were about to take. It is seldom that a sambur barks in broad daylight unless disturbed by either a tiger or leopard; I was accordingly in hope that the sound might be the signal of alarm, and that we might find the tiger between us and the neighbouring village by our camp, where a small stream might have tempted it to drink.

Having taken our positions – Mr Berry amidst a few trees which formed a clump in a narrow glade outside, and myself around the corner of a jungle – the beat commenced. I was in the howdah upon Moolah Bux, and from my elevated position I could look across the sharp corner of the jungle and see a portion of the narrow glade commanded by my companion Berry; upon my side there was a large open space perfectly clear for about 200 yds, therefore the jungle was well guarded upon two sides, as the drive would terminate at the corner.

In a short time the usual monotony of the beater's cries was exchanged for a series of exciting shouts, which showed that game of some kind was on foot. We had lost so much hope, that the presence of a tiger was considered too remote to restrict our shooting to such noble game, and it had been agreed to lose no chance, but to fire at any animal that should afford a shot. Presently, after a sudden roar of animated voices, I saw ten or twelve wild pigs emerge from the jungle and trot across the glade which Berry commanded. A double shot from his rifle instantly responded.

The line of beaters was closing up. This was a curious contrast to the dull routine which had been the character of the drives throughout the day; there was game afoot, and the jungle being open, it could be seen, therefore immense enthusiasm was exhibited by the natives. Another burst of excited voices proclaimed a discovery of other animals, and a herd of eight or ten spotted deer (cheetul) broke covert close to my elephant and dashed full speed across the open glade. They were all does and young bucks without antlers, therefore I reserved my fire. We could not now complain of want of sport, as all the animals appeared to be concentrated in this jungle; another sudden yelling of the beaters was quickly followed by a rush of at least twenty pigs across Berry's glade, and once again his rifle spoke with both barrels in quick succession. I was in hope that the sambur stag that I had heard bark in this direction might be still within the drive, but the beaters were closing up, and the greater portion of the line had already emerged upon either side of the acute angle.

I now perceived Berry advancing towards me, he having left his place of concealment in the clump of trees. "Did you see him?" he exclaimed, as he approached within hearing distance. "See what?" I replied; "have you wounded a boar?" "A boar! No; I did not fire at a boar, but at a *tiger*, the biggest that I ever saw in my experience! He passed close by me, within 20 yds, at the same time that the herd of pigs broke covert; and I fired right and left, and missed him with both barrels; confound it."

This was a most important announcement, and I immediately dismounted from my elephant to examine the spot where the tiger had so recently appeared. It must indeed have been very close to Berry, as I had not seen the beast, my line of view being limited by the intervening jungle to the portion of the glade across which the pigs had rushed.

I now measured the distance from Berry's position to the tracks of the tiger, which we discovered after some few minutes' search. This was under 20 yds. The question now most important remained – Was the tiger wounded? A minute investigation of the ground showed the mark of a bullet, but we could find no other. This looked as though it must have struck the tiger, but Berry was very confident that such was not the case, as he declared the tiger did not alter his pace when fired at, but, on the contrary, he walked majestically across the narrow glade with his head turned in the opposite direction from Berry's position. He was of opinion that the tiger had not been disturbed by the close report of the rifle, as the noise of 164 beaters shouting at the maximum power of their voices was so great that the extra sound of the rifle bore only a small proportion.

We looked in vain for blood-tracks, and having come to the

conclusion that Berry had fired too high in a moment of excitement, we now made the most careful arrangements for driving the jungle into which the tiger had so recently retreated.

This formed a contrast to all others that we had beaten during the morning's work, as it had not been burnt. The fire had stopped at a native footpath, and instead of the bare ground, absolutely devoid of grass or dead leaves, the withered herbage as yellow as bright straw stood 3 ft high, and formed a splendid cover for animals of all kinds. I felt certain that the tiger would not leave so dense a covert without an absolute necessity; at the same time it was necessary to make a reconnaissance of the jungle before we could determine upon our operations.

Mounting my elephant Moolah Bux, I begged Berry to take Demoiselle, and accompanied by a couple of good men we left the long line of beaters stationed in order of advance along the glade, with instructions to march directly that we should send them the necessary orders. I begged them upon this occasion not to shout, but merely to tap the trees with their sticks as their line came forward.

We proceeded about a quarter of a mile ahead, and then turned into the jungle on our left. Continuing for at least 300 yds, we arrived at some open ground much broken by shallow nullahs, which formed natural drains in a slight depression of grassy land between very low hills of jungle, through which we had recently passed. There was a small nullah issuing from the forest, in which I placed my elephant, and I begged my friend Berry to ride Demoiselle to a similar place about 200 yds upon my right. I concluded that should the tiger be between us and the line of beaters, he would in all probability steal along one or the other of these nullahs before he could cross the open ground. We now sent back one of the natives with orders for the line of beaters to advance. Mr Berry left upon Demoiselle to take up his position, while I pushed Moolah Bux well into the jungle in the centre of the small nullah, which commanded a clear view of about 20 yds around.

In a short time we heard the clacking sound of many sticks, the beaters having obeyed the injunction, and keeping profound silence with their voices.

There were no animals in this jungle, probably they had been frightened by the great noise of the beaters when shouting in the recent drive; at any rate, the beat was barren, and having waited fruitlessly until I could see the men approaching within a few yards of my position, I ordered the elephant to turn round, with the intention of proceeding another quarter of a mile in advance, and thus continuing to beat the jungle in sections until it should be thoroughly driven out.

I had hardly turned the elephant, when we were startled by tremendous roars of a tiger, continued in quick successions within 50 yards of the position that I occupied. I never heard either before or since such a volume of sound proceeding from a single animal; there was a horrible significance in the grating and angry voice that betokened the extreme fury of attack. Not an instant was lost! The mahout was an excellent man, as cool as a cucumber, and never over-excited. He obeyed the order to advance straight towards the spot, in which the angry roars still continued without intermission.

Moolah Bux was a thoroughly dependable elephant, but although moving forward with a majestic and determined step, it was in vain that I endeavoured to hurry the mahout; both man and beast appeared to understand their business thoroughly, but to my ideas the pace was woefully slow if assistance was required in danger.

The ground was slightly rising, and the jungle thick with saplings about 20 ft in height, and as thick as a man's leg; these formed an undergrowth among the larger forest trees.

Moolah Bux crashed with ponderous weight through the resisting mass, bearing down all obstacles before him as he steadily made his way through the intervening growth. The roars had now ceased. There were no leaves upon the trees at this advanced season, and one could see the natives among the branches in all directions as they were perched for safety in the tree-tops, to which they had climbed like monkeys at the terrible sounds of danger. "Where is the tiger?" we shouted to the first man we could distinguish in this safe retreat only a few yards distant. "Here, here!" replied the man, pointing immediately beneath him. Almost at the same instant, with a loud roar, the tiger, which had been lying ready for attack, sprang forward directly for Moolah Bux.

There were so many trees intervening that I could not fire, and the elephant, instead of halting, moved forward, meeting the tiger in its spring. With a swing of his huge head Moolah Bux broke down several tall saplings, which crashed towards the infuriated tiger and checked the onset; whether the animal was touched by the elephant's tusks I could not determine, but it appeared to be within striking distance when the trees were broken across its path. Discomfited for the moment, the tiger bounded in retreat, and Moolah Bux stood suddenly like a rock, without the slightest movement. This gave me a splendid opportunity, and the .577 bullet rolled the enemy over like a rabbit. Almost at the same instant, having performed a somersault, the tiger disappeared, and fell struggling among the high grass and bushes about 15 paces distant.

I now urged Moolah Bux carefully forward until I could plainly see the tiger's shoulders, and a second shot through the exact centre of the blade-bone terminated its existence.

The elephant had behaved beautifully, and I have frequently looked back to that attack in thick forest, and been thankful that I was not mounted upon such animals as I have since that time had the misfortune to possess. Moolah Bux now approached the dead body, and at the command of the mahout he pulled out by the roots all the small undergrowth of saplings and dried herbage to clear a space around his late antagonist. In doing this his trunk several times touched the skin of the tiger, which he appeared to regard with supreme indifference.

I gave two loud whistles with my fingers as a signal that all was over, and we were still occupied in clearing away the smaller growth of jungle, when a native approached as though very drunk, reeling to and fro, and at length falling to the ground close to the elephant's heels; the man was covered with blood, and he had evidently fainted. I had an excellent Madras servant named Thomas, who was behind me in the howdah, and he lost no time in descending from the elephant and in pouring water over the unfortunate coolie, from a jar which I handed from beneath the seat. In a few moments the man showed signs of life, and the beaters began to collect around the spot. Two men were approaching supporting a limp and half-collapsed figure between them, completely deluged with blood; this was a second victim of the tiger's attack. Both men were now laid upon the ground, and water poured over their faces and chests; but during this humane operation another party was observed, carrying in their arms the body of a third person, which was hardly to be recognised through the mass of blood coagulated and mixed with dead leaves and sand, as the tiger had dragged and torn its victim along the ground with remorseless fury. This was a sad calamity. There could be little doubt that when we heard the roars of the infuriated beast it was attacking the line of beaters, and knocking them over right and left before they had time to ascend the trees. The village was only a mile distant, and we immediately sent for three charpoys (native bed-steads) as stretchers to convey the wounded men. Demoiselle arrived with Mr Berry, who came into my howdah, while the tiger was with some difficulty secured upon the pad of that exceedingly docile elephant. In this form we entered the village as a melancholy procession; the news having spread, all the women turned out to meet us, weeping and wailing in loud distress, and the scene was so touching that I began to reflect that tiger-shooting might be fun to some, but death to others, who, poor fellows, had to advance unarmed through dangerous jungle.

The reason for this savage attack was soon discovered. As a rule, there is little danger to a line of beaters provided the tiger is unwounded, and no person should ever place his men in the position to drive a jungle when a wounded tiger is in retreat. In such a case, if no elephants are present, it would be necessary to obtain the assistance of buffaloes; a herd of these animals driven through the jungle would quickly dislodge a tiger. We now skinned our late enemy, while a messenger was started towards Moorwarra, 9 or 10 miles distant, to prepare the authorities for the reception of our wounded men in hospital.

The skin having been taken off, we discovered a small hole close to the root of the tail, which had not been observed. Upon a close examination with the finger, I found minute fragments of lead, resembling very small shot flattened upon an anvil. The hole was not deeper than 1 ¼ in in the hard muscle of the rump, and the only effect of Berry's .577 hollow Express was to produce this trumpery wound, which had enraged the animal without creating any serious injury. It is necessary to explain that the bullet of this rifle was more than usually light and hollow; but the want of penetrating power of the hollow projectile, and the dangerous results, were terribly demonstrated, notwithstanding the large charge of 6 drams of powder.

A comparison of the effect of my .577 with the same charge of 6 drams, but with a solid bullet of ordinary pure lead weighing 648 grains, was very instructive. The first shot, when the tiger was bounding in retreat after it had charged the elephant, had struck the right flank, and as the animal was moving obliquely, the bullet had passed through the lungs, then, breaking the shoulder-bone, it was found in its integrity just beneath the skin of the shoulder upon the side opposite to that of entry; it was very much flattened upon one side, as it had traversed an oblique course throughout, and had torn the inside of the animal in a dreadful manner. The second shot, fired simply to extinguish the dying tiger, passed through both shoulders, but was found under the skin upon the opposite side, flattened exactly like a mushroom, into a diameter of about 1 ½ in at the head, leaving about half an inch of the base uninjured which represented the stalk. This was a large tiger, and remarkably thick and heavy, with strong and hard muscles, nevertheless the penetration of the soft leaden bullet was precisely correct for that quality of game. If the .577 bullet had been made of an admixture of tin or other alloy to produce extreme hardness, it would have passed through the body of the tiger with a high velocity, but the animal would have escaped the striking energy, which would not have been expended upon the resisting surface. It is the striking energy, the knocking-down power of a projectile, that is so necessary when hunting dangerous game. I cannot help repetition in enforcing this principle: there is a minimum amount of striking energy in a light hollow projectile, and a maximum amount in a solid heavy projectile; keep the latter within the animal to ensure the effect of the blow; this will be effected by a bullet made of pure lead without admixture with other metal, to flatten upon impact, and by the expansion of surface it will create a terrific wound; at the same time it will have sufficient momentum from its great weight to push forward, and to overcome the resistance of opposing bones and muscles. A very large tiger may weigh 450 lbs; a .577 bullet of 650 grains, propelled by 6 drams of powder, has a striking energy of 3520 foot-pounds. This may be only theoretical measurement, but the approximate superiority of 3500 lbs against the tiger's weight, 450 lbs, would be sufficient to ensure the stoppage of a charge, or the collapse of the animal in any position, provided that the bullet should be retained within the body, and thus bestow the whole force of the striking energy.

We did all that could be done for our wounded men. The strength of caste prejudices was so potent that, although in pangs of thirst from pain and general shock to the system, they would accept nothing from our hands. I made a mixture of milk with soda-water, brandy, and laudanum, but they refused to swallow it, and the only course, after washing their wounds and bandaging, was to leave them to the treatment of their own people.

One man was severely bitten through the chest and back, the fangs of the tiger having penetrated the lungs; he was also clawed in a terrible manner about the head and face, where the paws of the animal had first made fast their hold. This man died in a few hours. The others were bitten through the shoulder and upper portion of the arm, both in the same manner, and the sharp claws had cut through the scalp from the forehead across the head to the back of the neck, inflicting clean wounds to the bone, as though produced by a pruning-knife. They were conveyed in litters to the hospital in Moorwarra, where they remained for nearly a month, at the expiration of which they recovered. The seizure by the claws was effected without the shock of a blow.

This serious accident was entirely due to a hollow bullet: if a solid bullet had struck a tiger in the same place it would have carried away a portion of the spine, and the animal would have been paralysed upon the spot.

In the absence of a dependable elephant we should have been helpless, and the tiger might have wounded or killed many others.

WILD BEASTS AND THEIR WAYS
(Macmillan 1891)

A Week with the Bears

MAJOR-GENERAL E. F. BURTON

ovember 16th – Truly, Veeranoor is a great place for bears. I sallied out, at the first blush of dawn, with about twenty men; and, after a hurried tramp, arrived at a small hill overlooking the river, and surrounded with deep and thickly-wooded ravines, and fantastic masses of rock, which crop out in all directions on the base of the hill: the hill itself is a mass of caves, and snug retreats beneath overhanging granite ledges, sheltered from the garish light of day by matted brambles, and creeper-festooned cactus bushes, cool and shady nooks after Bruin's own heart. Arriving on the ground shortly before sunrise, I climbed up to a good central look-out place, and sent the beaters, in the capacity of scouts, in parties of twos and threes, to mount guard on high rocks, and to telegraph the approach of Bruin whenever he might make his appearance. In a few minutes the posts were all occupied by dusky, cumbley-wrapped figures, squatting on the topmost rocks, and looking exceedingly like a congregation of vultures of magnified dimensions.

After ten minutes, no signs having been made by any of the scouts, I moved on to the head of a deep scarped ravine, on the river side of the hill; and had scarcely got there, when one of the look-out men near me slid down from his post and brought word the two bears were coming up from the river. The other semaphores now began to work their arms, and soon every digit was pointing to a thicket on the border of the ravine. One bear had lain down in the thicket, and another had gone into a smaller ravine which ran into the large one. I now advanced cautiously, under guidance of a man who had seen the bears, and, while advancing on the lair, and not more than half-way to it, the guide suddenly stopped on the edge of a smaller, but very precipitous ravine, and then crept back, and whispered that two more bears were standing in the nullah.

I stole to the side of the ravine, and saw a bear standing, like a statue, near some thorny creepers. He was evidently listening, having heard our movements, quiet as we had been. I fired my right barrel, and the bear fell into the midst of the creepers, with a ball through his back, and roaring hideously. I fired another shot at the black mass as it rolled about in the thicket. At the same moment another bush, only a few paces off, shook violently, and another bear rushed out, with an angry grunt, and scuttled down the ravine. Snatching up my single rifle, which, with a double gun and my shikarry's rickety single barrel, composed our whole armament, I sent a two-ounce bullet after the fugitive, but missed. I then extinguished my wounded bear with a shot in the head from my shikarry's gun; and, after loading again, descended into the ravine, and found the bear to be a fair-sized male.

Other scouts now came, and said that the two bears first seen had moved off at the sound of the firing, and that, as far as they could tell, one of them had got into a small cave about a quarter of a mile farther on: so away we trundled, and found very recent and evident signs of Bruin's presence at the cave's mouth. The den was almost half-way up a pile of rocks, more or less broken, and had but one entrance, and that very narrow and low. I shot a bear in this very cave a year ago, and therefore knew the place right well. Stones were thrown in at all the crevices; but the bear refused to come out and be killed, though he moved occasionally, puffing angrily.

I now took up my post at the mouth of the cave, and ordered a rocket to be put in at a promising crevice; and this was accordingly done, but without effect. Bruin snorted, and moved; but only into a deeper recess of his den. All this time a heavy fire of abuse had been kept up, and the Ursine family was dishonoured up to its remotest progenitors. Several other rockets were thrown into the cave, but to no purpose; the bear stirred not. Sticks were also rattled in all the crevices; and I began to fear that we were to be beaten by Bruin's passive resistance, when a beater, who had removed some stones from a crevice in the rock, put his bamboo down as far as it would go, and, by great good luck, clapped it right upon the bear's back, and stirred him up roundly. This was too much for Bruin's equanimity: he instantly fell into an extremity of rage, jumped about, bit the bamboo in a most vicious manner, and roared at the top of his lungs. At this welcome sound, and the no less welcome noise of scuffling and hustling up to the mouth of the cave, I cocked my gun, and put the muzzle within a foot of the entrance. Out came the grey head, with an ominous twinkle of the eye; the neck and shoulders were following, when I fired, and the bear fell dead, half in and half out of the cave: the ball had broken the neck.

It was very evident that the people would do no more after this success; so, leaving them to tie the two bears on long poles, on which to bring them to my camp, I returned quietly through the jungle, only stopping, for a few minutes, at a beautiful stream of water, which rushes down to join the Cauvery, fretting over the rounded basaltic rocks, and gladdening the jungle glades with its perennial bounty. Soon after I reached my tent the bears came in, borne in solemn procession, and followed by an admiring tail of herd-boys and idlers from the neighbouring hamlet. The usual process of skinning and cutting up was gone through with great *éclat*; and, in the first bear, we found a bullet which I had fired at it a year ago; the ball was under the skin of one shoulder, and embedded in a thick white cist of leathery texture. There being very little small shooting to be had in this place I did nothing more to-day, but retired to bed early, to dream of more luck for to-morrow.

November 17th – I went this morning to the hill where we had such good sport yesterday; but though we sat on the rocks till near 8 o'clock, and also had the hill beaten as far as this could be done, nothing appeared. Yesterday's rumpus had evidently put the bears on their guard, and they had evacuated the premises for the present. I therefore set off, over the shoulder of a large hill, from the top of which a most lovely view of the Cauvery valley is obtained, and beat up a cluster of caves, from one of which I turned out no less than three bears a year ago; now, however, the cave was untenanted, and there was no recent trace of Bruin, but there were fresh marks of a panther. After putting in some rockets, without result, we moved on to two large hills, separated from each other by a narrow pass, which gradually deepens into a tremendous ravine, running into the Cauvery, which flows immediately beneath.

Establishing myself in the pass, the people beat one of the hills, but nothing larger than a lizard made its appearance, and I began to think that this day would prove blank. The other hill remained to be beaten, and scarcely had the people got to the top of it, when a cry arose of "The bear! the bear!" After a minute's suspense, I heard that the bear had skirted round the opposite side of the hill; so I set off at a great pace to meet it, plunging into the ravine already mentioned, until I came to a place where another deep nullah, with a stream of water trickling down it, joined the main gorge. Then we rushed, panting and toiling, up this nullah, while ever and anon a violent shout, "It is coming! it is coming! it is coming round the hill! it is in the nullah!" arose. At last we heard a clattering of loose stones in front of us, and, in a few seconds, saw the bear coming down the nullah at a good canter. Shaking its head from side to side, and with its long black hair waving up and down as it came on in a clumsy gallop, it presented a formidable appearance, and, the heat being excessive, its temper was, undoubtedly, soured and cranky. However, the unfortunate beast had scant time to show off any freaks of temper; for, at the very moment that it appeared to see me, standing, as I was, on a small rock on the side of the nullah, an ounce ball crashed through its head, and it rolled over, struggling and gasping, into a pool of water, which soon was crimsoned with Bruin's blood. Another ball put an end to its struggles, and it was dragged out of the water, tied to a pole cut from a jungle tree, and carried off by six men to the tent, the distance being a good three miles.

After this adventure, we went about a mile further, and explored a great many caves and ravines; but, though it was pretty certain that there were bears in more than one of the dens, we could not induce them to show themselves. The caves which we thus visited were of enormous extent; and the riven and shattered masses of rock which stood out, piled in strange confusion, on the top of each little hill, were covered with marks of bears, and, in smaller degree, of panthers. Clearly, too, they were the favourite abodes of innumerable porcupine; but these shy nocturnal animals seldom show themselves in the light of day. At about 2 o'clock, I turned my steps to camp. The sun was excessively hot, and the rocks so heated that it was difficult to keep the hand on them for more than a few seconds at a time; even the natives complained that their feet, necessarily denuded of sandals in climbing up and down the bare and slippery granite, were inflamed and painful. I was not sorry when I arrived at the tent, after a very tiring trudge of near three miles over the plain. In cutting up the bear, which was a female, and fat, yielding twelve bottles of grease, a *young one* was found. It is rare to find a fœtus in a bear. I have never before met with one, though I have been at the "flinching" of so many. This young one was about the size of a kidney bean, quite white, and semi-transparent, with eyes perfectly developed; and its toes also, easily distinguishable, as it lay coiled up in a ball; the mouth, too, was distinctly marked by a dark line, but had no opening.

November 18th – We went to the hills which we had already twice visited, but this day's attempts upon Bruin ended in a failure. A bear was marked down into a deep and thickly-wooded hollow, and I endeavoured to get a close shot at it from the top of some rocks; but the jungle was so thick that, when the beast took alarm, which it very soon did, I could not see it till it had gained the skirts of the hill, all round which people were posted. As the bear was making off at a great pace, at some eighty yards distance, when I caught sight of it, and as I did not doubt that my scouts would mark it down again, I refrained from taking the long shot; but, upon moving round the hill, I was disgusted to find that not one of the lookouts had seen the bear. Nothing remained but to follow it up, in the direction in which it had disappeared; and, on passing the cave where the affair of the 16th had come off, we found that Bruin had been to it; but, warned by the smell of blood and of rocket powder, had, after most unmistakably testifying his disapproval of the unusual odours, passed on. We then tracked him to a huge cave which I had not before seen, and we endeavoured to turn him out; but to no purpose, though we heard him, now and then, scuffling about inside. Our attempts to get him out occupied so much time that I had no opportunity of retrieving our bad luck at any other hills; so, after beating a few deep dells without success, I returned to my tent, and issued orders for a move across the Cauvery the next morning. Iyanah Gounden took leave this evening, after having made violent love to my shikarry for a new clasp-knife which I had lately bestowed upon that long-legged biped, but which he would not, on any terms, surrender; so the zemindar went away baffled.

November 19th – I struck my tent this morning, and moved off to the Cauvery, shooting a partridge and a brace of rock pigeon on my way. At this point the river is seldom fordable, and I crossed over in a basket-boat of raw hides, stretched upon a round bamboo frame, about nine feet in diameter and two in depth. The river runs swiftly between high banks, on a rocky channel; and, when in flood, cannot be less than twenty feet deep, by three or four hundred yards wide. On the opposite or right bank of the river is a plain, covered with low jungle, very thick in places, and dotted with many craggy hills of the same character with those already described by me as being at Veeranoor. I amused myself with shooting some rock-pigeon (sand-grouse) on the bank of the river, while my tent and baggage, in many trips, was passed over; and then selected an open space in the jungle, for my camp, about two miles from some promising-looking hills. We got hold of a wild-looking fellow, rejoicing in the name of Pyreney, from the neighbouring village of Samapully, and he promised to show me several bears; he made honourable mention, in particular, of an old lady and two cubs, which cubs, he declared, had been with her for two years; if so, they must be fine youngsters! With Pyreney came two or three other villagers, but they did not seem to be much of shikarries; being, in appearance, very mild men indeed. This afternoon, I went out, under guidance of one of the mild men, and shot several rock-pigeon; I also went to a heavy thorn jungle on the bank of a tolerably large stream, which runs, on a low sandy bed, into the Cauvery; but I was soon tired of crawling under tangled creepers, and being held back by the hair of my head by "wait-a-bit" thorns, of which, and of other varieties, there is a most plentiful supply in these jungles; seeing plainly, all the time, that nothing in the way of shooting was to be effected without a strong gang of beaters to drive out the spotted deer and hog, which undoubtedly abound.

I passed the sites of several deserted villages this evening, in one or two of which stone seats were still to be seen under umbrageous tamarind trees; and could fancy to myself the assembly, years ago, of grey-bearded patriarchs, solemnly squatting on those seats, in the cool of the evening, like a herd of superannuated monkeys; discussing the price of grain, the best way of getting up a story of short crops, by which to *do* the collector, and, through him, the Government; or, perchance, forming themselves into an extempore jury, to try the merits of a row between Mrs Luchmee and her not unreasonably jealous husband, who, having been caught with his bullock cart, and pressed into the service of a marching regiment, had been passed on, by his first masters, to the relieved corps; from them to a third, and so on, till, at the end of many months, poor Ramasawmy, falsely reported to have died of cholera, returns to his native village, only to find his fields let out to others, his household goods wasted, and nothing flourishing except his family, miraculously fat and well-looking under the protection of some kind friend, who had taken possession of his vacant place during his absence on his enforced journey to see the world! Now, however, all this is completely changed. Ramasawmy has been sedulously taught his rights, and something more, by a new school of governors, &c., and it is as much as the life of the commandant of a regiment, or the collector of a district, is worth, to attempt to press Ramasawmy, and his cart, into the service at all.

November 20th – At earliest dawn did I sally forth this morning, and arrived at the foot of a low range of hills, about two miles from my tent, soon after daylight. I climbed up a steep rock, from which I could command a wide view over a stretch of rugged country, overspread with a thorny jungle, and broken up by innumerable deep nullahs, and wooded groups of low, time-worn, hills; and I felt very certain of an encounter with Bruin, and already took off his skin in imagination; but a defeat should be chronicled, as well as a victory, and, for my own part, I always look with suspicion upon an account of a shooting expedition in which good luck, and good shooting, are not sometimes chequered with their reverse. The sun rose, bright and fiery, as I sat on the rock; and each hillstone became tinted with red as it emerged, to all appearance, from the grey mists of the morning; still nothing came in view. I was just thinking of getting down from my post, when a scout came round from the other side of the hill, and said that he had marked a bear into a cave, about half-way up the rocks which crowned its summit. Up we all went, and a stiff climb it was over the *débris* of the ancient granite; at last we reached a ledge of rocks high up, lying under some beetling crags, which stood out, in bold relief, against the rosy sky on the apex of the hill. And now the guide began to crawl, with warning hand upraised, towards a rock-bound narrow den, in which the bear was sleeping. The affair was badly managed on all sides. Though I had, in a previous year, climbed up this hill, I was not acquainted with this particular den; moreover, I did not descend, as I should have, and examine its several outlets; and when, walking on to its roof, the guide pointed to a large chink between two rocks, and told me that, if I looked in, I should see the bear lying in a corner; I thought of nothing but of, most unfairly, blowing it up where it lay.

After these confessions, I will proceed with my story. I looked into the den, which was lighted, partly through the crevice, and partly through a lower aperture; and, when my eyes got accustomed to the imperfect light, I saw the bear, or, rather, part of it, lying on a ledge of rock, at three or four paces distance. I could not tell what part of his body was in view; it looked like a patch of black fur only, among the stones. I fired at the middle of the object, and the bear roared furiously. As the lower opening of the den was darkened by his retreating form, I fired another barrel, and, from the nature of the ground, over which nothing but a cat, or a bear, could move with any reasonable speed, I could not get sight of him again as he plunged down the hill. On descending to the point whence he had emerged, large patches of blood were visible, and by the blood we tracked him into a very large cave, under some enormous rocks, near the foot of the hill. On arriving at the entrance of this den, a greater smear of blood showed that Bruin had taken refuge inside; and the natives, especially Pyreney, began to walk over the steep and slippery rocks, peeping into every cranny, and coolly tripping over places the very sight of which made me feel giddy.

Presently, Pyreney came up, and said that he had found the bear, and took me to a chink between two perpendicular walls of rock, between which my portly body, portly by comparison with his attenuated carcase, could by no means pass. By dint of squeezing myself sideways, I managed to get my head and neck round a corner, and, about ten feet below, in a sort of open tunnel, I saw a small opening, between the stones, of about four inches square; and, after looking at it for some time, I made out that the bear was lying there, with a small portion of some part of his body pressed against the opening. What now to do I knew not; I could not find room to level my gun, as I had to fire *round the corner*. I got my gun handed to me over my shoulder, and laid it for the bit of fur, as well as I could, and fired. The fur disappeared, but I could not tell whether I had hit it or not, but there was no splash of the bullet visible on the rocks. Now another search after poor Bruin commenced. After some time, during which several rockets were put into the den, I heard the bear move, and presently it was discovered that he had gone out of the lower cave into another and higher den, to all appearance unassailable; it was a narrow cleft, between two huge rocks, ending in a den which turned at right angles from its entrance; accessible only by climbing a rock by which, and a drop beyond, the cleft was gained. I felt, I think reasonable, doubts of the wisdom of putting myself into a position from which retreat, *in a hurry*, would have been quite impossible. Acting, therefore, upon the better part of valour, I threw rockets in at the mouth of the den, but they fizzed idly in the entrance. I then had a pile of grass and branches thrown on the aperture, and a lighted brand tossed on them, and very soon there arose a tolerable blaze; but the bear would not come out, though he growled continually. At last, much to my disgust, I was obliged to leave him, for I hate to leave a wounded beast to languish and die; not to say that such imperfect success is exceedingly vexing. So I turned tentwards, tired and savage, blowing up the natives, and taunting my long-legged shikarry most unmercifully. So ended this day's work.

November 21st – This day's sport, being probably my last attack upon Bruin for some time to come, has been signalised by a very prodigious row. I determined to devote this morning to the bear and cubs, and accordingly went out long before dawn, and sat at the foot of a hill, close to the scene of yesterday's adventures. I remained on this hill, perched on the top of a heap of caves, till about 7 o'clock, but the bears did not appear, though it was quite evident that this was a favourite haunt of my greasy friends. We walked all over the rocks, disturbing a great number of spur fowl; and then I went to look at the cave where I met with defeat yesterday morning. I was leisurely walking, double gun in hand, along the foot of the hill, and was about climbing up its side, under a great collection of rocks covered, pretty thickly, with cactus trees and thorny creepers, and the natives who were with me were skipping from rock to rock, throwing stones into the thick bushes, when, suddenly, I heard a rustling sound behind me, and, turning round, saw the grey muzzle of a bear coming after me through the jungle. I had no idea that the bear would charge, and, consequently, waited for a clear shot; but, to my anger and astonishment, when she arrived within twenty paces of where I was standing, she came straight at me with a grand roar! I fired, and hit her in the shoulder, but she did not fall; and, at the same moment, I saw a second bear burst out of the bushes; and, in another moment, a third appeared – all in full charge at me, yelling furiously. The two last bears were as big as the first, which was their mother. There was no time to be lost – all three were within ten yards of me, jumping, open-mouthed. I fired the second barrel at the old bear, and, most fortunately, shot her dead; but the others came on, and were almost upon me. I had no time to take the rifle from my shikarry, who was standing behind me, so I threw down my empty gun, and bolted, as fast as I could, over the stones. Like "Sahela Selassie, King of Abyssinia", "I ran, and my men ran too." I verily believe that my legs were preter-naturally lengthened for the occasion. My shikarry thundered on in front, his long legs flying over the stones in a most ludicrous fashion, and the bears followed, like two savage dogs, at my heels. Fortunately they did not come very far, and I pulled up, and got my rifle from my shikarry. Content with their victory, the cubs moved up the hill; I got a snap shot, through the bushes, but did not hit; so I went back, picked up and loaded my gun, and found the old bear lying dead on her back; she was a very old bear, exceedingly thin and mangy.

After this scrimmage, I went to the cave of yesterday's wounded bear, and saw that it had managed to get out in the night. The two young bears had got into this cave; we heard them whining, but could not get them out; they were proof against rockets and everything else. While I was sitting here, Pyreney went up to look at another den, and presently shouted that a bear was coming out. The beast was coming right for me, though not, as yet, visible to me, when the villagers, who were sitting near me, jumped up, and the bear immediately turned off. From our position, it was impossible to follow his course; but I sent the natives over the top of the hill, and they came back with news that they had marked two bears down into a cave; that they imagined one of them to be that which had just gone round the hill, the other they thought to be the wounded animal of yesterday, as it seemed to crawl rather than walk. I went up to the place and saw a large den under a perfect chaos of rocks, and we tried hard to get the bears out, but without avail. Blank shots, stones, rockets, all were tried, and all to no purpose; so I had to abandon the assault, and return to my tent. Thus ended my "Week with Bruin"; four bears had been bagged and one wounded, out of eleven seen. Nearly a month's march, over a country barren to a sportsman's eye, lay before me, at the end of which I anticipated, with delight, eight or ten days of elephant-shooting in a jungle with which I am well acquainted, and in which I had enjoyed some good sport, and had experienced the pleasure of laying low more than one of the mighty pachyderms.

REMINISCENCES OF SPORT IN INDIA
(W. H. Allen 1885)

On the Track of Bears in Kamchatka

E. DEMIDOFF (PRINCE SAN DONATO)

eaving the horses in charge of one of our followers, we began ascending the right bank, which implied a couple of hours' continuous scramble through the dense zone of alder, dwarf cedars, and rhododendrons. We kept constantly sliding down the exposed roots, and one step forward often meant a downshoot of two or three yards. Moreover, the slope was uncommonly steep, at places almost perpendicular, while the mosquitoes, aroused from their slumber by our movements, took their revenge, and satisfied their appetites on our hands and faces. It was not until the sun was high over the opposite ridge that we finally emerged from that deadly zone and could see where we were. In spite of the recently endured struggle, it was not without an indescribable feeling of curiosity, mingled with an unsurpassed sense of freedom, that I set my foot on the timber-line of those unexplored wastes, which no one had as yet admired, no sportsman except our old guide had visited. Standing on a narrow ledge of rock, I commanded a view over a vast stretch of moor, slanting down from the Kamchatskaia Vershina and other lower pinnacles, with its innumerable patches of snow glittering in the morning sun, and higher up turning into large snowfields. It was a grand scene of silence and desolation, creating an impression which I shall never forget. I was roused from my contemplation of it by the gillie, who flatly declined to go any further, saying that he felt uneasy, being, I suppose, subject to giddiness, and it required no slight threats on the part of the General to induce him to proceed. Following a well-defined bear-path a little below the ridge,[1] we had hardly advanced a few yards when my companion suddenly crouched down, pointing towards a moving speck ahead of us. It was a huge bear, which I could plainly distinguish through a small gap in the rhododendrons; the beast was clumsily making its way down the

---

[1] It must be confessed that the paths made by bears greatly facilitated our getting through the thick covert, which otherwise it would have required superhuman exertions to penetrate.

slope some four hundred yards in front of us, probably on a fishing excursion. Turning back to get out of sight, and groping my way through the awkward and blinding brush, I crept in the animal's direction, and on peeping again over a rock I perceived Bruin at 150 yds, steadily advancing to meet us; a quarter of an hour brought me within shot. Taking a steady aim with my .303, I let go at him. The heavy mass pelted downhill, giving me a second chance for the other barrel before it disappeared in the depths of the ravine. A loud growl from below convinced me that at least one of the bullets had told. Both the General and I dashed wildly down the slope, nearly breaking our necks over a sheer fall, which it took us some time to turn. We soon struck the beast's spoor, leading straight to the bottom of the gully, where we found the animal lying stone dead half-way down a snow-slide, and with one push rolled him to the side of the stream. According to the General, he weighed over eighteen *poods* (a pood = thirty-two pounds), which meant a great deal more in September, at the end of the fishing season. The coat was of a lightish brown colour (dark ones, as I am told, being very rare in Kamchatka), and still in its winter condition, thick and well-furnished. My companion showed me the local method of telling the approximate weight of a bear, which they do by measuring the length from snout to root of tail with the outstretched hand; so many *tchetverts*, or hands, denote a corresponding number of *poods*. But since the weight varies considerably at different times of year, this calculation is not always correct.

We left the gillie to skin this, my first trophy, and continued up the ravine over steep, hardened snow till we reached the same ridge. A few minutes later two other bears came in sight to our left, apparently undisturbed by my shots. They were quietly playing together and rolling themselves on the moss; one of them would occasionally make a rush at his companion as if to frighten him, and both would then gallop downhill at full speed, stopping suddenly to begin the same game over again. Followed by the General, I slid out of view, and making a small détour to leeward, crept stealthily up a boulder, from the top of which I discovered the unsuspicious pair a hundred and twenty yards below me. Again the report of my rifle aroused the slumbering echoes of the mountains, bringing down the furthest animal, which dropped motionless on the snow. A second shot wounded the other, which dashed frantically uphill with a heavy growl. I let him approach, and then gave him his quietus at close quarters full in the chest. Both animals proved smaller than the first one, but their coats were darker and in good order. Three bears in an hour's time was no common quarry, and I began to think it was time to turn my attention to sheep.

Leaving our quarry to be skinned on the way back, we decided to pursue our course to higher ground in search of bighorn. We started accordingly ploughing our way through the light mosses, and carefully spying in every direction. The flora here was quite of the Alpine type: pink androsaces, saxifraga, violets, asters, and other plants of elevated regions grew profusely between the numerous patches of snow. As we advanced, we struck several sheep-paths with old tracks and droppings, but, though my Zeiss freely examined all the surrounding corries, which presented favourable aspects and afforded capital grazing, there was no sign of *Ovis nivicola*. In addition to this, it was perfect torture to use the binocular for spying on account of the mosquitoes, which would instantaneously settle on one's hands and unveiled face, mercilessly attacking any unprotected part. In this manner, after a couple of hours' walk, we reached the summit of a rounded boulder, commanding a view of vast tracts of moor and snowfields. My aneroid now showed an altitude of 4,000 ft. The scenery I had before me was of unsurpassed beauty. At my feet trickled from beneath accumulated masses of hard snow a small rivulet flowing into a lovely turquoise-blue lake, on which floated large glittering icebergs. Towering above the eastern shores of the lake rose the massive cone of the Kamchatskaia Vershina, with gloomy rocks piercing its snow garment; and lower, craggy ranges running east and west, all converging towards the main central peak. A majestic silence hung over this bright picture of northern magnificence, as yet unspoiled by the presence of man; to me it appeared like some fantastic country as described in tales of childhood, which rises in an instant and as quickly vanishes at a stroke of the fairy's wand. But alas! no well-meaning giant nor friendly dwarfs inhabited these lonely regions to welcome us.

The tiny stream which flowed beneath us was the source of the great Kamchatka River. It enters the lake from the east, and running out of its western extremity, joins another stream from the south, some three miles above our camp; gradually shifting round through the tundra, it eventually takes a direction due north, which is maintained across the whole peninsula to the mouth at Nijni-Kamchatsk. The lake, which it was proposed that very evening to call "Lake Sofka Demidoff", in honour of the only lady who had ever visited it, was about two miles long by three-quarters of a mile in breadth, and lay at an altitude of 3,500 ft above sea-level. Narrow at both its extremities, it widens towards the middle; its waters are wonderfully clear and, I imagine, very deep, as its banks are fairly abrupt on every side.

Seeing no trace of wild sheep, nor of any other living creature, I determined to return to camp after having skinned the two bears, for it was now late in the afternoon, and the prospect of a long struggle through the bush in the dark was by no means an attractive one. We luckily struck a useful snow-slide down a gully, and thus avoided part of the rhododendron zone. Heavily laden with the skins, we reached the bottom of the valley completely exhausted, and found ourselves in sight of the tents at 6 p.m. Camp was in a state of utter confusion; after the previous day's incessant rain there was not a single pack which had not been damped through, and everyone had hung up his belongings to dry: it reminded one of a gipsy encampment in the midst of the woods. My gillie had faithfully brought in the skin of the first bear, and we all eagerly awaited Littledale's arrival in order to know what might be expected from our first hunting-ground. It was not long before the familiar neighing of ponies, greeting their returning comrades, announced his approach. He brought back four average heads of *Ovis nivicola*, of which the best one measured 34 ins by 13½, and a large bear skin. That day's bag thus amounted to four sheep and four bears. Littledale had come across the sheep on the higher ridges, where they had probably betaken themselves to seek comparative protection from the mosquitoes. He had only spied the four rams he had shot as well as a couple of ewes, and, though our success seemed promising, he did not think that, with the exception of bears, game was plentiful in the district. Moreover, he said that sheep in these parts, unaccustomed as they were to human presence, were too tame to afford sport, and would let him come up to them in full view without attempting to escape; their ignorance of the rifle and curiosity at the sight of unknown beings placed them entirely in his power. My companion had failed to secure another bear at a long range on his way back to camp.

Next morning, accompanied by my faithful General and two men, I started before dawn towards one of the southern nullahs, with the firm intention of making straight for the tops, whilst Littledale took an eastern direction with the object of reconnoitring the slopes of the Kamchatskaia Vershina. The night had been chilly, and the mosquitoes in consequence gave us comparative rest as we rode through the woods and entered a fresh valley. The sky was perfectly clear, promising a fine day. Leaving the horses below the zone of scrub, we found a long, steep ravine, filled with hardened snow, which greatly facilitated our ascent. We could distinguish at the head of the valley rows of volcanic pinnacles, some 5,000 ft high, with precipitous snow-slides shooting down the gullies between them. They ran westward of the main peak, and appeared to be first-rate ground for sheep.

A distance of about 6 miles as yet intervened, and it took us at least

3 hours before we reached the more abrupt slopes of the towering crags. As we were preparing for the last scramble I spied a large bear some four hundred yards above us. As I watched him through the glass, digging the earth and slowly advancing at right angles from us, his coat seemed unusually light in colour, almost white. As he was on our way, I suggested a stalk, and, hiding from view, followed a lateral ravine in his direction. Unfortunately, on reaching the commanding ridge, alder bushes, on which we counted for concealment, had become scarce, and further advance in the open would have involved certain failure. Bruin was now two hundred and 50 yds off, and as he appeared to have no intention of coming any nearer, I had to take my chance. Out of five consecutive shots, the fifth at least reached its destination, for the beast, which had remained motionless, as if thunder-stricken by the cracks of the rifle, emitted a loud roar, and pelted downhill to my right into patches of dense brushwood, where we could locate him by the waving of the branches above him, as he forced his way through. Though we found blood on his tracks, he was strong enough to pursue his course through the thickly entangled scrub, in the midst of which it would be a dangerous matter to tackle a wounded bear. The rifle was of no avail, and the General proposed to abandon a chase which involved such risk. Time being precious, I agreed to this wise suggestion, and reluctantly leaving the animal to its unhappy fate, proceeded to climb a perpendicular slope towards the left ridge of the valley, along which we journeyed to a low saddle, where we settled down to spy. There mosquitoes again gathered round us in countless numbers; my companion, who wore no gloves, declined to use the spare Zeiss I had lent him and kept his hands in his pockets. As for myself, I was reduced to an occasional glance at the surrounding corries. I was soon destined, however, to catch my first glimpse of *Ovis nivicola*, for a small grey speck moving among the rocks of one of the lateral spurs presently came in sight; this proved to be a young ram. Hoping that he might be accompanied by others, I decided to approach him. Creeping cautiously below the ridge, in an hour we managed to get within a hundred yards of the place where I had spied him, and on peeping over a protruding ledge discovered him still standing in the same spot. I could plainly distinguish the remnants of his winter coat still clinging in patches to his back and withers. Crawling down to a small mossy knoll, I was over-anxious to get a shot, and the result was I scored a clean miss at 80 yds! The ram did not give me a second chance, for he disappeared like lightning round a boulder, and I never saw him again. So far success had not crowned my efforts that day. We returned disappointed to the saddles we had just left, and thence started towards the higher crags of that volcanic ridge, encountering on our way

many a "gendarme" round almost vertical rocks, parts of which treacherously gave way under my grip. At places it was necessary to advance in a riding position over the narrow ledge, with precipices of several hundred feet on either side of us.

The aspect of the country beyond, at an elevation of about 5,000 ft, had entirely changed. Odd-shaped rocks of volcanic formation stood out of the ground like rows of disjointed fingers, between which lay scattered everywhere rough heaps of porous stones and sharp débris of old lava. There were no more signs of grass or vegetation whatever in this place of dark desolation. In addition to this a heavy mist came on unexpectedly, preventing us from proceeding further. It was not until a whole hour had elapsed that we were able to resume our course over the broken ground, peeping here and there through the small gaps into the deep corries below. We passed along numerous paths of sheep, which to judge by the tracks seemed to frequent these places in preference to the lower pastures, and whose habits, in this regard, resembled those of ibex.

Presently, as I was peering down through a clearing in the mist, I perceived two animals on my right coming up a ravine in our direction. Creeping cautiously down the sharp stones, which yielded under my feet, I made for a mass of rock, and on looking over found that the mist had again filled the gully. I waited motionless, the wind being favourable, for that aggravating veil to lift, and as it partially thinned down I vaguely distinguished two sheep advancing quietly 100 yds below me; I could just tell that they were young rams. Taking my chance, I fired at the nearest one, which rolled over, while the other ran a few yards, and, stopping to look back for his companion, received my second bullet, which knocked him head over heels into the abyss. I found them to be both four-year-old rams, and though the heads were by no means trophies to be proud of, I enjoyed the illusion of a success. One of these animals had entirely shed its winter coat, the other still carried thick brown patches of hair. I was specially struck by the shortness of their skulls and prominent eye-bones. Their summer coat is of a dull grey hue, lighter on the legs, rump, and under the belly; their height at the shoulder is about 40 ins. An average ram weighs from 200 to 250 lbs (six to seven *poods*) without the gralloch. With regard to their ways, it appears to me, as I have said before, that during the two warm months in Kamchatka they betake themselves to the highest ground and adopt the habits of wild goats, living in the tightest rocks, unlike wild sheep in the other parts of the world, that rely more on their sight for safety, and prefer rolling hills. Whether this peculiarity be due to natural inclination, or to a legitimate horror of mosquitoes, it is difficult to say; their tracks seemed more numerous along the ridges than on the lower pastures.

How they can survive the severe winter months of that northern climate, and find shelter or food when snow covers everything several feet deep, is a mystery. There can be no doubt that *Ovis nivicola* is considerably more plentiful along the coasts, where life is made easier for them, both on account of the constant breeze, which blows away mosquitoes in summer and carries off the snow in winter, as well as for the capital grazing, partly due to the sea salt. The well-known Normandy *prés-salés* owe their celebrity to the same cause. I am inclined to believe that Kamchatkan bighorn, for the same reasons, grow larger and stronger along the sea coast than in the interior of the peninsula. The fact remains that the heads obtained by me, or picked up by the natives near the coast, proved finer than any of those which we obtained in the Ganái region.

Taking the horns and some meat, we now retraced our steps in the direction of camp. It was no light job, heavily laden as we were, the General and I, to reascend the ridge; luckily on the other side we were able to slide down the steep snow-shoots almost the whole way back to the place where the ponies awaited us, and reached the tents in three hours, at 7 p.m. Littledale had already returned with three fair heads, one of which measured 33 ins, the other two being smaller. He had only seen these three rams together with a herd of ten ewes on the top of a high ridge, west of the Kamchatskaia Vershina. He said he might have bagged the lot, for they all stood about five minutes round him after his shots; he availed himself of the opportunity to secure one of the ewes, whose skin and bones he brought back for the British Museum.

An amusing adventure befell him that day. While climbing a slope with his hunter, they suddenly met face to face a large bear which had come up from the opposite side. Bruin's amazement was great; he got up on his hind legs at first, then crouched down again intently gazing at the intruders. Not wishing to disturb the ground, Littledale picked up a stone and threw it at the beast, hitting him on the snout; whereupon Bruin ran a few yards and stopped again to look back, when another stone was hurled at him, till he eventually decided to be off. On his way home Littledale shot a bear close to camp. Exchanging that evening our respective impressions, we concluded that few sheep were distributed among those hills, and that one or two more days' hunting would well-nigh exhaust the remaining stock.

Next morning, a thick mist having set in, it was decided to make it an "off-day", and enjoy twenty-four hours' rest. We spent our time skinning the heads and taking numerous photographs round the camp. The incessant struggle against mosquitoes could not be abandoned, and fires were constantly kept up round the tents to smoke out these troublesome foes. The afternoon was quite warm, and dinner was laid out-of-doors, Vasska doing wonders with roast fillets of sheep. Before turning in I found that the barometer had risen and promised a clear day for the morrow.

A SHOOTING TRIP TO KAMCHATKA
(Rowland Ward 1904)

A Buffalo Hunt in Central India

CAPTAIN J. FORSYTH

y mission for the succeeding six months was to explore this vast region of sál forest, lying to the north and east of Amarkantak, and stretching far beyond and to the south of the plain of Chattis'garh, in the semi-independent country called the Garhját States.

Over all this country roams the wild buffalo, and in the forests north and east of Amarkantak were then found large herds of wild elephants, which descended at the ripening of the crops of Chattis'garh to the skirts of the forest, doing immense damage, and forming a serious obstacle to the cultivation of the country. To penetrate to their haunts, ascertain their numbers, and propose means for their destruction, was another object of our expedition.

In the end of January I descended the Rajádhár pass from the Mandlá district, and marched across the Chattis'garh plain, where antelope, ducks, snipe, etc., afforded perpetual occupation for the gun, to the station of Rái'púr, where I met the Chief Commissioner's camp and my future companion in this expedition – Captain B., of Her Majesty's ―― Regiment. Thence we proceeded to the eastern and southern forests, marching rapidly to get from one portion of these forests to another, where days and weeks would be passed in tramping about the hills and making notes, the great part of which would possess no interest for the general reader. We never allowed ourselves to linger for sport; but the herds of buffaloes are in some parts of this country so numerous that it would have been almost impossible to avoid encountering them.

The extreme western range of the wild buffalo[1] in Central India is almost exactly marked by the 80th meridian of longitude, or in physical features by the Wyn-Gangá tributary of the Godávarí river, and below their junction almost by the latter river itself. I say *almost*, because in a trip down the Godávarí river which I made during the rains, I saw the tracks of a herd of buffaloes on the western side of

[1] *Bubalus arni.*

that river, at the "third barrier"[1] south of the station of Chándá, that is, a short distance to the west of the 80th meridian. The natives, however, told me there that they only cross the river in the rainy season, and that they do not penetrate very far to the west, so that so slight an exception may fairly be held to prove the general rule. So far, then, from the common adage of the sportsman being true that the wild buffalo does not extend *south* of the Narbadá, the truth is that the animal is unknown to the *north* of it, in the longitude of that river. It has been stated that the feral buffaloes of these parts are only the descendants of tame ones run wild, an idea that will not hold water for a second. They have all the habits of fully wild animals, are extremely numerous in the parts they inhabit, and exactly correspond in size and every particular with the aboriginally wild buffaloes of eastern Bengal. Two varieties are recognised in India, differing chiefly in the length and shape of the horns. They have been called by Hodgson, *B. Macroceros*, and *B. Speiroceros*, the horns of the former being long, straight, and more slender, and of the latter, shorter, thicker, and more curved. All the Central Indian species that I have seen pertain to the latter race, the average length of the horns of a mature bull being three-and-a-half to four feet. No animal has changed so little in domestication as the buffalo. In appearance the wild animal is extremely like the tame one, but fully a third larger, and showing fine, plump, sleek condition, instead, of the slouching, scraggy appearance of the domestic "buff", and possessing the free action and air of a denizen of the wilds. I have never heard an authentic case of their interbreeding with the domestic race, though individuals of the latter sometimes join the wild herds, and become difficult to reclaim. In height I have never seen a wild buffalo exceed sixteen hands; but though thus less in stature than the bison, the buffalo stands on much shorter legs, and is altogether a heavier built animal, so that in bulk and weight he must a good deal exceed the wild bull of the hills. They never interfere with each other, the bison adhering to hilly tracts, while the buffalo is essentially a lover of plains and level plateaux, where the extensive swamps he delights in can be found. The very different structure of their hoofs would suffice of itself to indicate this, those of the buffalo being broad and platter-like, to support him on soft ground; while those of the bison, who has to pick his way among rocks, are wonderfully small for his

---

[1] These "barriers" are points in the course of this river where its otherwise still, lake-like character is broken by spaces in which the river assumes more the character of a mountain stream. They interrupt what would otherwise be an unbroken stretch of waterway into the heart of the country, and are now being dealt with by a staff of skilful engineers. Probably a herd of buffaloes would find it easier to cross at one of these barriers than elsewhere.

size, as neat and game-like and little larger than those of the sámbar deer. The buffalo is also much less intolerant of man and his works than the bison, invading the rice cultivation, and often defying all attempts to drive him from the neighbourhood of villages. They are altogether very defiant of man, and, unlike the bison, will generally permit a close approach without any concealment, where they have not been much molested, trusting apparently to their formidable aspect to secure the retreat of the invader, which is usually successful. If the attack be followed up, however, they almost always make off at last, and are then not so easily got at again. The favourite resorts of the buffalo are on the skirts of the lower sál forests, where they run out into the open plain, and between them and the rice cultivation of these regions, in the great open, swampy plains, where long rank grass affords the sort of cover they like.

Our first introduction to the wild buffalo in this trip was near the high-road between Rái'púr and Sambalpúr, when B., who had the shot (in stalking a herd together we always arranged by turns who should have the first shot), killed a cow. We followed the herd a long way, and wounded another, but could not bag. For a long time after this we were employed in the forests, and though we saw a few, never had time to hunt them, until, near the Mahánadí river, we came out on a cultivated plain, of which a large bull and four cows had completely taken possession, devastating the rice, and charging indiscriminately at all who approached. A Baboo from the nearest police station had come out a little while before to rid the place of the invader, but contented himself with firing away all his ammunition at half a mile's distance from the top of a house, and the bull remained monarch of all he surveyed. We had scarcely entered on the plains when the owner of the ruined rice-fields pointed out his enemy, looming out against the horizon as large as an elephant, and we at once made preparations for the attack. The place was as level and open as a billiard-table, so we had to rely on our rifles alone. We were both heavily armed with two-ounce rifles, however, and several smaller guns in reserve, so we marched straight on the foe, with our very miscellaneous pack of dogs under orders to be let go at the first shot. The bull and his harem came boldly down to meet us, and as we approached commenced his usual demonstrations to put us to flight – pawing the earth with his feet, tossing his mighty horns, and making short runs in our direction. But we steadily advanced, and when within about 80 yds separated a little, so that one should get a flank shot, the full front of the buffalo being practically proof against lead. It was my turn for first shot, and when about 60 yds intervened I knelt down and brought the heavy rifle to bear on the point of his shoulder. Crash went two ounces of lead, propelled by eight drams of powder, against his tough hide, and he fell upon his knees. Bang went several more of our shots, and he stumbled off dead lame and very much crestfallen. Following him up with the dogs, who were now baying round him, we overhauled him in an open field, and repeated the dose again and again till he fell heavily against the embankment of a rice-field, and then, stepping up, I put a three-ounce shell behind his shoulder, and with a quiver of the limbs he gave it up. He was a fine animal, in the prime of life, and we were amazed at the bulk and strength exhibited by his massive form. The horns were each three feet ten inches long, which is nearly the extreme length they ever attain here.[1] He had sixteen bullets in him before he died, several of large calibre, and at close quarters. We were, however, shooting with bullets of plain lead, and I found that my first two-ounce ball, propelled by eight drams of powder, had flattened out on his shoulder, pulverising the bones, however, and completely laming him. After this we shot with hardened projectiles.

Next day we embarked in a long canoe, hollowed from the stem of a mighty sál tree, on the bosom of the Mahánadí and sailed down to Sambalpúr in two days and a night. It was mighty exciting work, the stream passing at intervals over long rapids, where the water, broken into many channels, rushed between narrow banks overhung with bushes, the boatmen steering the canoe with long poles in the most dexterous manner, now warding her bows from a rock on which the stream broke in a sheet of foam, then prostrating themselves at the bottom of the boat to avoid the sweep of the branches, while the canoe shot through some narrow passage, and presently emerging, after a final shave against a sunken rock, into a deep and silent pool, where the splash of huge fish, and the eye-knobs and serrated backs of crocodiles sailing about, showed that we had entered one of the long, silent reaches that break at intervals the torrent of these mountain rivers. My companion had got a severe attack of fever, which marred what would otherwise have been a sufficiently jolly trip. After resting awhile at this most secluded of stations (they get their supplies from Calcutta, several hundreds of miles away, on men's heads, and a convoy had just been trampled up by wild elephants before we arrived), we started again for the Garhját States, where the next month was spent in unremitting toil among their rugged hills. Here we were among the Khónd aborigines, famous for the Meriá sacrifices of human beings to the dread goddess Kálí. How they can have been confounded with our Central Indian Gónds I

---

[1] Fossil horns of much larger size have been found in the Narbadá gravels, along with bones of the hippopotamus, etc.

cannot imagine. They are much blacker and more negro-like in their physique, and speak a wholly different language, a few words only of which approximate, like Góndí, to the Támil of the south. Their country is wholly beyond the limits of the Central Highlands; and it would be out of place to enter here into a detailed description of the tribe, even did the few weeks I passed among them justify such an undertaking. We returned from this trip with most of our following severely ill of fever, contracted in these close jungles, where water is so scarce and bad at the time of year (April) that we rose, like river gods, from our daily bath hung with the green slime of the fetid pools from which our supplies were drawn. As we marched northward again we entered the valley of the Jónk river, a tributary of the Mahánadí, and here we fell in again with great herds of buffaloes, and halted for a day or two to recruit our followers and shoot. Our camp was pitched below a great spreading tree at the deserted site of the village of Jildá. Eaten up by the buffaloes, the people had moved off to a less open space. Around us was a sea of long grass, bounded by low hills and sál forests on the far horizon. Here our poor fever-stricken people paraded themselves in rows to let the sun into their shivering bones, and three times a day got a dose of quinine all round, a course of treatment (preceded by a smart dose of jalap) which soon frees a native from this hot-weather fever.

When marching in the morning, about a couple of miles from camp we saw a herd of fifty or sixty buffaloes standing up to their knees in a swamp among long grass. It was B.'s turn for the shot, and we spent several hours trying to get near enough to shoot. The buffaloes were very wild, having been much fired at a few weeks before by a sportsman with long-range small-bore rifles. As we approached on one side they waded through the swamp and went out on the other, reversing the process when we changed the direction of approach. At last I got on my horse, and took a light breech-loading gun, to try and get round and drive them across to B. They now got alarmed, and made off towards the head of the swamp; and on our following them on either bank, left it altogether, and started at their best pace across a rising ground. The ground seemed very favourable for riding for that country, so I could not resist the temptation to breathe my little nag at them, and was soon galloping full speed in their rear. My animal was an Arab pony, about thirteen three in height, but game as a bantam, and wonder-fully sure-footed over bad ground. To my surprise and delight, I found myself ahead of them in less than half a mile; and, shooting past, looked out for a worthy quarry among the labouring mass. I fixed on a bull with long horns, whose shining tips danced in the sunlight conspicuous above them all, and was just ranging alongside to fire when a tremendous bound of my little nag nearly unseated me, and we just escaped the long pointed horns of a lean brute of a cow that shot past my quarter, and then pulled up beyond me, shaking her head and looking very wicked indeed. I sheered off, and let her proceed to rejoin the herd, giving her a broadside of two barrels as she passed, which was followed by another end-on charge for several hundred yards. Eventually she went off again towards the retreating herd; but, though the ground had now become very bad, cut up in all directions by deep rifts in the black soil and pitted by the old footmarks of the buffaloes, I was not going to decline the challenge of this fighting cow. So after reloading my breech-loader, which was a very light snipe gun pressed into ball service, and wholly unfit for this sort of work, I cantered after her, and, when within distance, made a rush past, intending to fire into her at close quarters. But she was too quick for me, and we almost met, my gun going off, I believe harmlessly, in her face. I had another narrow shave as she again charged me, the little horse stumbling heavily several times in the frightful ground. Again she sheered off, and once again I rode up, though not so close as before, and gave her both barrels, holding the gun out like a pistol. She felt these, and, though shaking her head in a threatening manner, did not charge again. She now held on slowly behind the herd; and as I felt I could not kill her with this weapon, I waited behind, hoping she would lie down and the heavy rifles come up. Presently she slackened her pace to a walk, and I watched her from behind a bush. Peering cautiously all round, she went on a little further, and then, after standing about five minutes watching, lay down in the long grass. I marked the spot carefully, as I thought, by a bush, and then rode back full split for a heavy rifle. About a mile behind I met B. with the rifles and dogs, and we proceeded together to finish off the cow. My large rifle had got bulged on one barrel some time before, being unable to bear the proper charges for buffalo-shooting, so I had only one barrel to depend on. We walked up through the grass close to the spot I had marked, but she was not there. I soon lost the bearings, there being fifty bushes just like the one I had marked her by, and we wandered about, a little apart, looking for her. I had stood up on an ant-hill to get a better look, when just below me up started her savage-looking head and long horns, and she plunged towards me in the grass. A ball from the heavy rifle in the neck turned her, and she passed between B. and me, preventing both of us from further firing. The dogs now tackled her, "Tinker" in particular (whose deeds of valour in the wolf line have already been recorded) striving to seize her by the nose as she tore along. A couple of 100 yds further on she stopped in another patch of grass, the dogs baying round her, and Tinker, exhausted by the great

Inspired by Gordon Cumming's bestseller The Lion Hunter of South Africa, William Charles Baldwin (1826–1903) set off for Durban, making three hunting trips in Zululand between 1852 and 1856.

A narrow escape for Baldwin.

Sir Samuel Baker (1821–1893) and his intrepid Hungarian-born wife, Florence, who rode with him on his celebrated expedition to the sources of the Nile. A Major-General in the Ottoman Army and Governor-General of the Equatorial Nile Basin, Baker, a man of great physical strength and character, was the most famous of the 19th century big game hunters.

The hunter hunted . . . R. G. Gordon Cumming (1820–1866) shot huge quantities of game between 1843 and 1848. He usually hunted in South Africa in a kilt and deer stalker; he is today widely regarded as the classic example of a big game hunter who shot anything in sight. It has to be remembered that the vast herds of game must have seemed almost limitless to a mid-19th century big game hunter.

A professional elephant hunter of great skill, Arthur H. Neumann (1850–1907), was known to the Africans as 'Nyama Yangu' (my meat) because of his ability to kill any animal he selected as a target. An intensely shy man, he could hardly bring himself to walk through a crowded street.

Neumann pounded by an elephant during a safari near Lake Rudolph. An impression by E. Caldwell.

Abel Chapman (1851–1929) and his brother, Walter, taking cover as a column of forty elephants divides. They shot four huge bulls. At Rugby with F. C. Selous, Chapman is now regarded as one of the outstanding naturalist/hunters; he was also a gifted wildlife artist. A drawing by E. Caldwell.

James Sutherland (1872–1932), with an elephant shot in 1907. Sutherland shot more than a thousand elephants, many of them in German East Africa where he was allowed to shoot freely, having worked with the German colonial troops before the Great War.

...rick Courteney Selous DSO (1851–1917).
...s set sail for South Africa in 1871 and spent much of his life in the bush. An authentic British
...he sympathised strongly with the Boers whom he had learnt to respect during his hunting
...ditions. His exceptionally strong physique enabled him to continue his rugged life-style until he
...hot dead by a German sniper in 1917, aged 66. He bequeathed his fine collection of trophies to
...ritish Museum (Natural History).

King George V out shooting with the Maharaja of Nepal. This was big game hunting on a grand scale. The King, with his uncle the Duke of Connaught, presided over the Shikar Club, an elite society of big game hunters.

charge of a wounded tigress. A scene which cannot have been uncommon in India where from a howdah was calculated to disturb even the steadiest aim. A drawing by the illustrator, Stanley Berkeley.

Five Khandeish Bheel shikarees (India c. 1865).
Without the local knowledge of the shikarees, very little game would have been shot in India.

Captain C. R. E. Radclyffe (1873–1953) with a moose shot in Alaska. Perhaps the finest all-round
sportsman of his time, he excelled in shooting, fishing and falconry. He founded the Shikar Club
with Lord Lonsdale and travelled widely from the Arctic to the Equator in search of sport.

heat, lying down in the shade of a bush, but flying at her the moment she tried to move. We marched up, at a short interval from each other, and, arriving first on her blind side, I saw her glance at B., shake off the dogs, and creeping forward in a stealthy manner like a tiger, watch for him, with horns laid back, behind the screen of grass and bushes that intervened. Before he arrived, however, I took a steady shot at her neck with the little double fourteen-gauge rifle, dropping her stone dead. We found she had an old bullet wound in the flank, which was full of maggots, accounting for her extremely poor condition and unusual savageness. The small-bore rifle of our predecessor in these hunting-grounds was probably the cause. Her horns were of full cow length, the pair measuring eight feet four inches round the curve and across the skull.

The herd was now clean gone, of course, in the meantime, and we turned towards camp. On the way B. shot a cow, and I wounded a bull, and lost him in the long grass. While smoking our pipes after breakfast, one of the men who had remained to look after the wounded bull came in to say that he had been found lying down in an open plain about a mile away, looking very savage. We sallied forth immediately to encounter him, and found him lying close to a little ridge that had been the embankment of a rice field when the country was cultivated, and was now overgrown with tall grass. He had taken up a position which commanded all approaches, and, as there was no cover, there was nothing for it but to march up on foot. When within about 60 yds I took a shot with a small rifle, on the accuracy of which I could rely, at his broad forehead reclining on the bank. But the angle was wrong, and the ball glanced off without injury to the bull, who sprang on his feet and retreated to the middle of the field. The dogs were now loosed, and bayed round him till he began to chase them all round the field; but as soon as our heads appeared over the fringe of grass, he left them and charged down at ourselves. There was no sort of shelter, and every one had to look out for himself. I stood till he was within about half-a-dozen paces, and then jumped out of his course in the grass, not a moment too soon, my rifle being whirled out of my hands and its ramrod broken. Recovering it, I fired the undischarged barrel into the back of his shoulder, and at the same time the report of B.'s rifle in front of him rang in my ears. Next moment I saw B. fall spinning to one side, while the bull came down on his knees, Tinker, who had dashed past along with him, clinging nobly to his nose. Neither spare gun, gun-bearer, nor the dog-boy was in sight, as I dashed about, looking for the wherewithal to finish the struggling bull. At last I saw them, shrunk into nothing, in a shallow hollow in the black soil, and, seizing a couple of the guns, was hurrying up to the scene of action, when I met B., safe and sound, though rather pale, and at the same time heard the report of a rifle, and saw the bull fall over dead. My Mahomedan shikárí, a man accustomed to shoot, had fortunately ensconced himself, with my spare rifle, close to where the bull stopped after knocking B. over; and, putting the muzzle to his head, had pulled the triggers of both barrels at once! Tinker was covered with mire and blood from the bull, but otherwise uninjured, while the nose of the buffalo showed how determined had been his grip. B. had been caught fortunately with the *outside* edge of his horns, and but slightly, in the arms and ribs, and was not hurt beyond loss of wind and the shock of his fall.

The next day B. had fever, and was so shaken as to require a rest, and I went out alone in another direction. I came on a herd of about forty, grazing in an open plain some two miles south of the camp, and proceeded to stalk them. I had an elephant with me, and sent him round a long circuit to attract their attention while I crept in. Getting within about a hundred yards, I saw that the buffaloes had a bull nílgái along with them, which maintained a sharp outlook all round, while the buffaloes gazed stupidly at the elephant. I was crouched in grass about 3 ft high, and could not get any nearer for this singular sentinel. So I remained still, and presently the elephant disappeared in some low jungle, and the herd began again to graze. They fed down towards me, and when about 70 yds off I fired at the leader, who was standing end on to me, and was raked fore and aft by the heavy hard ball, falling prone, toes upwards, on the ground. Instead of retreating, the herd now gathered about their comrade, and trotted round, snuffing the blood, and looking about for their concealed enemy. The wreathing smoke of my rifle betrayed our position, and it was not without some alarm that I saw them draw up in a semicircle of pawing hoofs and snorting nostrils, surmounted by forty pairs of monstrous horns. My gun-bearer, Peer Khán, and I thought discretion the better part of valour under such circumstances, and espying, some way to our right, the pollarded trunk of a sáj tree, we retreated, snake fashion, through the grass, and clambered up it. Getting to the top, I sat on its smooth summit, while Peer Khán roosted crow-like on a branch, the only one, a foot or two lower down. I now opened fire on the herd, the first shot from the large rifle almost knocking me off my perch with the heavy recoil; I believe Peer Khán, who had reloaded it, had put in a double charge of powder. I then fired two rounds from the fourteen-bore, the herd pausing irresolute, and finally breaking into a panic-stricken flight. The balls had knocked the dried mud in clouds from their hides, and one remained standing on the ground, while another lagged, very lame, behind the retreating herd. I went up and finished the first, and then tracked up the other a long way till it went with the herd into a heavy swamp, when I returned to camp. I did not see, in the confusion, what became of the nílgái; but he was not with the herd when it retreated.

Our experience of the wild buffalo was thus different from that of some, who have reported it to be a timid, inoffensive animal. As is the case with most wild beasts, it all depends, I believe, on whether you press them hard or not; and probably many might be slaughtered at long ranges without even eliciting a charge. If followed up on foot, I believe the buffalo to be a much more dangerous opponent than the bison, being less timid, and also found in country where there is usually no protection to be derived from trees or rocks. In Bengal they are scarcely ever shot in any way but from elephants; and then have been known to prostrate an elephant in their charge. The prime sport with the buffaloes is on horseback; but it is rare that ground is found fit to ride them on with any degree of safety, and I never heard of its having been accomplished excepting on the occasion above related. I am sure, though, that with a horse clever over rough ground, and a light, breech-loading carbine, capital runs at buffaloes might often be secured by watching them into favourable ground. To kill them with the spear wound, I conceive, be utterly out of the question. We cut open one bull down the chest with an axe, to see what stopped our balls so strangely in front shots, and found that a bullet fired into the chest has to pass through more than 2 ft of hide, bone, and gristle before reaching the cavity of the lungs. Nor is the brain more accessible, the animal holding its head either elevated till the nose is level with the eyes, or, if charging, down between its fore-legs, and quite protected from a shot. A plain leaden bullet of an ounce weight, with three drams of powder, will go clean through the skull if hit perpendicularly, which, however, it is nearly impossible to do. The best places to fire, both at bison and buffalo, are through the point of the shoulder, if the rifle be powerful enough, or, if not, then behind and a little above the elbow. The centre of the neck is also very deadly, if the aim be true; natives almost always fire there with their matchlocks. The skull and horns of a bull buffalo are so large and heavy as to form a considerable encumbrance as a trophy to the sportsman marching fast with a light camp. Its value is completely spoilt, however, by sawing off the horns and throwing away the skull, as is often done. The better way is to boil away the flesh, and wait a few days till the horn-sheaths loosen on the bony cores, when they can be taken off, and the cores sawn down, leaving only a few inches to give the set of the horns. In doing this, the wonderful provision for giving requisite strength to the structure, without undue weight, by constructing the bony cores like hollow cells, crossed by stays in every direction, will not fail to be perceived.

THE HIGHLANDS OF CENTRAL INDIA
(Chapman & Hall 1889)

Tiger Shooting near Bareilly

J. PESTER

arious accounts having reached us of some tigers having committed horrid depredations at a village in the jungles about sixteen miles from Bareilly, at daylight this morning our elephants, guns and servants were despatched, and Peyron, Anderdon and myself left Macan's at twelve at night, and about two we crossed the Rham Gungah; a curious circumstance occurred in crossing the river! *One* of the party felt quite exhilarated by the wholesome quantity of champagne and claret we had partaken of, and in crossing our boat touched on a sandbank, and it was some minutes before we could get her off! My friend felt quite indignant at being detained, and, mounting his horse in the boat, he clapped spurs to him, and the horse immediately leaped the boat's side, and they plunged together into the river, from which they reached the banks with no other inconvenience than a sound ducking, and that to our great amusement! We soon after reached our tents, escorted by a strong party of armed villagers with torches, to conduct us in safety through the woods which at many parts were hardly penetrable! We were well assured that the intelligence of tigers being in the neighbourhood was *perfectly correct*, for about mid-way between the river's side and our tents we heard them roaring, and howling hideously, and that at no very great distance from us. Some of the villagers who were conducting us left us, and took to the tops of trees. The men carrying the torches remained with us! We drew our pistols, and at the head of a party of Matchlock men we advanced, and got safe to our tents, which were pitched at the village end. Went immediately to bed, and the villagers remained all night, and promised to take us at daylight in the morning immediately to the spot where the tigers always harboured during the day.

May 1   At four this morning we mounted our elephants, and within the distance of half-cannon shot from our tents, the villagers pointed to a brake of briars, in which they assured us there was a tigress and four half-grown cubs! The brake was not 300 yds round, and we instantly encircled it with our elephants! To penetrate it was

impossible, and we commenced shouting and firing into the jungle, but all in vain, no tiger making its appearance! The villagers who for safety had, according to their usual plan, mounted to the tops of the trees near us, persisted in assuring us that the tigers were yet in the jungle, and one of the drivers attached to my elephant dismounted and looked under the cover, which we were unable to do from our elephants. The man instantly remounted, and in a terrible funk declared that he saw one of the young tigers stalking along under the briars. We commenced again every stratagem we could invent to draw the tigress out to charge us, but she would not come, and I suspected that fear had got hold of the man who dismounted to reconnoitre, and was therefore induced to go down to look myself! I had no sooner reached the ground than I discovered two of the young tigers, and plainly saw the immense feet and paws of the tigress. I instantly ran up the elephant's side by a rope, and communicated this glorious intelligence.

We all loaded a double barrel each with small (buck) shot, and fired in the direction I pointed out. This had the desired effect. The young ones bellowed out a ghastly noise, and the crashing of the jungle soon convinced us what was coming. The tigress, on hearing the cubs roar, instantly sprang forward, bore down everything before her, made a most savage and desperate charge on us. The roar was really like a clap of thunder when she attacked us. Peyron and Anderdon both fired, and wounded her, but she sprang upon the elephant nearest to her, and shockingly wounded three of the people; one of them died almost immediately! She was fairly fast on the elephant's poll with her teeth sticking in her neck, and the hind claws fast deep in the poor elephant's trunk and face. This was a subject which the best artist would have been puzzled to have done justice to. The tigress was nearly the size of a Bengal bullock, and presented a fair mark to me although closed with the elephant, and I immediately fired my two-ounced double barrel at her; she instantly quitted her hold, dropped from the elephant (which I firmly believe she would have brought to the ground in an instant more), and slunk back, apparently stupefied, into the jungle, all of us saluting her as she returned. She staggered into the briars, evidently mortally wounded.

We now prevailed upon the villagers to come with fire, and soon had the brake in a blaze. The young tigers now came out, and although not half-grown, attacked the elephants with all imaginable fury, and evinced that savage and desperate nature born with them. They afforded us excellent diversion, and we despatched the whole party. The tigress was stone dead in the jungle, and such a monster my eyes never beheld! The poor villagers threw themselves at our feet, calling us the saviours of them and their cattle.

We returned with our glorious spoils to our tents, as much gratified with the morning's sport as men ever were.

The inhabitants of the village, men, women and children, came to express their gratitude, and to put up their prayers for us. We had a delicious breakfast on mutton chops, cold fowls, tongue, eggs, and all sorts of good things, and slept till two in the afternoon; walked out upon the banks of the river, and shot two immense alligators. The Rham Gungah swarms with them, and we wounded at least a dozen. In the heat of the day every sand is covered with these monsters; they come up to bask in the sun. At four we mounted our horses and crossed the river about five miles above our tents, at a good ford. Reached cantonments soon after sunset, dressed and dined with Becher, passed a glorious evening, detailing to our friends the sport of the morning, and aiding our repetition with a comfortable quantum of most excellent claret.

May 5 Anderdon, Peyron, Middleton and myself went this morning to breakfast with Becher; we found them exceedingly agreeable, and after breakfast the lady played and sung us a great number of songs and fine pieces of music. Hers was a grand piano, braced with brass to preserve it from the scorching winds, and was one of the most elegant instruments I ever beheld, and her superior skill and taste did it real justice. At noon we commenced shooting with Becher's air gun. Killed a "minor" with a ball from it on the top of the house, and broke several kedgeree pots at a great distance. We returned to tiff at home with Middleton, and I took with me Becher's double-barrel ball gun, by Nock, to carry with me on our next tiger party, with which, in addition to five double barrels and a rifle, all of my own, I considered myself well equipped in arms. Becher declined accompanying us, on account of the scorching sun and winds which prevail at this season of the year. Our guns, elephants, servants, with a good store of claret, Madeira, fowls, hams, etc., etc., left cantonments to-day, with orders to remain at the ground we last shot at (in the jungles) till we should come up.

Met Becher, W——t, Colonel Powell, Nuthall, Guthrie, Anderdon, Thornhill, Vernor, Boileau and Montague at dinner this evening at Doveton's, who gave us a sumptuous entertainment. Doveton was Middleton's senior captain in the 3rd, and as friendly a fellow as ever lived. After passing a most sociable pleasant evening, and as the clock struck twelve, Major Middleton, Anderdon, Peyron and self mounted our horses, and rode off for our tents in the jungles, with proper guides, and a good escort of troopers.

About four in the morning we arrived safe at our tents, and went immediately to bed, agreeing to halt to-morrow to take rest, and shoot alligators.

May 6   We slept till ten this morning, and after taking a hearty breakfast we left our tents to talk on the banks of the river for an hour with our rifles. The alligators were innumerable, and we made some fine shots, and left several of those monsters dead upon the sands, and wounded many more. If an alligator is not struck either in the head or behind the fore leg where the scale is more tender than at any other part it is a thousand chances to one against its penetrating, or giving a mortal wound. They sleep very sound on the edges of the water, and by making a circuit on the banks you may easily come directly upon them; the banks in general are so steep that there is little fear of their being able to come up the sides to annoy the sportsman.

In the afternoon some villagers came to our tents with news of tigers near a village called Sullamy; we immediately sent on one of our tents, took an early dinner and a bottle of claret each, went to bed, and at two in the morning mounted our horses, and rode on for Sullamy, leaving directions for our equipment to follow immediately. Our breakfast apparatus had been ordered on with the first tent.

May 7   We reached our breakfast tent at daybreak, and got on the elephants instantly on our arrival. The Jemadar (chief) of the villages had assembled all his people (himself we put on a spare elephant) to attend us, and we set forward, all keen for the expected sport. We agreed to fire at nothing but a tiger, and in consequence the deer and hogs, which we found in greater abundance than I could have believed, all escaped. We beat in vain till nearly twelve o'clock, and although we saw their tracks and dens in the deep part of the cover we could not find. The jungle was so very extensive that if inclined to avoid us they could easily effect it, and the grass was sufficiently high to conceal them from our sight, unless they came, like the deer and hogs, close under our elephants' trunks. At twelve we left the cover, and I shot a deer (the longest shot I ever made with a ball) on our way to the tents, Middleton and Peyton also killed a boar each in returning.

At breakfast other villagers came in with intelligence of tigers, and we determined to try for them in the morning, but the jungles in this part of the country were so exceedingly strong that it was next to an impossibility to see them. The ground we beat over this morning was a perfect forest, so lofty and thick was the jungle that we could see nothing ten yards in our front, and the elephants with great difficulty moved very slowly through it. Tigers there were beyond a doubt, in great numbers, and we traced them on the sands by the river's side, where their prints were in thousands, and it was evident that at night they frequently crossed the river in quest of prey, and returned to lie in the strong cover. Shot with rifles at a mark after breakfast, and the natives, who many of them had never seen a European before, were much amused at our firing, and showed us every civility, bringing us presents of goats, eggs, milk, etc., etc. Tiffed at two, and a little before sunset I mounted "Major" and went to try for a hog in a short piece of jungle close to our tents. Many of the villagers, with their chief, accompanied me, and we had scarcely formed our lines and began to beat when a large herd of hogs got up. I gave chase to the boar, and a noble fellow he was. He soon separated from the others, and took across the country towards a strong jungle. The ground was very bad, and full of holes (which kept the rest of the party at the tents), and my horse was several times on his face with me. I could not choose my ground nor pull up for a moment, but with every prospect of losing him. We had a most complete race of it for full two miles, when I came near him, and the instant he heard me at his heels, and found that he could not reach the jungle (about 150 yds in his front) he turned upon me, and made a most furious charge. I well knew that if I missed my first spear he would be in the high jungle before I could again recover it, and as I was single-handed at him, I could afford to risk nothing. At the distance of about 20 yds, when he was coming down, he increased his speed, and made a most desperate push at me, and was almost close to my boot top before I could give him the spear, and turn off to avoid him. The spear entered just behind the shoulder blade, he staggered a few paces, when the blood poured out of his mouth, and he dropped upon his haunches, and in the act of exertion to tear the spear from him he fell as dead as a stone. He was an immense boar, and had not mine been a tractable horse with an excellent mouth he would probably have destroyed us both. The horse would assuredly have been upset had he struck us, and as there was not a soul at hand we should both have been at his mercy, and in nature I do not imagine anything can be more desperately furious than a wild boar charging. (I have actually seen a *young one*, not half grown, come voluntarily down to charge a complete line of elephants!) I was as much gratified with my evening's sport as a man ever was on any occasion, and it proved more than a compensation to me for our disappointment in the morning after tigers. A camel was sent out to bring in my *prize*, and they all agreed that it was as noble an animal as was ever seen. Our tents we sent on at sundown to the village of Russanpore, and dined under a mango tree. Drank our bottle of wine, and at ten o'clock mounted our horses to proceed to Russanpore for to-morrow's shooting. We came up with our elephants and baggage upon the banks of the river, where they were detained for boats. The river here was very deep and wide, but as there was no prospect of the arrival of boats, and as we had news of tigers, we had no inclination to lose our day's sport, and therefore determined to cross. We got on our elephants, with our guns and ammunition, and in the dark they swam the river with us. Our saddles we took with us in the howdahs, and each took his horse in tow, and all got safe over, leaving the baggage to cross when the boats should arrive. Our breakfast tents had gone to the proper passage, and found their way with our beds and breakfast things to Mungarah. Placed our cots in the open air, under some trees, as the night was very close, and slept soundly till nearly five in the morning.

May 8   Mounted our elephants this morning at half-past five, and commenced shooting at a cover within a mile of Mungarah, in which they assured us they had very lately seen tigers, and several people and many cattle had recently been destroyed by them. We were not long in finding, and after several desperate charges, and nearly twenty shots fired, we dropped an immense tigress. Almost every shot struck her, and she fought with much desperation, bleeding most furiously. At last a ball from Middleton, just as she was in the act of springing on his elephant, gave her a brain blow, and rolled her completely over – several shots from the rest of us, aimed at her heart, despatched her before she could again recover herself. We loaded the tigress, and were proceeding towards our tent, when one of the elephant drivers discovered in the jungle three tiger cubs, apparently but a few days old, and lying close by them was an immense buck, which appeared to be but just killed. We were back to our tents, had bathed, and dressed for breakfast before eleven o'clock, the morning vilely hot indeed. We had a good tiffin on some excellent fish, and at three o'clock again mounted the elephants.

Going out, and not one hundred yards from our tents, which were pitched upon the banks of the river, I being nearest the water, shot an immense alligator; the first shot was through the head with the rifle; he struggled off the sand upon which he lay sleeping, but could not remain under the water, which was quite discoloured with his blood. The second and third shots which I fired from Becher's gun completely finished him, and the villagers, who were always in great numbers attending us, brought him to shore, and one of the baggage elephants with a strong rope dragged it to our tents! He was a tremendous beast, and weighed as much as a couple of good horses. We proceeded into the jungles, and had excellent deer and hog shooting. My horses were out, and I dismounted from the elephant to ride after a hog, but the cover was so strong that I could not keep sight a moment. This evening I am convinced that besides hogs innumerable, we saw at least a hundred deer, seven of which we killed, and might easily have shot twice that number had we been inclined. The villagers told us that they never recollect to have seen the game disturbed before. They themselves were deterred from pursuing it, on account of the tigers, of which they are never free. Dressed and dined at seven o'clock, passed a very happy evening, drank to our friends in Old England, and wished only for the society of some of them to complete our happiness. A day never passed that we did not talk of them, and fox hunting was always drank in high glee.

MAY 9   Went from our tents this morning at four o'clock to a jungle which the villagers recommended as likely for tigers. After beating a considerable time and rousing a great many deer and hogs, our elephants began to roar and to beat their trunks on the ground and spuming in such a manner as left little doubt of tigers being at hand, and the driver of Anderdon's elephant positively affirmed that he saw two large tigers dart past in the jungle.

We were exceedingly annoyed at not being able to get a sight at them; the jungle was absolutely higher than our tents, and we could scarcely move in it. In this situation were we, surrounded with tigers, and our elephants, by winding them so constantly, became quite furious, and apparently were as eager to get at them as ourselves.

We had not a glimpse of each other for some hours, and kept our direction in the forest entirely by hearing the rustling of our elephants and their roaring, which we could not prevent.

We went directly through the depth of the wood, as there the tigers lay, but did not get a *single shot*. On passing a low jungle attached to the stronger one we picked up two cubs, and saw the tigress slink in a most unusual cowardly way into the deep cover. I never before either saw or heard of a tigress quitting her young but with their lives. On the contrary, they generally advance the moment you get within their hearing. We saw her and fired at least twenty distant random shots at her, but it only seemed to accelerate her movements.

On our way to the tents we shot a hog and three deer, and arrived to breakfast about twelve, which, after taking a bath and a *dry shirt*, we relished much and stood greatly in need of, as the morning was very hot, and we were a good deal fatigued. Slept till nearly three o'clock. In the evening our people fishing caught a younger alligator in their nets, and we spoilt half-a-dozen swords in trying them on the scales of its back, which the best metal and the strongest arm could not cut through.

MAY 10   At four this morning we went off to the jungle in which we yesterday saw the tigress, and took up the cubs. We made our disposition to interrupt as much as possible her retreat to the deep cover. On drawing near the spot we were gratified with a sight of her, not skulking away as yesterday, but the instant she heard us she came on most desperately and evidently determined to rout us, or die herself in the trial. She came down, roaring and lashing her tail in a truly glorious style, apparently frantic with rage. It is impossible to conceive anything more furious than she was, and the sight was really enough to strike terror into the system of any one not confident in his gun and the resolution of his elephant. On approaching us at the distance of about thirty paces in our front we gave her the contents of four double barrels, loaded with a couple of balls in each barrel. The tigress trumbled completely over, and in a moment recovered her legs again, and closed with the elephant nearest her, which she tore almost to pieces about the face, trunk, and the breasts. She was, however, enfeebled very considerably by the wounds we had given her, which was much in favour of the elephant, and after a most furious fight (which drove us almost *mad* with the pleasure it afforded us) the elephant shook the monster off, and struck it so violent a blow with the trunk that quite stupified it for a moment. The elephant instantly, and in a most sagacious manner, took the advantage of this, and immediately knelt upon the tigress's breast, and endeavoured by all means to crush it to death. It was impossible for us to take a shot, although we were completely round them, so close and entangled were they in each other.

The tigress at length extricated itself, and was advancing to renew the combat when we brought her down, and twenty balls were in or through her before she could get herself again on her legs, and we settled her, after a fight of at least a quarter of an hour from the time we first saw her. The elephant attacked, and its driver (who firmly kept his seat), behaved most gallantly. The man with his sabre (which they always carry on tiger parties) made many good cuts at the tigress, whilst they were engaged. Our elephants were bellowing, and shewed every inclination to join in the combat; they seemed almost as furious as the parties engaged; in short, we were *all mad together*, and the roaring and shouting might have been heard for many miles in the woods. Loaded the royal game upon an elephant, and returned by eleven to our tents to breakfast, having first taken a good bathe and dressed. It was quite *the thing impossible* for a small party to be more happy and comfortable than we were. We had *noble sport*, and every luxury at command that the country afforded, besides which we were doing no small service to the poor wretches who, with their little property, so constantly fell victims to the merciless monsters we destroyed, and they, poor devils, were most grateful to us in return for the good we did them, calling themselves "our slaves", and bringing us in everything their country produced, which they thought would be acceptable to us. We slept till four in the evening, and then walked out with our rifles to shoot alligators on the Rham Gungah. Peyron, Anderdon and myself fired at one tremendous brute within 20 yds of us. Each shot went through his head, and he died almost without a struggle. We sent out the elephants to drag him to our tents to shew to Middleton, who was a good deal fatigued with the morning's sport, and did not accompany us.

We dined at seven, and drank "Tiger Hunting", "Fox Hunting", and "Hog Hunting" with each three times three!

WAR AND SPORT IN INDIA
(Heath, Cranton & Ouseley 1913)

The Iyenpoor Man-Eater

G. P. SANDERSON

iger-shooting on foot is very generally condemned, but as in most matters of choice there is something to be said for, as well as against, it. It is never followed systematically by any man, but circumstances occasionally arise when it must be resorted to, or sport be sacrificed. At this point some men abandon their quarry, some stick to it. Those without experience of their game do well to pause; but one who knows the beast he has to deal with, may kill many dangerous animals on foot without accident or even serious adventure. Almost every accident that occurs is directly traceable to ignorance or carelessness. The sportsman is a tyro, and overventuresome; or due precautions are not observed when a wounded beast is on foot, and some one, moving about where he does not think the animal can possibly be, is seized.

Tiger-shooting on foot can never, of course, be safe sport; but a sportsman is not supposed to look for absolute safety on all occasions, any more than does a soldier. Risks must be run, but if properly conducted dangerous game-shooting on foot is not the mad amusement usually supposed. Speaking for myself, I have been fortunate enough to kill several tigers and panthers, and a large number of bears and other formidable beasts, on foot, so I will venture to state what I think are the chief precautions to be observed.

It makes all the difference in the world whether the animal to be attacked is wounded or not. The sportsman occasionally comes upon a tiger when after other game, or one is driven from a cover without being much bullied. There is no danger to speak of in firing first shots at a hundred such beasts. But if a tiger has been much harassed and irritated, and imagines himself unable to escape – or wounded, and is followed up whilst pain and exhaustion have forced him to stop – he proves a very different beast to the retiring animal he ordinarily is, though he is always an abject coward if firmly faced. It is true that in shooting with elephants tigers frequently get on board some of them; but a tiger fears man more than any other being, and though he will charge pluckily enough to all appearances, he always shirks the last ten feet if boldly received. In netting tigers I have seen this so constantly that I am quite sure a few determined men, keeping together, are quite safe from any tiger in open ground.

Whether a tiger should be attacked on foot or left alone depends greatly on the nature of the jungle in which he is found. In the grass plains and thick undergrowth of such parts of Bengal as I have seen, tigers can only be shot from the elevation of elephants' backs; but in many parts of Southern India the jungle is clear inside, and the ground is broken, so that rocks and ravines may afford advantageous positions. The tiger can also be shot even without such aids when he can be seen at some distance.

None but the utterly ignorant would think of following a wounded tiger into long grass or close cover, where it has every advantage, and the sportsman may be seized before he has time to use his rifle. As well might one follow it on a dark night. In such cover the tiger rarely makes any demonstration from a distance, seeking to avoid observation, but when almost stumbled upon he attacks like lightning. In doing this he is seldom seeking to make a reprisal, and only acts in self-defence when he thinks himself discovered.

One of the most powerful elements in the tiger's attack is his voice if the attack be commenced very near. The startling, coughing roar is almost paralysing to the coolest in such cases. But if the tiger has to come on from any distance he rarely does more than grunt, and the sportsman's attention is concentrated on the beast himself, and his demonstrations pass unnoticed. The power of the tiger's voice at close quarters may be understood by any one who has an opportunity of seeing a newly-caged tiger. It is almost impossible to watch a charge against the bars, if standing within a yard or so of them, without flinching; but if seen at twenty yards' distance it is nothing.

If a moment's time be given for preparation, a tiger's charge loses much of its power. In following any dangerous game the excitement felt when the beast is known to be near, but not visible, amounts to positive nervousness. A quail rising at his feet startles the man who the next moment faces an elephant or tiger with *sang froid*. As soon as the game is seen, nervousness gives place to the most perfect coolness, and if a tiger's charge can be anticipated it loses most of its danger.

I never myself hesitate to follow wounded animals on foot if the ground be favourable. In such cases the chief precautions to be observed are: to trust no place as not holding the tiger till it has been ascertained not to do so; never carelessly to approach thick cover from which a beast may make a sudden attack; and, if possible, to have men who will all stand firm. Under no temptation should the sportsman's last shot be fired at a retreating beast.

I will now recall, with the aid of my hunting-journal, some scenes in tiger-shooting, and will endeavour to select occurrences illustrative of the nature and peculiarities of the animal. Amongst them I will relate one or two incidents in tiger-shooting on foot, to show how I consider the sport may be managed when occasion demands.

When I pitched camp at Morlay in September 1873, to commence the elephant kheddahs, the country-side was in a state of considerable alarm from the attacks of a man-eating tigress. This tigress's fits of man-eating seemed to be intermittent, as after killing three or four persons some months before, she had not been heard of till about the time of my arrival at Morlay, when she killed two boys attending goats. I anticipated some trouble from her in our kheddah work, as it would be unsafe for one or two men to go alone through the jungles; but whether it was from the disturbance caused by seven or eight hundred work-people, or other reasons, we heard nothing of her for some time.

On November 30th, when the work-people had dispersed, news was brought in that a man, returning to the village of Nágwully (about 6 miles from Morlay) with cattle, had been carried off the evening before. From an account of the place where the mishap had occurred I knew it was useless to look for the tigress after the lapse of eighteen hours, as she would have retired to impracticable jungle. I urged the people to bring news of further losses at the earliest possible moment.

On December 19th another man was carried off close to the village of Iyenpoor, 5 miles from Morlay, but I did not hear of this till two days afterwards.

On Christmas-day I thought I would look up the jungles in the Iyenpoor direction, so took an elephant and some trackers in hopes of learning something of the tigress's habits. The unfortunate man's wife, with her three small children, were brought to me as I entered the village. The woman, with the strange apathy of a Hindoo, related what she knew of her husband's death without a tear. I gave her some money, as she would have to expend a small sum in accordance with caste usage to rid her of the devil by which she was supposed to be attended on account of her husband's having been killed by a tiger, before she would be admitted into her caste's villages; and then, accompanied by the headman and others, went to the scene of the last disaster. A solitary tamarind-tree grew on some rocks close to the village; there was no jungle within 300 yds, only a few bushes in the crevices of the rocks; close by was the broad cattle-track into the village. The unfortunate man had been following the cattle home in the evening, and must have stopped to knock down some tamarinds with his stick, which, with his black blanket and a skin skull-cap, still lay where he was seized. The tigress had been hidden in the rocks, and in one bound seized him, dragged him to the edge of a small plateau of rock, from which she jumped down into a field below, and there killed him. The place was still marked by a pool of dried blood. She had then dragged her victim half a mile, to a spot where we still found his leg-bones.

After walking about for two hours with the trackers, in the hopes of seeing recent marks of the tigress, but without success, the village cattle were sent for and herded into the jungles in the hope of attracting her if near. The poor beasts were, however, so frightened by the constant attacks of tigers, that we could scarcely get them to face the jungle, and a partridge rising suddenly was too much for their nerves, and sent them, tails up, to the village before they had been out half an hour. After some time they were got back. About 1 p.m., as they were feeding near a cover in a hollow encircled on three sides by low hills covered with bamboo, and a very pretty spot for a tiger, a wild scurry took place as a large tiger rushed amongst the foremost of them. Strange to say they all escaped, two only being slightly wounded; a few plucky buffaloes were in advance, and interfered considerably with the tiger's attack, as these animals never hesitate to do.

Up to this time I had been walking, rifle in hand, amongst the cattle, but the heat was considerable, and at this unlucky moment I was some little distance behind getting a drink, or I might have had a shot. As the herdsmen were not certain that the tiger had not secured something in his rush, we went in force to look through the cover. We only found footprints, however, and knew they were not those of the man-eater, but of a large male who was a well-known cattle-killer about the place. We shortly heard a spotted-deer bark over the saddle of the hill to our left; the tiger had moved off in that direction upon his discomfiture. We saw nothing more of him that day, or of the man-eater, and I returned to camp by moonlight. It was so cold that I was glad of an overcoat. A good camp Christmas dinner was awaiting me; and had I only been lucky enough to bag the man-eater, I should have been able to enter this amongst my red-letter days.

After this nothing was heard of the tigress for a week, when the trackers and I were going to look after some wild elephants, and at the ford in the river below the Koombappan temple found a tiger's pugs that were immediately pronounced to be hers. I sent back two men on my riding-elephant to warn the people of Morlay that the tigress was in our jungles, as her usual hunting-grounds were to the east of the river, and the people on our side were liable to be off their guard. We tried to follow her, but she had crossed open dry country, in which tracking was impossible, and we had to give her up. During the day I made arrangements for hunting her systematically next day should she still be in our jungles.

Whilst at dinner that evening, I heard voices and saw torches hurriedly approaching my tent, and could distinguish the words "*naie*" and "*nurri*" ("dog" and "jackal") pronounced excitedly. The Canarese people frequently speak of a tiger by these names, partly in assumed contempt, partly from superstitious fear. The word "*hooli*" (tiger) is not often used amongst jungle-men, in the same way that, from dread, natives usually refer to cholera by the general terms of *rōga* or *járdya* (sickness). The people were from Hurdenhully, a village a mile and a half away, and had come to tell me that their cattle had galloped back in confusion into the village at dusk, without their herdsman. Only one man had been with them that day, as there was some festival in the village. We suspected he had fallen victim to the tigress, but it was useless to attempt a search that night. The cattle had been two or three miles into the jungles, and we had no indications where to look for the unfortunate herdsman, who was, moreover, probably now half devoured. So ordering some rice for the men, I sent them to Morlay to tell the trackers, and to sleep there and return with them in the morning.

At dawn we started on the back-trail of the cattle from Hurden-hully till we found the point where they had begun to gallop, just below the embankment of a small channel drawn from the river near Atticulpoor, and supplying the Hurdenhully tank with water. The ground was hard and much trodden by cattle, and we looked for some time for the tigress's tracks in vain, till the distant caw of a crow attracted us to the place where we found the man's remains; only the soles of his feet, the palms of his hands, his head, and a few bones were left. We lost no time in taking up the tigress's track, and used every endeavour to run her down, as we had over a hundred men ready at camp to beat her out could we but mark her into some practicable cover; but though she had eaten so much she had recrossed the river as usual, and had gone into the jungles towards the hills, where there was no chance of finding her.

About a week after this the priest of a small temple ten miles due west from Morlay, and in comparatively open country where a tiger had not been heard of for years, was jogging along on his riding-bullock one morning, to sweep out and garnish the small jungle-temple in which he officiated, and to present to "Yennay Hollay Koombappah" the offerings of the simple villagers whose faith was placed in that deity. Suddenly a tigress with her cub stepped into the path. The terrified bullock kicked off his rider and galloped back to the village, whilst the tigress – for it was the dreaded Iyenpoor man-eater, far out of her ordinary haunts – seized the hapless *poojáree* (priest), and carried him off to the bed of a deep ravine near.

Upon hearing next day of this, my men and I thought it must be some other tiger, as this fiend had managed with such cunning that we did not then know that she had a cub; and it was not till we found this out subsequently that we traced this death to her also. Up to this time she must have left her cub in the thick jungles along the hills, making her rapid hunting forays alone, as the cub had never been with her before; and this accounted for her invariably crossing the river and making for the hills after a raid. The absence of the tigress from the vicinity of Morlay during September and October was probably caused partly by her keeping out of the way when this cub was very young.

The next death was of a horrible description. Several villagers of Rámasamoodrum were grazing their cattle in a swampy hollow in the jungle near the temple, when the tigress pounced upon one man who was separated from the others. She in some way missed her aim at his throat, seized the shoulder, and then, either in jerking him, or by a blow, threw him up on to a thicket several feet from the ground. Here the wounded and bleeding wretch was caught by thorny creepers; whilst the tigress, as generally happens when any *contretemps* takes place, relinquished the attack and made off. The other men and the cattle had fled at the first alarm. The village was some distance away, and there was not time before nightfall for a party to search for the man, whose being still alive was not known.

Next morning the lacerated wretch was found. In his mangled state he had been unable to release himself; he was moaning and hanging almost head downwards amongst the creepers; and he died soon after he was taken down.

Before long the tigress visited my camp, but fortunately without doing any mischief. Close to my tent (my bungalow was not built then) was a large banian-tree: every night a fire was kindled near it, and here I sat and discussed plans for work or sport with my men. One morning when the trackers came to wake me early, they found the man-eater's tracks leading down a path close to the banian-tree in question. As we thought she might still be on our side of the river, I accompanied the men to examine its vicinity, and to ascertain if she had recrossed it towards the hills; if not, we intended to hunt the different covers on its banks during the day.

Upon reaching the river we walked down the sandy bed overshadowed by drooping *hongay* (the Indian beech, *Pongamia glabra*) trees. The scene at early morning was very pleasant. Gaudy kingfishers fluttered and poised over the pools and shallow runs of clear water into which the river – a considerable stream in the rains –

had now shrunk. At a bend we came upon a troop of lungoor monkeys (*Presbytis priamus*) feeding upon some fallen fruit; these ran nimbly across the sand to the sanctuary of the large trees when we appeared. In one stretch a spotted stag and several graceful hinds were drinking at the cool stream, perchance admiring their shapely forms in nature's mirror; but for the nonce they passed unheeded. The soothing cooing of doves, the scream of the toucan, the cheery and game cry of the jungle-cock (*Gallus sonneratii*) perched aloft, whilst his ladies ruffled themselves in the sand below, combined to make one of those tranquil phases of beauty in nature which are such a contrast to the wildness and grandeur of other scenes.

The trackers moved quickly and silently along. We passed two or three pugs, but these elicited no notice, except one into which Dod Sidda drove the butt-end of his spear without a word; this was the night's track of the tigress to our side of the river. We had nearly got to the temple, below which it was not likely she would have crossed, and were in hopes of not finding her out-going trail, when a single track across an unblemished stretch of sand caused an exclamation of disappointment, and one glance showed it to be the unmistakable small oval pug of the man-eater. We felt our chances of finding her that day were very small, but there was nothing like trying; so sending for an elephant to come to the temple and there await my return, we cast ahead towards the hills, and again hit off the trail. After several hours' work, finding tracks now and then in the sandy beds of ravines, but all leading up to a country where the cover was continuous, we were obliged to give it up as useless, as we could neither keep the trail nor have done anything towards driving such extensive cover had we even found where the tigress lay hidden. We were forced reluctantly to return, consoling ourselves with the hope of finding her in more favourable country soon, and vowing to leave no stone unturned till we bagged her. It had become quite a point of honour with the trackers; we had never been played such successful tricks before by any animal, and they said the tigress was "throwing dirt into their mouths".

We got back to the temple late in the afternoon; here I found the elephant and several of my people, and a man with a note from Captain C., of the Revenue Survey, who was in camp a few miles from Morlay. I started the messenger back with a reply, and though we were pretty certain the man-eater was miles away, it was a nervous job for him to get through the jungle till he reached open country on the far side. He left us, already casting furtive glances around him, to the great amusement of my men (who had not the job to do themselves!). Before he had got far, one of them, who was a bit of a humorist, called him back. The man came, when the wag, assuming a concerned air, said: "You know, *keep a good lookout ahead of you* – never mind the *rear*; if a tiger seizes a man from behind, what could any of us do? but, you know, *you can see her if she is coming for you from in front*, and you might try a run for it. Good-bye! Koombappah be with you! *Don't* delay; it's rather late as it is!" The poor villager grinned painfully at the joke, which the rest enjoyed immensely; but I saw he was in such a fright – and reflected that, with the uncertainty of her class, the tigress might as likely be near as far away – that I sent half-a-dozen men (the joker amongst them) to see him safely into the cultivated country on the other side.

Shortly after this, work took me to Goondulpet, twenty-five miles from Morlay, on the Neilgherry road, and I returned on the 14th January 1874. As I rode into camp about mid-day the trackers were waiting for me, and informed me that they had heard the "death-cry" raised at a small village called Bussavanpoor below the Rámasamoodrum lake, and some two miles from Morlay, that morning; and that on inquiry they found a woman had been carried off by the man-eater out of the village during the night, but that they had not followed the tracks, as I was not with them. Bussavanpoor was a small hamlet situated in the middle of open rice-fields, then bare as the crop had been cut. There was no jungle to cover the man-eater's advance, and a tiger had never hitherto been heard of near the village. This attack was therefore the more unlooked for and terrifying to the villagers.

Immediately breakfast was over and an elephant ready I started and soon reached Bussavanpoor. The attack had been most daring. At one end of the single street of the village stood a shady tree, round the base of which a raised terrace of stones and earth had been built as a public seat; within 10 yds of this tree the houses began. From the marks we saw that the tigress had crouched upon this raised terrace, from which she commanded a view of the street. The nearest house on one side was occupied by an old woman, the one opposite by her married daughter. The old woman, it appeared, sometimes slept in her own house, sometimes at her daughter's. The night before she had been going to her daughter's, and as she crossed the street, only a few feet wide, the tigress with one silent bound seized and carried her off. No one heard any noise, and the poor old creature was not missed till morning.

When I arrived the son-in-law came forward, and with the other villagers gave an account of the mishap. The son-in-law's grief was really painful to witness; and when he told me how all his efforts to find any trace of his mother-in-law had been unsuccessful, he gave way to the most poignant outbursts. Now, knowing pretty well how little store is placed upon an old woman in India, I could not but regard this display of feeling by the fat young son-in-law as rather strange. A mother-in-law is not usually so highly esteemed (amongst natives) that her loss is deemed an irreparable calamity; and when I further noted that the afflicted youth could only give a shaky account of his exertions in looking for the body, I thought something was wrong, and had him taken along with us.

The tigress had gone towards the river; and though cattle and people had been over the fields, and it was now afternoon, the sun hot, and a strong wind blowing clouds of dust about, the trackers carried on the trail very cleverly, and pointed out that several footmarks had followed it before us, for which the prostrated son-in-law found some difficulty in accounting. After passing through a field of standing rice in which the broad trail was very distinct, and where in the soft mud we got a fair impression of the tigress's pugs, and through some bushes where strips of the woman's blue cotton cloth were hanging, we came to a cocoa-nut garden near the river, and here, amongst some aloe-bushes, we missed the drag. There was a place which looked as if the tigress had lain down, probably to eat, as there were marks of blood; but there were no remains, and her trail continued across the river, whither we followed.

The trackers soon thought something was amiss, as no trace of the body's being dragged could be found. One of them remarked that the tigress would hardly eat the whole at once; whilst, had she carried off the remainder in her jaws, she must have laid it down at the pool in the sandy bed where she had drunk. There was no trace of her having done this. We returned to the aloe-bushes. After examining these for some time, one of the men looked inside a thicket, and with an exclamation turned upon the son-in-law, and giving him a sound box on the ear asked him "what he meant by it". "It" was that the villagers had followed the track with horns and tomtoms (as we subsequently learned) in the morning, and had burnt the remains to avoid police inquiry, the dejected son-in-law acting chief mourner. The ashes of a fire which the tracker now pointed to inside the thicket sufficiently explained the affair.

The woman was of good caste. Had her death been reported, the remains would have been handled by out-castes, and have formed the subject of a sort of inquest by the police at Chámráj-Nuggar; to avoid this, the relatives had burnt the remainder of the body as soon as found. What could be done when the foolish villagers either brought us news too late, or acted in this way? We sent the now truly smitten son-in-law back to the village, bewailing his mother-in-law more sincerely probably than before; and finding that the tigress had gone east we returned to Morlay, it being useless to follow her in that direction.

This death caused great consternation. The villagers concluded that they would now not be safe in their houses at night, and some of the outlying hamlets would have been temporarily abandoned had the tigress lived much longer. But this was to be her last victim; though our chances of killing her seemed still as remote as ever, a few more hours were to end her bloody career.

Next day, the 15th January, I determined upon a more organised plan of hunting her. I arranged that Bommay Gouda and three trackers should go to Iyenpoor, at one end of her usual range, whilst I remained at Morlay. In case of any one being killed near Iyenpoor the men were to let me know immediately; and I supplied them with strychnine, and a gun charged with powder, as a safeguard in their jungle wanderings. The four men started early in the afternoon. About an hour afterwards one of them came running back, pouring with perspiration and covered with dust. I feared some accident had happened until he found breath to say that the party had met the tigress, and that she was then in Kárraypoor Guddah, a small hill two miles from camp. This hill rose to a height of about 200 ft out of a level cultivated plain. On three sides it was almost bare granite, a few bushes and boulders being the only cover, and the country was open all round it. On the east face there was a little more cover, and the main jungle was distant 500 yds, but between it and the hill was open ground, so that the tigress was in an isolated position.

I ordered a pad-elephant at once, whilst I thought over the best plan for hunting her. Such a chance as getting her into a detached hill could hardly be hoped for again, and the present situation offered a fine opportunity of extinguishing her. The only plans were to drive her out, or to watch for her return to the carcass. The first I saw would not do, as all the Morlay men – the only ones amongst the villagers who would have been useful for this service – the others were too terrified – were at their fields, and time would be lost in collecting them; and though this might possibly have been effected, and the tigress have been driven out, as there was no doubt she would flee readily from a hunting-party, it would be impossible for one rifle to command the entire east side of the hill, at any point of which she might break. I therefore decided to watch for her return to the carcass, and hastily securing a bottle of water and some bread, and an overcoat in case of night-watching, I started.

On the way the tracker told me how the party had met the tigress. They were going across open fields and saw an object moving over the bare ground which they could not at first make out, but presently discovered to be a tiger on the far side of, and partly hidden by, a bullock, which it was half dragging, half carrying towards the hill. They immediately divined it to be the man-easter, and ran shouting towards her, obliging her to drop the bullock at the foot of the hill, up which she sullenly trotted. One tracker then hastened to camp; the others remained to prevent her returning to the bullock before I arrived.

I need here hardly say, except for the information of those who have had no experience of man-eating tigers, that they never refuse a bullock or other prey, if such offers, and that when opposed by man they give way at once. Their tactics in attacking man may be described in one word – surprise; and if discovered in their attempt they generally abandon it. The most confirmed man-eaters never lose the innate fear with which all inferior animals regard human beings, and unless they can stalk and catch an unwary cow-herd or wood-cutter in their own fashion they are not to be dreaded. When the tables are turned on them they flee as readily as other tigers.

When we got near the hill we left the elephant and joined the trackers. The only cover near the carcass was a large rock, but the wind was wrong for watching from that quarter. About 70 yds away in the plain was one solitary bush, not sufficiently large to hide a man; there was neither tree nor other cover within a couple of 100 yds. The situation certainly presented difficulties, and it was not easy to decide what to do. At last I hit upon a plan, and sent the men to bring leafy branches and creepers; when these came we walked past the bush in a body, and the branches were thrown on to make it larger; at the same time Bommay Gouda and I hid behind it, the others going on in full view from the hill. By the manœuvre, should the tigress be watching, she would not perceive that we had concealed ourselves.

We sat till evening. The sinking sun threw a strong light from behind us upon the granite hill, whilst in the distance the Billiga-runguns were bathed in purple light, deepening to blue in the gorges. The smoke of evening fires began to ascend from the small hamlet of Hebsoor away to our left, and a thick white cloud of dust moving slowly along the riverbank towards the village marked the return homewards of the village herds. There would only be sufficient light to shoot at so long a range as 70 yds for half an hour or more, and I was beginning to fear the tigress might not return during daylight. The afternoon had been hot, and I had drunk all the water in the bottle, whilst patient Bommay Gouda, who being of good caste could not drink from my bottle, had sat with his bare back exposed to the grilling sun, watching without a movement. At this time of the year – January – the change in temperature in Mysore, and, in fact, the whole of India, between day and night, is very considerable, sometimes upwards of thirty degrees, and as the sun neared the horizon the evening quickly became chilly; but this disturbed Bommay Gouda no more than the heat in his imperturbable watch. A couple of hares appeared from somewhere and gambolled in the space between us and the hill; and a peacock perched himself upon a rock, and with his spreading fan of purple and gold opened to the full, turned slowly round and round, courting the admiration of a group of hens who pecked about, more intent upon their evening meal than the admiration of their vain swain. Satisfaction with himself, however, rendered him oblivious to the want of homage in his harem.

We had been whispering quietly, as we were out of earshot of the cover, and Bommay Gouda had just said, after a glance at the sinking sun, that it was the time, *par excellence*, for a tiger's return to its prey, when a peahen which had been hidden amongst boulders on the hillside to our right, rose with a startling clamour. This signal, as well known as unmistakable, made us glance through the leafy screen, and there we saw the man-eater, a handsome but small tigress, her colour doubly rich in the light of the sinking sun, walk from behind a rock across the side of the hill, here a bare sheet of blue granite, and come downwards towards the carcass. She halted now and again to look far out into the plain behind us. Was the beast dreaded by thousands, hunted by us so long, and which we had never even seen before, the guilty midnight murderess, really before us? Could nothing but some untoward failure now avert her fate?

I followed her with my rifle so eagerly that Bommay Gouda whispered to me to let her get to the carcass before I fired. When she reached the bullock she stooped, and at the same instant I fired at her shoulder, broadside on, with my express. Bommay Gouda could contain himself no longer, and jumped up before I could stop him; I did so also, but could see no tigress! It was extraordinary, certainly; we looked up the hillside, but she was not there. Was she really a devil as all believed, and had she vanished in air? Just then up went a tail on the far side of the bullock in a convulsive quiver; she had fallen exactly behind the carcass.

THIRTEEN YEARS AMONG THE WILD BEASTS OF INDIA
(W. H. Allen 1879)

NORTH
AMERICA

The First Run at the Bison

HON. G. F. BERKELEY

blivious, then, to every unpleasant sensation that the fever had left, I mounted Taymouth, Prince's breech-loading carbine in hand, and joined Mr Bayard and Major Martin, and very soon set my eyes on about thirty huge old bull bisons grazing quietly at the distance of a mile. Beyond them, again, there was a much more numerous herd. Prepared as I had been to see a large animal, these bulls loomed infinitely more magnificent than my fondest imagination could have depicted, and, instead of being lost or lessened in the infinity of space around them, they stood forth out of it in such black, bold relief, their long manes and beards flowing in the wind, that in size they seemed to resemble elephants more than bisons, and were, indeed, to me a most novel as well as a splendid picture of the largest and wildest-looking game!

Bayard and myself (I confess to have been in a charmed delight) then set off towards them gently and without noise, availing ourselves of any inequality in the ground there might be to cover our approach, and in order to give the bisons as little the start of us as possible; but when we came to within about half a mile of them, off they set in that peculiar up-and-down canter in which they invariably commence their retreat. This canter of theirs gains its appearance of height from the hump on the shoulders and the tossing up of the long mane, more than from any high action in the legs. The instant we set off at a gallop in our run to the game, Taymouth was all on fire to keep ahead, and when he saw the retreating mass of beasts flying from him, ignorant of what they were, it increased his anxious desire to overtake them. Having heard that horses were terrified at even the smell of as well as the sight of bisons, I drew Taymouth into the wake of the retreating animals, in order to encourage his approach, and to let him know they were in retreat. He soon overtook them; but when he came up to within about 50 yds of the rearmost bull, while he slackened his pace a little, he pricked his ears and made such a stare that I knew, as well as felt, he was very much scared, and inclined to go to the right-about. A slight touch of the spur, however, and that clasp of the knees which horses so well understand, put all direct refusal out of his head, and we came up at three parts' speed alongside the bulls, though he swerved from them infinitely further than I desired. But for the rein and heel, he would have gone clear away; with these adjuncts, I managed to keep him, though fighting against me, to within about 25 yds of the bulls. His so much over-pacing the bisons enabled him, when restrained, to change his legs and fling his head and shoulders in such a way from side to side, that to aim and fire with the carbine was for some time impossible. Oh! what an exciting wild sight it was, thus close up with them, to see these thirty rusty black monsters, flying two or three abreast, or else close in each other's wake – the last old bull (generally the king of the herd) leering out from side to side beneath either horn, as much as to say to the pursuer, "I *don't* like you, and I *am* retreating; but just you get into *my* way, that's all, and then see what I'll do." Bayard, I am sure, did not run for a shot at first, himself, but rather waited to observe me, for not until a large bull that I had pressed left the herd was I aware that he was close to me, and then too I saw that Mr Canterall also was in company. As Bayard seemed to be holding back for me, I called out to both of them to go at the bull, when Bayard, on his steady nice horse, ran alongside, and, with his heavy revolver, slightly struck the bull, but not in a spot to stop him. The bull then became mischievous, and prone to charge anything that came in his way – of this he made both Bayard and myself well aware – and as bisons often do, when stricken or in a fighting humour, he took no more notice of the direction of his herd, but went away sulkily by himself. I shot at him without effect, and then Mr Canterall, as I found afterwards was his usual custom, fired two or more shots at the bison with an army carbine, and missed him clean, my horse Kansas, which Mr Canterall rode, being beautifully steady.

We now came to a creek that intersected the plains, down the steep bank of which, without the least pause in his long gallop, the buffalo went in the oddest and most reckless way I ever saw, getting a complete summersault into the water at the bottom, at which I was immensely amused. Bayard and myself then halted on the brink of the creek, and waited for a steadier shot at the bull as he climbed the other side. Bayard fired with his revolver, at a long distance for that weapon, and I got my second shot, and saw that it took effect in a slanting direction on the back of the bison. We then rode over the creek, and my third shot, at some distance, broke the shoulder of the huge beast, proving the strength of the shooting of Prince's carbine, and brought him at once to bay. We then drew up at a respectful distance, as the victory was sure; the monster, lame as he was, being ever ready to charge, when, drawing a little closer, Taymouth being somewhat quieted by the length of the chase as well as his fractious exertions, I opened my left side for the facility of a shot, and hit the bison close behind, and a little above, the elbow, when he swayed from side to side for a moment, and then fell dead. Making much of my horse, I rode him up as near as he would go and dismounted, when, giving my hunting-knife to Mr Canterall, I bade him cut off the peculiarly immense beard of this bull, which, with his tail, now ornaments my rooms at Beacon Lodge – the tails of the bisons, handsomely set in an acorn the size of a small pine, by Harvey, of Lambeth House, Westminster-bridge road, append from and make a sporting finish to the bells of drawing-room, dining-room, and study. Mr Bayard then, in the most scientifically sylvan way, took out the tongue, while Mr Canterall availed himself of some of the meat; when, as we were too far removed to get either his skin, the best of the meat, or his marrow-bones to camp, very reluctantly I left such a waste of good things to be eaten by wolves, or to enrage the aboriginal redskin of the soil at the wasteful destruction, by the white man, of the animal from whose herds were derived the chief subsistence of Indian tribes.

A more splendid beast of chase than the one in question could not be, nor can there well be an animal of greater muscular power and bone than is the bison on the western prairies. Added to an enormous depth of carcase, the ribs are immensely expansive, while the quarters of the animal are indeed "rounds of beef", as circular as they can well be. His hocks are peculiarly strong, while between the hock, knee, and fetlock, the leg is short, and the bone very large. The head, neck, and hump are so very heavy that the animal gives a sort of lift with his head to assist the action of his fore legs when he starts into a canter. By way of proving the immense width of chest and roundness of figure that the bison has, I cannot do better than tell the reader that in all the bulls we killed during our hunt, when lying dead on their side, the uppermost fore leg stood straight out, in a direct line from the body, the foot not even inclining to the ground. During this run at my first bison, in crossing a small creek of water, Mr Canterall said he rode over an otter in the rushes. He might have done so, but, as I crossed within 10 yds of the same place at the same time, and saw nothing like an animal of any sort, I do not believe it. It was impossible for this fellow to stumble on the truth, even by accident.

After the excitement of this splendid run was over I began to find a return of great lassitude and stiffness all over my limbs; but, as we returned towards our waggons, we saw another herd of buffaloes at a considerable distance from us, and on ground of which we could take no advantage in our approach; the consequence of this was, that when we were scarce within a mile of them, that peculiar toss of their heads and apparently high action denoted that they had seen us, and were off. Between us and the herd there intervened a little rill of water, in the midst of high grass and rushes, the latter some 30 ft broad; the little creek itself, scarce 4 ft wide, but worn into the soil perhaps 5 ft deep, and lapped over and completely disguised into a sort of pitfall by the grass and reeds that grew so many yards on either side of it, was completely hidden. This obstacle intervened just at the start; Bayard was leading, and his steady horse walked through the stuff, put his head down to peer into the water, and got over; Taymouth, however, now that he had been made aware that a race was the order of the day, on seeing the grass, and guessing at the obstacle, for he could not see the water, and knowing that Bayard was on ahead, tried to rush blindly after the other horse, which I prevented, as to let him thus rush into it was to come to perfectly certain grief. On being checked, he turned his tail to it and commenced restiveness and a succession of jibbings and rearings, to which I had to drop my hand to prevent the chance of his going backwards. At this time I felt so giddy and weak that I could hardly retain the saddle, and was at last obliged to dismount. After a little time Mr Canterall and one of Bayard's men came up, when I led my horse through the obstacle, and then, with their assistance, re-mounted, but I was much too exhausted to take up the running, even if there had been time for me to do so.

Away in the hills I then heard Bayard's heavy revolver, when, on proceeding steadily towards the spot whence the report proceeded, a wolf crossed me, but on pointing my carbine, Taymouth, now knowing what that meant, plunged so that he prevented my fire, and constrained me seriously to vow that the day should come when I would try to cut out work enough to make him glad to stand still. I then found Bayard standing over the body of a fine four-year-old bull bison, up to which his steady, splendid, and smooth-going buffalo horse had taken him as straight as a line, and, if I recollect right, he disabled the bull at the first shot, but it charged him very viciously ere he received his death-wound. Before he killed the bull he made a dash at a heifer, but she shut him out in the ruck. This fine young animal being pretty fat, Bayard and Mr Canterall set about taking as much of his meat as they could carry, and I took his horns, as they were very smooth and evenly grown.

Pretty well laden with spoil we were on our way to camp, when we saw several bulls at feed, one of whom was so situated that he might be approached on foot. To this bull I approached to about a 100 yds, and shot at and hit him, as my ear told me, but he went off, as bisons will go off, if not hit in some spot that is almost fatal, and I was too weak and tired to attempt the run. On reaching camp we found that some bisons had crossed so near the line of march that the men had had a volley at one, and had succeeded at first in only wounding him and then in killing him, so that my servant George Bromfield had helped to despatch a bison for the first time in his life. We found the camp pitched on a creek of running water, on which the waggons were ordered to march when we commenced hunting, but they had selected a spot not very well provided with fuel. Of beef we had now plenty, for on this the first day of sighting buffalo we had killed three, besides a few prairie grouse picked up in the morning. From first to last I had also viewed two wolves. We needed a good supply of fresh meat, for in all we were, if I recollect rightly, four or five and twenty men.

On reaching my tent, I divested myself of my belt and ammunition, and lay down for half an hour on my bed, drinking at the same time a large glass of very fair sherry, and before dinner was ready I felt greatly refreshed and as hungry as a man could be who had no more of a fever left than weakness and the appetite which such attacks when surmounted very often occasion. I was still in my tent when Little Willie came to ask me to come and look at Bayard's horse, who was very lame, and I hastened out accordingly. To my deep regret I saw that nice steed with a knee swollen to twice its size, the effects, as I at once declared, of a severe kick. "Oh, no," the men said, "it could not be a blow, it must be a strain"; of course they said so, because their orders were, never to let the animals reach each other from their respective picket-pins. We, Bayard and myself, however, decided that it was a blow from the heels of a mule – they are always handy in that way – so orders were given for an immediate hot fomentation with vinegar. Mr Bayard also bled his horse from the mouth, breathing a vein elsewhere not being understood. We then dined in my tent, and did ample justice to bison soup, broiled hump rib, grouse, and other good things, washed down with sherry, brandy, or whiskey, which we liked best, and talked of the events of the day, till the time for rest arrived. Brutus slept in my tent that night, an indulgence of which he was very fond.

Having arranged my bed, and in a chair at the head of it put my revolver, breech-loading carbine, and Pape's breech-loading double rifle, all loaded and ready for use, feeling heated, I resolved to go my rounds to cool myself, as well as to ascertain that my sentinel over my portion of the camp was doing his duty. The first thing I came to was a loose mule, which had pulled up her pin, and the next two mules put so near together that they had got their larriets entangled. I went then to the watch-fire, where one of my men named Tom was supposed to be on the look-out, and roused that gentleman from a listlessly sedentary attitude, and asked him "What use he was of, if he could not attend to the animals during his watch?" On this he replied most insolently, so I at once told him if he gave me any more of his impudence I would that instant turn him out of camp, pay him up the day of his discharge, and leave him to find his way back to Kansas city the best way he could. He said something about a constable when we got back if I did; but I told him that out on the plains there were no constables but myself, when, on finding that I would put up with no sort of American independence, he became more civil, and said he did not wish to displease me, and the mules were then forthwith better attended to. After this little episode in the history of a prairie camp, I went to bed, and, in spite of the yellings of wolves, slept till daylight the next morning, although the night was disagreeable, cold, and windy, and my tent had not been well pitched; it was too slack, and the wind not only flapped it about, but, though I had taken the precaution to tread down the long grass within into a sort of carpet round its walls, sundry draughts came up and found their way to my head in spite of my endeavouring to bury it in the pillow. It did not prevent my sleeping, though, and on the next morning, after broiled bones, hot coffee, and some nicely-baked soda rolls, also hot, I felt considerably stronger than I was the day before.

In the chase of the previous day I had seen enough to know that Bayard was a fine and resolute horseman, as well as a good shot, and that whatever I might succeed in doing there was no beating him; it would be quite as much as I could expect, on fractious and unsteady horses, to be anywhere by his side. On inspecting his horse, for the second time a terrible ill luck attended his stable; the swollen knee, though slightly better, still offered so severe an impediment to work, that it was resolved to send both his lame horses back to Fort Riley: so our party sustained the loss of a man, and Bayard the use of his two best steeds. My bay horse Kansas, which Mr Canterall had been riding, was then put at the service of Mr Bayard.

Ere we left camp on Monday, the 10th of October, a considerable flock of wild geese passed over our heads, flying high, although the wind was very strong. On this day I rode my brown mare Sylph, and suspecting, in spite of her beautiful and temperate temper, that she might be afraid of the bisons, I asked Bayard to lend me a heavy, six-barrel, army-revolver, such as the one he used, as I thought that it would be more handy on a terrified horse than a carbine. On this day we desired some men and a waggon with six mules to keep us in sight, in order to bring home such trophies as the sport afforded; and we were not long in viewing a large herd of bisons, but at some distance; they soon saw us, when just as we started at them, and were going at full speed, Bayard riding a horse of Major Martin's, again one of those old winter watercourses intervened, grown up with long grass, but having no great rill of water in the middle. Bayard and myself came at a close together; I kept my mare well in hand, but he went into it at tip-top pace, and by the continuation of his speed was a few lengths in front of me, when I was pained to see his horse, from the blind inequality of the ground, throw a complete summersault on his rider, who was cumbered with a second heavy pistol in his belt, and then, in rising, tread on his hand and leg. Sylph, held well in hand, made no mistake, and ere Bayard's horse had gone 20 yds I caught him, when, on seeing that Bayard, though apparently shaken, was not seriously hurt, and that Mr Canterall had come up, I handed him Mr Bayard's horse, ordered him to attend to him, and then gave Sylph her fling at full speed to overtake the herd of bisons, who had thus gained a considerable start. How pleased I was with her fast smooth action, though she was neither so fast nor so well up to my weight as Taymouth, and oh, how beautifully she gained and reached the herd, consisting entirely of large old bulls! but when she began to close with them, at first she was more frightened than Taymouth. However, I forced her to within 25 yds of the long string of retreating beasts, and delivered my six barrels from my revolver, as close as I could induce Sylph to get, to a sly-looking old bull, who more than once slackened his pace with a very wild leer at me, and that ominous crook of the tail as I came near him which ever portends a charge. I could not see that my shots took any effect, though I felt sure I had hit him, but the noise of a hundred bulls in their gallop over the prairies prevented my distinguishing a hit by ear; however, the bull suddenly gave indications of distress by slackening speed and leaving the herd, and I am sure that one or the other of my shots had done the office. At this moment, and when I had fired my last barrel, I was delighted to be joined by Bayard, followed by Mr Canterall, when the latter missed the bison with an army carbine twice, and Mr Bayard fired at him and hit him hard.

On reaching a small creek, the bull there stood stock still and turned to bay, though neither myself nor Bayard could see where he was wounded; nevertheless, it was very obvious that the game was dying. Mr Bayard shot at him again, and I took the carbine from Mr Canterall, and fired at him twice, Sylph standing fire rather more steadily than Taymouth, when the great bull reeled slightly and dropped down dead. Having taken his tongue and tail, &c., we returned to the waggon, deposited our spoils, and then, finding that Sylph was more manageable than Taymouth, I took in hand my double breech-loading rifle, made by Pape of Newcastle, the cartridges ready capped with the needle, so that it loaded without the least additional delay; and Bayard mounting my bay horse Kansas, we set off to search for further game. Bisons were all round us, and we soon viewed nearly two hundred in a herd, and on them we immediately ran. The herd separated into detachments, and myself and Bayard ran buffalo in different directions, while Mr Canterall followed other beasts we knew not where. The section which I followed and came up with was a large one, and I passed to the right of the string at about 30 yds, Sylph at that distance giving very little trouble, and then, when I came up with the leading buffalo, taking very good care to watch that the rear of the route did not deploy and get me in line, I pulled up, and thus got, if an unsteady shot, still such a shot as enabled me to take some aim and hit one beast or the other. My first shot told, but struck the bull, as I very well saw, too far back, or, as we should say with a deer, paunched him; my second shot I could see nothing of, and then I slackened speed to reload. Alas! the exploded cartridges neither of them would withdraw, by the purchase of the exploded needle. My hunting-knife was too large to permit of a hold on the edge of the cartridge itself, and I pulled up, terribly chagrined at seeing the herd, with the wounded one falling to the rear, keep on in their persevering gallop till they got out of my sight. There was nothing left for it, then, but to return to the waggon.

In going back, however, my eyes detected Bayard standing over a two-year-old bull, which he had killed, and Mr Canterall also joined me with an assertion that he had killed two large bulls and a calf. On my asking where they were, he replied, "Oh, there away, that's a fact, guv'nor, t'other side the hills." "Where are their tongues and tails?" I asked. "Oh," he replied, "I did not stay to take them, I came on after you." "Very well, then," I said, "*I believe the calf*, for at starting I caught a glimpse of that; but as to the bulls, I don't believe a word of it; come on to Mr Bayard." We then went, and got the excellent meat, &c., of the two-year-old; that done, in some amusement I asked Mr Canterall "to take me to his two bulls". To that desire he made evasive answers; first "they were too far", then "they were very old, and not worth going after", and at last he abandoned the idea of them altogether, the truth being that he had hit nothing but the calf. The whereabouts of the calf I knew myself, so, followed by one of my men, I think by Philip Smith, one of the best of them, carrying my old favourite muzzle-loading single John Manton rifle, I went to look for it. The calf was only wounded, and had lain down in some long grass, and I rode by the spot without seeing him; not so my man, who was on foot with my rifle; he nearly trod on the calf, which, when it got up to run away, he fired at and killed, for which he got a good reproof for using my rifle without orders, as I could have ridden the calf down without the waste of ammunition.

The waggon having been laden with the spoils, we turned our heads towards camp, and very soon after beheld a fresh herd of bisons, full two hundred strong. Bayard and myself and Mr Canterall immediately charged – they were considerably to my left, and went at a wing of the herd in that direction; while I, seeing the inclination of the leading animals, and having Pape's double rifle in hand reloaded, with a penknife to disengage the cartridges after future explosion, was making my way to the head of the retreating column, in the hope of some part of the string passing me, after I had reached the front and come to a momentary stand-still. Sylph was at tip-top speed flying in this direction, when, some way ahead of me, only to my right hand, I saw rise from his lair in some longer grass than usual a beautiful male antelope, who, not seeing me, fixed his full eyes in a steadfast gaze on the ruck of buffaloes and their two pursuers. A very little inclination in my line would bring me within distance of the new game, while at the same time I should lose very little of my position in regard to the bisons, and I hoped to escape the notice of the antelope till notice would be too late. Before I reached within shot, however, the beautiful beast turned his head, looked at me, and then darted off at tip-top speed in a contrary direction from the bisons. To follow him was useless, so, never having slackened speed, I again went at the buffalo.

Just before I reached them, a calf sprang out of some grass in an endeavour to overtake the herd, and it being all in the line I put Sylph to her utmost speed to get a shot at the calf. At first the calf was on my right, which was not easy for a rifle shot, so I charged right on the little game, Sylph more steady, and not caring for a creature of that size; when I was immensely amused by this buffalo in miniature, when she found I was almost on her, drawing up, crooking her tail, and charging right at the mare, narrowly missing her quarters! The calf thus passing behind me, then came up on my left, which was just where I wanted her, both going at full speed, when, with the first barrel, I rolled her over with a bullet through the heart. By this time I had heard several shots at the herd, so thinking that there would be wounded bulls to deal with even if I delayed a few minutes, I jumped off Sylph and took the tongue and tail, without the production of which we made it a rule never to believe in the death of game. Major Martin saw me make this shot, which, as a successful attainment, was a brilliant one. I was soon on Sylph again, and to my great joy met eleven old bulls coming back upon me. On seeing me they veered off. To these I immediately gave chase, and reached them close enough to deliver two shots, but without any visible effect, when, on finding that Sylph, who had had a very hard day, so soon after her illness at Fort Riley, was very tired and unable to continue the pace, I pulled up, and went slowly in the direction of Bayard. In meeting these scared buffaloes retreating from Bayard, I at once learnt that when we are in chase of a large herd the herd never goes as fast as it can go, and for this reason: the leading buffaloes, always the cows and calfs and barren heifers, are not at first aware of the immediate presence and pressure of danger, when, as the bulls always follow in their wake, taking the pace from them, and acting as their rearguard, we overhaul them easily in a hand-gallop. Not so with these eleven old bulls – they had been made aware of danger; and it was with a great struggle that Sylph, tired as she was, outpaced them; and as to my pony, which my man Phill rode, carrying my stalking rifle in case I should need it, he found that he could scarce keep near enough to see which way we went, and expressed his wonder at the speed of the buffaloes.

Soon afterwards I came in sight of Bayard, standing by the body of a fine old bull, excessively disgusted with Mr Canterall, who as usual, having failed to kill a bison himself, came up just as Bayard had mortally stricken his bull and brought him to a dying bay, when, instead of leaving Bayard to finish him, Mr Canterall shot into the foe already half slain, and seemed to think he had done a clever thing. As to this, he got a caution from me for the future. The etiquette among hunters is, never to interfere with an already safe animal unless told to do so. It was dark when we reached the camp, horses and men all tired; but my strength improved, though the lassitude from which I had suffered for some days still hung about me, but it did not prevent my enjoying my dinner. At night, before it had long been dark, the chorus of wolves began, to thank us, perhaps, for the dinners we had left them on the plains; and ere long the muttering of thunder and a pitchy horizon, its jet blackness advancing against the wind, occasionally enlivened by forked lightning, warned the camp that a terrible storm was coming. It came! with wind and such rain and hail, lightning and thunder, as I had even never yet seen nor heard. I thought my tent would have been blown away, while the deluge of drenching rain sounded precisely as if my locality had been situated under a portion of the Falls of Niagara. I had a light in my tent at first, and it amused me to see the effect the storm had on Brutus, and his awe-stricken look. He sat bolt upright listening to the elements, and occasionally turning his eyes anxiously on me to ask for explanation. Storms and unrest, however, cannot last for ever, and with the retreating thunder, but still amidst the rush of the descending rain, I fell asleep, but not to a very refreshing slumber, for I was over-tired and again prone to feverish sensations, so that sleep came to me by fits and starts. Pour, pour, pour – spatter, spatter, spatter – the rain continued all night, and in my waking moments I had very grave doubts if the state of the plains would permit us the next day to go in search of what the Americans call elk on the Far West plains, but which are really the American red, or the wapiti, deer, as proved by the shape and nature of their antlers.

THE ENGLISH SPORTSMAN IN THE WESTERN PRAIRIES
(Hurst & Blackett 1861)

HON GRANTLEY F. BERKELEY

A Huge Brown Bear

CAPTAIN C. R. E. RADCLYFFE

n May 29, Glyn decided to make an expedition down the river which flowed towards the Bering Sea, and with this purpose in view he and the two natives set out down stream in the bidarki, taking with them supplies for five or six days. There were at least hopes that he might meet with some caribou, as we could see none round the lake, and the food supply promised to become ere long a serious question. I remained near the lake with Little, where for two days and nights we were treated with samples of what the wind can do on the Alaska Peninsula. It blows there in a peculiar way of its own. The wind seems to come simultaneously from all four quarters of the globe, rushing up and down the valleys, and even if you think you have defeated it by getting on the leeward side of a mountain, it comes rushing round the corner and still hits you in the face. No matter what you may be doing, nor in which direction going, the prevailing wind of the Alaska Peninsula is always a head wind, that is, excepting when stalking an animal, and for that purpose the wind seldom seems right. The only engine of discomfort approaching it, which I have ever seen, is a dust storm on the veldt in South Africa; but in Alaska rain takes the place of dust. In both countries I have remarked the surprising ease with which the wind will flatten the best-pitched tent, and compel its unwilling occupants to face the elements in their futile attempts to fix ropes, etc., securely.

May 31 dawned at last, a fine warm day, a harbinger of the long-expected spring, which was then some three or four weeks overdue. I remarked to Little before leaving camp in the morning, that if we were going to kill a May bear we must make haste about it; and furthermore, that as it was now some five weeks since we first set foot on Kodiak Island, during which time we had not seen a bear at all, I felt rather like my Norwegian boatman and gaffer on the Namsen River, Norway, who has a quaint saying when the river is in bad fishing order. His morning greeting on such occasions is, "I have generally a good hope, but I have not a good hope to-day."

We took our daily tramp across the desolate plain in front of the camp, and sat down on a small sand-hill to scan the hills with our glasses. After looking in every direction without success, and being on the point of returning to camp, about 2 p.m., I saw with the naked eye what appeared to me to be two foxes playing on a snow patch high up on the face of a hill opposite where we sat. Turning our glasses on them, one beast appeared to be nearly white, and we said at once, "They are only caribou," and too high up to be worth going after. This seemed more particularly true as there were a wide river and several streams to wade which lay between us and the hills. After watching them closely for some time, the animals began to walk along the hillside, and with such an unmistakably clumsy gait that we both jumped up, exclaiming, "Bears at last." Such was undoubtedly the case, but we were over two miles from the foot of the hill, and the bears were some 1,000 feet or more above us. They might go miles ere we could reach them. However, it was worth a trial, and not hesitating to think of the cold, we rushed down the bank of the river and plunged into it. It was here a raging torrent about 60 yds wide and as cold as the ice and snow from which it sprang in the mountains far above. With some difficulty in keeping on our legs, we crossed it; then, running fast across the level plain, panting and blowing, we started up the mountain side, still keeping the bears in sight. By the irony of fate, it had now of course turned very warm, and when half-way up, I thought I should burst a blood-vessel. Throwing myself on the ground, I asked Little, who was in better condition than I was, to go ahead and try to keep the bears in sight, as they were gradually going higher. This he did, and as I laboured painfully after him, he located them in a hollow some 500 ft higher than where we first viewed them. How I managed to get over this last 500 ft I don't know, but I repeatedly sat down utterly beat, and urged Little to go ahead and shoot at the bears. This he refused to do, saying if I could not get up to them, he would not take the honour of killing our first bear. It was fortunate for us that the two beasts were so occupied in their attentions to each other that they did not travel very fast. It was soon obvious to us that they were a male and she bear which had paired off, and although the opportunity of studying them was freely given us, I feared there ere long they would receive an unexpected interruption to their amorous gambols. At last, on reaching a ridge whence we could look down on a hollow below, we saw the two bears about 80 yds away, and slightly below us. We had previously arranged that Little should take the dark-coloured animal, whilst I had a predilection for the light-coloured male. So utterly beat was I, and so afraid of a further repetition of our climb if the bears got over another ridge, that, without stopping to get my wind or a steady aim, I fired hurriedly, putting in two shots from my

Mannlicher as fast as I could load. It appeared to me that I hit my beast with the first shot, as, startled by the report of the rifle, he almost fell. Subsequent examination, however, proved that neither bullet touched the bear. Little, on the other hand, did better, as with his first shot he broke the hind leg of the she-bear, and turning he put a shot into the other bear, thinking it was going away wounded. As the latter was still going, but pretty sick, I gave him another shot, this time in the neck, and he fell like a log without moving. We afterwards found that this bullet had smashed a bone of his neck clean in half. Little then started pumping lead after the other bear, which was shuffling off downhill at a good rate with a broken leg, and giving forth terrible snarls and groans. Five or six shots seemed to have no result, except one bullet which, we could see, hit the bear in the nose. Finally, taking my rifle, in which there still remained two cartridges, Little gave her a bullet in the shoulder which settled her. On examining the bear, we found that nearly all the bullets had gone through her feet and legs, and this was owing to the fact that after firing the first shot, the back-sight on Little's rifle had fallen down, and in the excitement of the moment he had not noticed that he was shooting without it.

Both bears were small ones, the female being the larger, but her skin, when taken off and spread on the ground, only measured 7 ft 8 ins; and the actual body, from nose to tail, was much shorter. No measurement of the skin alone can give an accurate idea of the size of the beast from which it was taken. The male was a few inches smaller, but carried a remarkably fine coat, which was of a very light fawn colour, and looked in the distance almost white. Both skins were in fine order, and we judged the male to be a two-year-old, and the female one year older. Their bodies were rolling in fat, and as they could not have been long out from winter quarters, it showed how remarkably fat these animals keep all through the long winter months when they "hole up" and eat nothing during the entire period.

Our day's work had been satisfactory but was by no means over. We had next to skin both bears and pack home the pelts on our own backs, as the only two natives were away with Glyn. The skinning was one of the coldest jobs I ever remember. The wind was blowing bitterly cold off the ice and snow around us, and we were standing in snow slush many inches deep, with our boots already full of water and wet to the skin above the waist. To make matters worse we had but one skinning knife between us, no whetstone, and no rope or straps with which to make a neat pack of the skins. The packing of them afterwards, with the skulls and feet, etc., back to camp, was no child's play.

The picture of two weary men, covered with blood and grease, toiling slowly down the mountain side with their burdens, through swamps and rivers, five or six miles to camp, to a constant accompaniment of the smell of bear's grease, lingers yet with me in a vividness which is only possible to one who actually took part in the scene.

Next day Little and I were busy cleaning and "fixing up" the skins and skulls. This is a job, essentially for natives, but being also one which will not wait, we had to do our best, which was by no means bad.

The following day Glyn returned from his trip down the river. He reported that the river ran down a great valley which was one vast swamp, and that to cover a distance of some twenty miles straight the river flowed nearly twice that distance. He had been unable to reach the sea owing to lack of provisions for the return journey, but as he drew nearer to the coast, there were many fresh tracks of bears on the hills and river-banks. He had not actually seen a bear, but all the signs tended to show that the bears from the mountains and the neighbourhood of the lake were making their way towards the Bering Sea. This was indeed what we had surmised after a few days spent near the lake. There is little doubt that the favourite food of these bears is salmon, and as soon as the fish are due at the river-mouth in the early part of June, most bears work towards the sea, there to await the run of fish and follow them up as far as they go. Distance is no object to a bear, and it is surprising how far these beasts will travel in a day, even in such mountainous country as this, especially early in the season, when all kinds of food are scarce.

Glyn had managed to bag two caribou, which put the meat question at rest for some time, and although rather thin at this season of the year, they were excellent eating and a pleasant change from the inevitable bacon and Yukon strawberries (as beans are called in Alaska), which form the staple food of a hunting party there.

As we were convinced that we had bagged the only two bears that had lived within a radius of many miles from the camp, nothing then remained but a sorrowful return to the coast to await the arrival of the schooner *Alice* from Kodiak. For a wonder we were favoured with bright sunshine and a pleasant day for our trip down, which was easily accomplished in a day and was a very different matter, as we floated down the stream in the dory and bidarki, from the tedious undertaking of towing the boats up the river.

On the way down we happened on the camp of two Aleuts, who had come up the river from a neighbouring settlement to hunt for meat. They had just killed a small caribou, the skin and flesh of which lay by their tent. They were a quaint-looking couple with their small figures, rather large heads, and a peculiar likeness to the Japanese. Their language was different from that of our two natives from Kodiak and Afognak, who had great difficulty in making them understand. But we gathered that they had seen no bear up the river, and they thought our best chance to see one would be to visit the next bay to the westward, where they had seen some bears a short time before. On this Glyn, who was now getting desperate, at once engaged them to take him round to this bay in their bidarki for a few days' hunting until our schooner arrived.

I decided to remain in Aniakchak Bay and do a bit of hunting round a large salt marsh and lake there, where we thought it possible a few bears might come to prospect for salmon and clams along the shore. Leaving Little and one native in our base camp at the river-mouth, I crossed the bay some 5 miles with the native Nicolai, and camped near the shore on the edge of the salt lagoon.

Two days later I heard from Little, to the effect that whilst walking along the shore he had caught sight of a wolverine on the beach. Having nothing but a shot gun with him, he ran to cut off the animal from the only place where it could get away up the rocks. He managed to get near enough to bag it with a charge of buckshot. This was a stroke of luck, as, although fairly numerous in those parts, a wolverine is not often seen in daylight.

I spent several days without seeing anything, regularly scanning the bay in the early morning and evening in the hopes of spying the schooner. It was a performance which constantly recalled to my mind the title of the well-known old song, "Alice, where art thou?"

On June 13 I saw the first fresh traces of a bear which we had come across for a fortnight. We struck the tracks of a very large one leading back towards camp. As these were quite fresh and evidently made during the day, we followed them three miles, hoping in vain to see the bear which must have passed close by the camp during our absence. He had followed a well-worn trail leading past my tent within full view of it, and only about 200 yds away from it. The next day it rained so hard, and the fog was so thick, that it was impossible to see 500 yds. I spent the whole day until 9 p.m. watching the trail in the hopes of seeing my friend returning along it. A faint hope, but one which might have been realised, as my rage was great when I found early next morning that the brute had actually passed back again on the trail during the night. His huge hind feet had left a track which exceeded 14 ins in length – truly a beast worthy of sitting up for all night on the bare chance of getting a shot at him. Another day of fog and rain followed, and I had given up all hopes of ever seeing this bear. On the 16th, however, the fog lifted a little in the afternoon, and taking Nicolai, I walked about four miles from camp to a small hill, where we sat down to look round. The persistent attentions of mosquitoes soon brought out my pipe. Shortly afterwards, happening to glance at the side of a steep mountain opposite, I saw, about 500 yds away, a huge bear galloping along the side of the hill away from us, evidently having caught the scent of my tobacco smoke in a large patch of alders where he had been lying down wind of us. I was furious, as it looked hopeless to follow him, but there was just one chance. The mountains along which the bear travelled were so precipitous that he could not get up more than a few hundred feet, and the range ran in a V-shape. There was a low neck in the hills somewhere about a mile and a half distant, in a straight line from where we sat. To get there, following the hillsides, the bear would have to travel nearly twice that distance, and as it appeared to be the only spot he was making for, I decided to race for it. I am at the best an indifferent runner, and was then in a pair of high gum-boots reaching to the thigh, probably the most uncomfortable things on earth to run in. But, quickly telling Nicolai to follow, I started at a run, both of us throwing away coats and waistcoats as we went. My object was to get as far ahead as possible at first, since we started with a cross wind blowing from us to the bear, which only served to make him go faster. Our pace could not have been great through swamps, streams, and scrub willows, but it seemed to me like record-breaking; and soon we had the satisfaction of seeing the bear gradually slacken his pace, then stop and look round. By that we knew that we had got a point on the right side of the wind, but we had to strive hard to keep it, as he was soon off again though not moving so fast as before. The bear was much hampered by low and thick alders, and numerous deep gullies running down the mountain slopes. In the distance lay the neck which we strove to reach, and here the valley along which we ran ended abruptly in a cup-shaped basin. At this spot there was a narrow open clearing across which it appeared that the bear must travel if his object was, as we surmised, to reach the top of the hills. Putting on a final spurt, I dashed up to within 20 yds of the high alders on the edge of this clearing, and threw myself panting on the grass in the open. Nicolai, who was hopelessly done up, arrived a few seconds afterwards and followed my example. We had beaten the bear by about 200 yds, and could hear him coming crashing through the bushes towards us. Very soon I saw the high alder-tops moving, about 40 yds from where we sat, and we knew then that the bear was coming straight towards us. When about 10 yds from the edge of the clearing, he stopped and remained perfectly motionless, evidently listening and trying to wind us. He was perfectly invisible in the dense brush, and this was the critical moment, since, if he turned round and retraced his steps, we could not possibly see him or get a chance of a shot. For fully two or three minutes we remained sitting perfectly still, scarcely daring to breathe, and then we saw a huge head slowly emerge into the open. Taking a couple of paces forward, until he stood at a spot (which we afterwards measured) only 18 yds from where we sat, the bear stopped and looked at us fairly face to face. I had previously raised my rifle to fire on first seeing his shoulder, but curiosity to find out what he would do, mastered my murderous intentions. Slowly lowering my rifle on to my knees I sat watching him, and bitterly regretted the absence of my camera in camp. Keen as I was to obtain his skin, I would have gladly risked the chance of killing him, could I but have got a good picture of this magnificent brute as he then appeared. He looked splendid, standing there in the full glare of a bright sun, against a dark background of alders. Nicolai thought I had gone mad, and kept whispering frantically in my ear, "Hurry up, hurry up, shoot quick, he run soon." But I wanted to see which way he would run, as we had heard so many conflicting yarns about the Alaskan brown bears charging on sight, and the reverse. This one seemed in no hurry to run either way, and after looking steadily at us for a few seconds, he slightly raised his head and gave vent to his surprise by uttering a deep "woff". Whether this was a token of rage or fright I cannot say, but the noise was deep and loud enough to scare anything. Once more he repeated this deep growl, and then took one step towards us, evidently bent on making a closer inspection. This was more than Nicolai could stand, and he fairly shouted in my ear, "Shoot, shoot." Thinking "discretion the better part of valour", I gave the bear a bullet right in the centre of his chest. He turned a complete somersault towards us, and, getting on his legs a few yards away, gave out some of the most appalling growls and snarls I ever heard, at the same time biting savagely at the small wound in his chest. I sat quite still, waiting a second till he turned sideways, and then planted a second bullet in his shoulder. This settled him, and the good little Mannlicher had inflicted the most frightful wounds in both places, as we afterwards found on skinning the body.

Of course I thought at once that we had secured a record, as this was by far the largest bear I had ever seen, alive or dead, but to make sure I said to Nicolai, "Have you ever seen a larger bear than this one?" After a short inspection he replied, much to my disgust, "He big bear all right, me see bigger bear killed Kodiak Island." Nothing remained to be done except to send back word to Little, who arrived in our camp that morning, reporting our luck and calling for his assistance to help skin and pack the hide back to camp. Whilst skinning the beast, we noticed that he had recently been fighting and had got badly mauled by another bear, as the scratches and fresh blood on his face and feet clearly showed. I remarked to Little that if there was another bear round that neighbourhood large enough to give this one a thrashing, I should like to meet him. Unfortunately we had no tape with us at the time to take the exact measurements of this beast, as Glyn had our only tape away with him, and although I took several measurements with string at the time, none of these can be accepted as accurate. This beast was, however, only a few inches smaller in every measurement than my largest bear, which we measured carefully with the tape soon afterwards. The actual skinning did not occupy much time, as Little and Nicolai were both adepts at the task. The biggest part of the undertaking was packing the skin and skull back to camp. It was a job that fell to the lot of Nicolai, and although only provided with some strong cord which must have cut his shoulders badly, he proceeded to make a pack of the skin and started off with it to camp.

I did not envy him the task, as the four or five miles back to camp lay over very rough ground, which entailed pushing our way through thick alders, wading several streams, and crossing long stretches of very boggy ground. In these latter spots I, without any pack, often sank in up to my knees, and what Nicolai felt like with his big pack I cannot say, but there is no doubt that his burden was not a light one. Although small in stature, and with no appearances of great strength, it is surprising what big loads a good Aleut can carry. It took this man some two hours to cover the journey back to camp.

The following day all hands in camp were busy cleaning the skin and skull. At this work the Aleut again excels, nor do I think it possible to find any natives better at the business, since long experience in preparing furs for the market, and the great number which they had handled for years, make them masters in the art of cleaning skins. Their method is to sit down like tailors, with the skin resting on their knees. They hold a corner of the skin in their teeth, and placing one hand beneath it, and using their knife in the other hand, with great rapidity and dexterity they soon remove every particle of fat and blood from the hide. No white man can compete with them, and I must confess that although I tried it myself on more than one occasion, I felt rather ashamed when I looked at the cleaned part of a skin which represented my own labours, and compared it with a piece cleaned by the natives in the same time. Not only did they do three times as much, but it was also twice as well cleaned as mine. A further damper to my own efforts was the taste of bear's grease, which lingers indefinitely in one's mouth after attempting to hold the skin in one's teeth according to the approved Aleut style.

The next day Little, Nicolai, and I went out in the direction of our last kill. When about two miles from the spot where the carcass lay, we saw a bear feeding on the young grass a few yards from the spot where I first saw the other bear two days before. Even at that distance this fellow looked enormous through the glasses.

It was evidently a case of another smart bit of running, and off we went, Little leading with his advantage of 6 ft 2 ins, and legs in proportion. Both of us were more than a match for Nicolai, who was very blown before we had gone half a mile. On reaching a small knoll about a mile from where we had viewed the bear, we were delighted to see that he was still in the same place, and were just in time to witness a most curious thing. After feeding some time, moving slowly along, the bear reached the exact spot where I had first seen the other one. Here he stopped suddenly, apparently smelling the ground. Taking a look all around, he suddenly whipped quickly to the right-about, and dashed off at a gallop over the brow of the hill. This manœuvre puzzled me, and I at first imagined he must have winded or heard us. This, however, was impossible, and I knew there must be some other reason for the brute's behaviour. I appealed to Nicolai for an explanation, and he said, "Me think he smellum other bear tracks. He run little way, then lie down." There was nothing for it but to make our way to a point whence we could see the ground lying on the other side of the hill over which the bear had gone. This we did, and on looking down from the spot where we last saw our quarry we could perceive nothing but a dense patch of alders, many acres in extent, covering both sides of a deep ravine through which ran a small mountain torrent. So dense was the brush that it was hopeless to push a way through it with a view of getting a shot at the bear, even if were fortunate enough to walk almost on top of him. At the head of the ravine, and on both sides, the hills towered up some 1,000 ft with steep sides. There was just a chance that, by getting to some high point which overlooked the ravine, it might be possible to spot the bear if he was still in the alders. Giving Nicolai my glasses, I told him to hurry up the mountain side, and if he could see anything, to wave his hat. He and Little both started climbing, whilst I remained on the look-out below. Shortly afterwards I saw Nicolai standing on a rocky eminence some 500 ft above me, and after a long scrutiny with the glasses he began waving his hat. The next move in the game was for me to get up to him, and after much puffing and blowing, and scrambling over rocks, I reached the *coin d'avantage*, only to find that I could see no sign of the bear, although both Little and Nicolai declared that he was lying down in a place which did not appear thick enough to hide such a big beast. Then the problem to be solved was how to get a chance of a fair shot at the creature. As the wind was blowing up the ravine towards us, I decided to send Nicolai round to the far side of the alders, to a spot where he could get up wind of the bear and within 150 yds of him, with instructions to light his pipe when there, and remain quietly smoking. This I hoped would have the effect of rousing the bear and make him take off up the hillside, in which case he would give me a good shot in the open. But I had not then, nor have I even to-day, mastered the principle on which the wind blows in Alaska, especially in the gullies along the mountain sides. On this occasion it appeared to be blowing from the low ground upwards, at an angle of about 45°, for after Nicolai had vainly smoked his pipe for five minutes without effect, he proceeded to make a large heap of dead grass and set fire to it, with the result that I could smell the smoke distinctly, but that it appeared to be passing too high over the bear, which never moved. It was clear that some other plan must be tried, and Little, who was some distance from me, shouted to know if he should throw down a rock from the hill. I shouted "No," as I feared that this would drive our friend in the wrong direction. However, our voices had the same effect, as a moment afterwards I caught sight of the head of the bear as he stood up for a moment listening, and then dashed off through the brush – but in the wrong direction for me, as he was heading straight for Nicolai and his fire. Seeing no hope of getting a shot in the open under 500 yds if he kept on in the same line, I lay down as best I could on the sloping ground, judging the distance at about 200 yds, and fired three shots at the small part of the animal's back, which I could see occasionally as he moved through the bushes. He gave a dreadful squeal after my first shot, rather like a pig with its throat cut, and at the third shot stopped on the edge of the stream below us, and appeared too sick to cross it. Here Little got a view of him from his position and fired a shot at him. After going a little farther through the alders, the bear lay down. Nicolai meanwhile, who could see nothing that was going on in the bushes (and presuming, I imagine, that because I had stopped shooting the bear must be dead), started to run into the brush. I shouted to him to stop, but was too far off to make him hear. I then shouted to Little, who was making his way down the hill, to go to the rescue of Nicolai in case the bear should have life enough in him to give chase. Whilst I was blundering down the hillside, I saw Nicolai come running out of the bushes, and momentarily expected to see the bear after him. Fortunately, however, the latter was so sick that he could barely stand, and on Little shouting to say that he could see the bear in the brush, I told him to finish the business, which he did with a bullet in the shoulder. On reaching the spot, I knew that I had got a bear at last, and one that any one might be proud of, even in Alaska. Little said it was the largest he had seen, and, turning to Nicolai, I repeated my question of two days before regarding his opinion, fully expecting the same reply as before, since I suspected Nicolai of having caught the American trick of not liking to be beaten on his former experiences. However, I was agreeably surprised when he at once said, "No, me never see bear so large before." The task of skinning this great brute was not easy; in fact it took us all we could do to haul the carcass out of a small hollow in the ground where it lay. When skinned, it looked like the carcass of some great bullock, and I guessed its weight at 1,400 lbs, since we had heard such tales about these Alaskan bears exceeding 1,600 lbs in weight. Little, on the other hand, said he thought the weight was under 1,200 lbs, but as I had provided myself with a weighing machine, in order to get some idea of the weight of the fabulous monsters inhabiting the country, we decided to return on the following day and then weigh the carcass. It was not, however, till two days later that we did return to do this, since it streamed so unceasingly with rain during the next day that none of us cared to face it. As soon as the skull and skin had been made into a pack, and the natives had removed part of the entrails for making cameleekas, we started for home. Nicolai fairly staggered under the weight of his pack, and on his arrival in camp some hours later, I could scarcely induce him to stand up with his pack and be photographed. On placing the skull and skin on the scales, we found the total weight to be 148 lbs, and I sympathised with Nicolai when he subsequently remarked that he hoped I should not get many more bears as big as that one. Two days after we returned to the scene of the kill, and, chopping up the carcass with axes, weighed it carefully. The weight, including the skin, etc., was 968 lbs, and allowing 40 lbs for the entrails removed, and blood lost during two days, this gives a total weight of about 1,010 lbs. I am told that my estimate, and allowance of 40 lbs for wastage, is well under the mark, but I prefer to err on the right side in such matters, since it is my earnest desire to get the weight of these great bears definitely determined, and as nearly as possible correct. There is no doubt that if this bear had been killed in the fall of the year, just before holing up for the winter, when rolling fat, he would have been heavier on the scales by at least a hundred pounds more than was the case then, when he was in very poor condition. Taking it for granted that this was a fair specimen of the largest Alaskan brown bear — since every one who subsequently saw the skull and skin pronounced it to be so — I assume that it is very unlikely that Alaska produces many bears which exceed 1,200 lbs live weight. One thing is certain, that this bear was of great age, as was evident from the worn and split teeth in his skull, and from the short thick coat which these brown bears only assume in old age. I am therefore certain that he would never have increased in measurements or weight.

As we returned to camp on the evening of our last successful hunt, my joy was great on seeing, far out in the bay, what was unmistakably the good ship *Alice* slowly beating her way towards us. She anchored near the shore that night, and early next morning Glyn arrived, with his two natives, in a bidarki from the next bay.

I was delighted to hear that he had at last broken his run of bad luck, and he produced the skins of a large she-bear and three cubs. The latter were evidently yearlings, as they were of considerable size, and were quite disposed to show fight after the death of their mother. Consequently Glyn was obliged, much against his sporting inclinations, to give them their quietus. The incident, as described to me by Glyn, was rather curious. It appeared that after leaving our camp about a week before, he had made his way in the bidarki, with his two natives, a distance of some thirty-five miles by sea into the next bay, where his men reported good prospects of finding bear.

Several days of fruitless search were the result, and Glyn reported the mosquitoes as being absolutely terrific in numbers and fierceness in the vicinity of his camp. There was a large tract of swampy ground which is always dear to the hearts of these venomous pests, and in fact is about the only place where they are found in great numbers along the Alaska Peninsula. It is a country bare of the timber and trees beneath which they swarm along the coast of Alaska. One rainy morning, during the dense fog peculiar to that district, which seems to hang like a sheet around your camp, Glyn was sitting in his tent when one of his natives ran up explaining that he could see several bears moving about at no great distance from the tents. Glyn, doubting the statement, and not clearly understanding his native, who could only speak Aleut, took his rifle and went to investigate. He soon saw two or three large cubs moving around some object lying on the grass, and on a closer inspection this proved to be a large she-bear fast asleep. He decided to bag her, and leave the cubs to their own devices, knowing that they were quite large enough to be capable of making their own way in the world. Consequently he got within easy range of the sleeping bear and planted a bullet behind her shoulder. She never moved or gave any signs of being hit, and Glyn was uncertain as to the result of his shot. He described how the cubs, on hearing the report, ran to the old bear and tried to rouse her, but without success. She was stone-dead, having been shot right through the heart. Glyn imagined that the cubs would soon leave her and take to the bush, but such was by no means the case. They appeared inclined to assume the offensive on his approaching their mother. He said afterwards that the idea of trying to capture them alive occurred to him, but on mature consideration he thought the proceeding too risky, and to save further trouble expended a bullet on each, which settled the matter.

BIG GAME SHOOTING IN ALASKA
(Rowland Ward 1904)

RIFLES

Fifty Years of Rifles

SIR SAMUEL BAKER

orty years ago our troops were armed with a smooth-bore musket, and a small force known as the "Rifle Brigade" was the exception to this rule.

The military rifle carried a spherical bullet, and, like all others of the period, it necessitated the use of a mallet to strike the ball, which, being a size larger than the bore, required the blow to force it into the rifling of the barrel in order to catch the grooves.

Sporting rifles were of various sizes, but they were constructed upon a principle generally accepted, that extreme accuracy could only be obtained by burning a very small charge of powder.

The outfit required a small mallet made of hardwood faced with thick buff leather, a powerful loading-rod, a powder-flask, a pouch to contain greased linen or silk patches; another pouch for per-cussion caps; a third pouch for bullets. In addition to this cumber-some arrangement, a nipple-screw was carried, lest any stoppage might render necessary the extraction of the nipple.

The charge of powder in ordinary use for a No. 16 bore (which carried an ounce spherical ball) was 1½ dram, and the sights were adjusted for a maximum range of 200 yds. Although at this distance considerable accuracy could be attained at the target upon a quiet day, it was difficult to shoot with any precision at an unmeasured range owing to the high trajectory of the bullet. Thus for sporting purposes it was absolutely essential that the hunter should be a first-rate judge of distance in order to adjust the sights as required by the occasion. It was accordingly rare to meet with a good rifle-shot fifty years ago. Rifle-shooting was not the amusement sought by Englishmen, although in Switzerland and Germany it was the ordinary pastime. In those countries the match-rifle was im-mensely heavy, weighing, in many instances, 16 lbs, although the bullet was exceedingly small.

The idea of non-recoil was paramount as necessary to ensure accuracy.

It will be at once perceived that the rifle was a most inferior weapon, failing through a low velocity, high trajectory, and weakness of penetration.

In 1840, I had already devoted much attention to this subject, and I drew a plan for an experimental rifle to burn a charge of powder so large that it appeared preposterous to the professional opinions of the trade. I was convinced that accuracy could be combined with power, and that no power could be obtained without a corresponding expenditure of powder. Trajectory and force would depend upon velocity; the latter must depend upon the volume of gas generated by explosion.

The rifle was made by Gibbs of Bristol. The weight was 21 lbs, length of barrel 36 ins, weight of spherical belted bullet 3 ounces, of conical bullet 4 ounces, charge of powder 16 drams. The twist was one full turn in the length of barrel. The rifling was an exceedingly deep and broad groove (two grooves), which reduced the difficulty of loading to a minimum, as the projecting belt enabled the bullet to catch the channel instantly, and to descend easily when wrapped in a greased silk patch without the necessity of hammering. The charge of powder was inserted by inverting the rifle and passing up the loading-rod with an ounce measure screwed to the end; this method prevented the powder from adhering to the sides of the barrel, and thus fouling the grooves

An extraordinary success attended this rifle, which became my colossal companion for many years in wild sports with dangerous game. It will be observed that the powder charge was one-third the weight of the projectile, and not only a tremendous crushing power, but an extraordinary penetration was obtained, never equalled by any rifle that I have since possessed.

This weapon was in advance of the age, as it foreshadowed the modern Express, and the principle was thoroughly established to my own satisfaction, that a sporting rifle to be effective at a long range must burn a heavy charge of powder, but the weight of the weapon should be in due proportion to the strain of the explosion.

When I first visited Ceylon in 1845, there were several renowned sportsmen who counted their slain elephants by many hundreds, but there were no rifles. Ordinary smooth-bore shot-guns were the favourite weapons, loaded invariably with a double charge of powder and a hardened ball. In those days the usual calibre of a gun was No. 14 or 16. A No. 12 was extremely rare. The charge for No. 16 was 2¾ drams of fine grain powder, and 3 drams for No. 12. Accordingly, the light guns, or "fowling-pieces", as they were termed, were severely tested by a charge of 6 drams of the strongest powder with a hardened bullet; nevertheless I never heard of any failure.

At a short range the velocity and penetration of an ounce spherical ball, with the heavy powder charge, were immense, but beyond 50 yds the accuracy was imperfect.

I believe I was the first to introduce rifles into Ceylon, which were then regarded by the highest authorities in the island as impractical innovations, too difficult to sight, whereas an ordinary gun could be used with ball more quickly in taking a snap-shot.

The rifles which I had provided were heavy, the 3 ounce already mentioned, 21 lbs, and a long 2 ounce by Blisset, 16 lbs. The latter was a poly-groove, the powder charge only 1½ dram when I originally purchased it. It was wonderfully accurate at short ranges with the small charge, which I quickly increased to 6 drams, thereby losing accuracy, but multiplying velocity.

Twelve months' experience with elephants and buffaloes decided me to order a battery of double-barrelled rifles, No. 10, two-grooved, with 6 drams of fine grain powder, and spherical-belted bullets. These were most satisfactory, and they became the starting-point for future experiments.

Shortly before the Crimean War, the musket was abolished, and about 1853 the British army was armed throughout with rifles. The difficulty of a military rifle lay in the rapid fouling of the barrel, which necessitated a bullet too small to expand sufficiently to fill the grooves; this resulted in inaccuracy. If the bullet were properly fitted, it became impossible to load when the barrel began to foul after a few discharges.

At that time I submitted a plan to the authorities which simplified the difficulty, and having left the pattern bullet at Woolwich, it quickly appeared with a slight modification as the "Boxer bullet". My plan designed a cone hollowed at the base. The bullet was a size smaller than the bore, which enabled it to slide easily down the barrel when foul. The hollow base fitted upon a cone of boxwood pointed at the insertion, but broad at the base, which was larger than the diameter of the hollow in the bullet. It may be easily understood that although this compound bullet was smaller than the bore of the rifle, a blow with the ramrod after loading would drive the conical bullet upon the larger diameter of the boxwood cone, which, acting like a wedge, would expand the lead, thus immediately secured within the barrel. The expansion when fired drove the boxwood into the centre of the bullet, which of necessity took the rifling.

The Boxer bullet superseded the boxwood plug by the use of a piece of burnt clay, which was less expensive and equally serviceable.

Before breechloaders were invented, we were obliged to fit out a regular battery of four double rifles for such dangerous game as elephants, buffaloes, etc., as the delay in re-loading was most annoying and might lead to fatal accidents.

In hot damp climates it became necessary to fire off and clean the entire battery every evening, lest a miss-fire should be the consequence upon the following morning from the condensation of moisture in the nipple during night. This was not only great trouble and a wasteful expenditure of ammunition, but the noise of so many loud reports just at the hour when wild animals were on the move, alarmed the country. Trustworthy gun-carriers are always difficult to procure, and it was by no means uncommon that in moments of danger, when the spare rifles were required, the gun-bearers had bolted from the scene, and the master was deserted.

The introduction of breechloaders has made shooting a luxury, and has obviated the necessity of a large battery of guns. For military purposes the breechloader has manifold advantages – as the soldier can load while lying down, and keep up a rapid fire from a secure cover. It was remarked during the Crimean War that a large proportion of wounded men were struck in the right arm, which would have been raised above the head when loading the old-fashioned rifle, and was thus prominently exposed.

It is not my intention to enter into the minutiæ of military rifles, but I cannot resist the satisfaction with which I regard the triumph of the small-bore which I advocated through the columns of the *Times* in 1865, at a time when the idea was opposed by nearly all authorities as impracticable, owing to the alleged great drawback of rapid fouling. There can be no doubt that the charge of 70 grains with a small-bore bullet, .303, will have a lower trajectory and higher velocity (equivalent to long range) than the heavier projectile, .450, with the additional advantage of a minimum recoil.

The earliest in the field of progress was the old-established firm of Purdey and Co. Mr Purdey, before the general introduction of breechloaders, brought out an Express rifle, No. 70 bore, with a mechanically fitting two-groove solid bullet. This small projectile was a well-pointed cone weighing exactly 200 grains, with a powder charge of 110 grains, more than half the weight of the bullet. The extremely high velocity of this rifle expanded the pure soft lead upon impact with the skin and muscles of a red deer. At the same time there was no loss of substance in the metal, as the bullet, although much disfigured, remained intact, and continued its course of penetration, causing great havoc by its increased surface. Nothing has surpassed this rifle in velocity, although so many improvements have taken place since the introduction of breechloaders, but in the days of muzzle-loaders it was a satisfaction to myself that I was the first to commence the heavy charge of powder with the 3 ounce bullet and

16 drams, to be followed after many years by so high an authority as Mr Purdey with a 200 grain bullet and 110 grains of powder, thus verifying the principle of my earliest experience.

This principle is now universally accepted, and charges of powder are used, as a rule, which forty years ago would have been regarded as impossible.

The modern breechloader in the hands of a well-trained soldier should be a most deadly weapon, nevertheless we do not find a greater percentage of destruction among the numbers engaged than resulted from the old Brown Bess. The reason is obvious: battles are now fought at long ranges, whereas in the early portion of the century fire was seldom opened at a greater distance then 200 yds, and the actual struggle terminated at close quarters.

A long-range rifle in the excitement of a hot action has several disadvantages. The sights may have been set for 600 or 800 yds when the enemy was at a distance, but should that interval be decreased by an approach at speed, the sights would require an immediate re-adjustment, otherwise the bullets would fly overhead, and the nearer the enemy advanced, the safer he would be. Troops require most careful training with the new weapons entrusted to their care. Although a rapidity of fire if well directed must have a terrible result, there can be no question that it engenders a wild excitement, and that a vast amount of ammunition is uselessly expended, which, if reserved by slower but steady shooting, would be far more deadly.

Although the difficulty is great in preventing troops from independent firing when their blood is up in the heat of combat, the paramount duty of an officer should be to control all wildness, and to insist upon volleys in sections of companies by word of command, the sights of the rifles being carefully adjusted, and a steady aim being taken at the knees of the enemy.

There cannot be a better example than the advice upon this subject given by the renowned General Wolfe (who was subsequently killed at the siege of Quebec) to the 20th Regiment, of which he was Colonel, when England was hourly expecting an invasion by the French:– ... "There is no necessity for firing very fast; ... a cool well-levelled fire with the pieces carefully loaded is much more destructive than the quickest fire in confusion." – At Canterbury, 17th December 1755.

This instruction should be sternly impressed upon the minds of all soldiers, as it is the text upon which all admonitory addresses should be founded. It must not be forgotten that General Wolfe's advice was given to men armed with the old muzzle-loading Brown Bess (musket), which at that time was provided with a lock of flint and steel. Notwithstanding the slowness of fire necessitated by this antiquated weapon, the General cautioned his men by the assurance, "There is no necessity for firing very fast," etc., etc.

The breechloader is valuable through the power which exists, especially with repeating rifles, for pouring in an unremitting fire whenever the opportunity may offer, but under ordinary circumstances the fire should be reserved with the care suggested by the advice of General Wolfe.

Small-bores have become the fashion of the day, and for military purposes they are decidedly the best, as a greater amount of ammunition can be carried by the soldier, while at the same time the range and trajectory of his weapon are improved. The new magazine rifle adopted by the Government is only .303, but this exceedingly small diameter will contain 70 grains of powder with a bullet of hard alloy weighing 216 grains.

For sporting purposes the small-bore has been universally adopted, but I cannot help thinking that, like many other fashions, it has been carried beyond the rules of common sense.

When upon entering a gunmaker's shop the inexperienced purchaser is perplexed by the array of rifles and guns, varying in their characters almost as much as human beings, he should never listen to the advice of the manufacturer until he has asked himself what he really requires.

There are many things to be considered before an order should be positively given. What is the rifle wanted for? What is the personal strength of the purchaser? In what portion of the world is he going to shoot? Will he be on foot, or will he shoot from horseback or from an elephant? Will the game be dangerous, or will it be confined to deer, etc.?

Not only the weapon but the ammunition will depend upon a reply to these questions, and the purchaser should strongly resist the delusion that any one particular description will be perfect as a so-called *general rifle*. You may as well expect one kind of horse or one pattern of ship to combine all the requirements of locomotion as to suppose that one peculiar rifle will suit every variety of game or every condition of locality.

In South Africa accuracy is necessary at extremely long ranges for the open plains, where antelopes in vast herds are difficult of approach. In Indian jungles the game is seldom seen beyond 50 or 60 yds. In America the stalking among the mountains is similar to that of the Scottish Highlands, but upon a larger scale. In Central Africa the distances are as uncertain as the quality of the animals that may be encountered.

Upon the level plains of India, where the black-buck forms the main object of pursuit, extreme accuracy and long range combined are necessary, with a hollow Express bullet that will not pass through the body. How is it possible that any one peculiar form of rifle can combine all these requirements? Rifles must be specially adapted for the animals against which they are to be directed. I have nothing to do with the purse, but I confine my remarks to the weapons and the game, and I shall avoid technical expressions.

The generally recognised small-bores, all of which are termed "Express" from the large charge of powder, are as follow:—

Small-bore Express.	Charge of Powder.	Large-bores.	Charge of Powder.	For all Game such as
.577	6½ drams	4 bore	14 drams	
.500	5½ drams	8 bore	14 drams	Elephants.
.450	5 drams	10 bore	12 drams	Rhinoceros.
.400	4 drams	12 bore	10 drams	Buffaloes.
.360 .295	Toys.			

The two latter rifles, .360 and .295, are charming additions, and although capable of killing deer, are only to be recommended as companions for a stroll, but not to be classed as sporting rifles for ordinary game. They are marvellously accurate, and afford great satisfaction for shooting small animals and birds. The .360 may be used for shooting black-buck, but I should not recommend it if the hunter possesses a .400.

It would be impossible to offer advice that would suit all persons. I can therefore only give a personal opinion according to my own experience. For all animals above the size of a fallow deer and below that of a buffalo I prefer the .577 solid Express – 648 grains solid bullet, – 6 drams powder, *not* 6½, as the charge of only 6 drams produces greater accuracy at long ranges.

The weight of this rifle should be 11½ lbs, or not exceeding 12 lbs. For smaller game, from fallow deer downwards, I prefer the .400 Express with a charge of from 85 grains to 4 drams of powder – solid bullet, excepting the case of black-buck, where, on account of numerous villages on the plains, it is necessary that the bullet should not pass through the body. The important question of weight is much in favour of the .400, as great power and velocity are obtained by a weapon of only 8½ lbs.

I should therefore limit my battery to one .577, and .400, and one Paradox No. 12, for ordinary game in India, as elephants and other of the larger animals require a special outfit.

The Paradox,[1] invented by Colonel Fosberry and manufactured by Messrs Holland and Holland of Bond Street, is a most useful weapon, as it combines the shot-gun with a rifle that is wonderfully accurate within a range of 100 yds.

It is a smooth-bore slightly choked, but severely rifled for only 1½ in in length from the muzzle. This gives the spin to the projectile sufficient to ensure accuracy at the distance mentioned.

The No. 12 Paradox weighs 8¼ lbs and carries a bullet of 1¾ ounce with 4½ drams of powder. Although the powder charge is not sufficient to produce a high express velocity, the penetration and shock are most formidable, as the bullet is of hardened metal, and it retains its figure even after striking a tough hide and bones. The advantage of such a gun is obvious, as it enables a charge of buck-shot to be carried in the left barrel, while the right is loaded with a heavy bullet that is an admirable bone-smasher; it also supersedes the necessity of an extra gun for small game, as it shoots No. 6 shot with equal pattern to the best cylinder-bored gun.

There are many persons who prefer a .500 or a .450 Express to the .577 or the .400. I have nothing to say against them, but I prefer those I have named, as the .577 is the most fatal weapon that I have ever used, and with 6 or 6½ drams of powder it is quite equal to any animal in creation, provided the shot is behind the shoulder. This provision explains my reason for insisting that all animals from a buffalo upwards should be placed in a separate category, as it is frequently impossible to obtain a shoulder shot, therefore the rifles for exceedingly heavy game must be specially adapted for the work required, so as to command them in every conceivable position.

I have shot with every size of rifle from a half-pounder explosive shell, and I do not think any larger bore is actually necessary than a No. 8, with a charge of 12 or 14 drams of powder. Such a rifle should weigh 15 lbs, and the projectile would weigh 3 ounces of hardened metal.

The rifles that I have enumerated would be all double, but should the elephant-hunter desire anything more formidable, I should recommend a single barrel of 36 ins in length of bore, weighing 22 lbs, and sighted most accurately to 400 yds. Such a weapon could be used by a powerful man from the shoulder at the close range of 50 yds, or it could be fired at long ranges upon a pivot rest, which would enable the elephant-hunter to kill at a great distance by the shoulder shot when the animals were in deep marshes or on the opposite side of a

[1] Since this was written Messrs Holland have succeeded after lengthened experiments in producing a Paradox No. 8, which burns 10 drams of powder, and carries a very heavy bullet with extreme accuracy. This will be a new departure in weapons for heavy game.

river. I have frequently seen elephants in such positions when it was impossible to approach within reasonable range. A rifle of this description would carry a half-pound shell with a bursting charge of half an ounce of fine grain powder, and the propelling charge would be 16 drams. I had a rifle that carried a similar charge, but unfortunately it was too short, and was only sighted for 100 yds. Such a weapon can hardly be classed among sporting rifles, but it would be a useful adjunct to the battery of a professional hunter in Africa.

There can be little doubt that a man should not be overweighted, but that every person should be armed in proportion to his physical strength. If he is too light for a very heavy rifle he must select a smaller bore; if he is afraid of a No. 8 with 14 drams, he must be content with a No. 12 and 10 drams, but although he may be successful with the lighter weapon, he must not expect the performance will equal that of the superior power.

It may therefore be concluded that for a man of ordinary strength, the battery for the heaviest game should be a pair of double No. 8 rifles weighing 14 or 15 lbs to burn from 12 to 14 drams of powder, with a hardened bullet of 3 ounces. Such a rifle will break the bones of any animal from an elephant downwards, and would rake a buffalo from end to end, which is a matter of great importance when the beast is charging.

Although the rifle is now thoroughly appreciated, and sportsmen of experience have accepted the Express as embodying the correct principle of high velocity, I differ with many persons of great authority in the quality of projectiles, which require as much consideration as the pattern of the gun.

The Express rifle is a term signifying velocity, and this is generally accompanied by a hollow bullet, which is intended to serve two purposes – to lighten the bullet, and therefore to reduce the work of the powder, and to secure an expansion and smash-up of the lead upon impact with the animal. I contend that the smashing up of the bullet is a mistake, excepting in certain cases such as I have already mentioned, where the animal is small and harmless like the blackbuck, which inhabits level plains in the vicinity of population, and where the bullet would be exceedingly dangerous should it pass through the antelope and ricochet into some unlucky village.

As I have already advised the purchaser of a rifle to consider the purpose for which he requires the weapon, in like manner I would suggest that he should reflect upon the special purpose for which he requires the bullet. He should ask himself the questions – "What is a bullet?" and "What is the duty of a bullet?"

A bullet is generally supposed to be a projectile capable of retaining its component parts in their integrity. The duty of the bullet is to preserve its direct course; it should possess a power of great penetration, should not be easily deflected, and together with penetrating power it should produce a stunning effect by an over-powering striking energy.

How are we to combine these qualities? If the projectile has great penetrating force it will pass completely through an animal, and the striking energy will be diminished, as the force that should have been expended upon the body is expending itself in propelling the bullet after it has passed through the body. This must be wrong, as it is self-evident that the striking energy or knock-down blow must depend upon the resistance which the body offers to the projectile. If the bullet remains within it, the striking energy, complete and entire, without any waste whatever, remains within the body struck. If, therefore, a bullet .577 of 648 grains propelled by 6 drams of powder has at 50 yds a striking energy of 3,500 foot pounds, that force is expended upon the object struck, — provided it is stopped by the opposing body.

We should therefore endeavour to prevent the bullet from passing through an animal, if it is necessary to concentrate the full power of the projectile upon the resisting body.

This is one reason adduced in favour of the hollow Express bullet, which smashes up into minute films of lead when it strikes the hard muscles of an animal, owing to its extreme velocity, and the weakness of its parts through the hollowness of its centre.

I contend, on the contrary, that the bullet has committed suicide by destroying itself, although its fragments may have fatally torn and injured the vital organs of the wounded animal. The bullet has ceased to exist, as it is broken into fifty shreds; therefore it is dead, as it is no longer a compact body, – in fact, it has disappeared, although the actual striking energy of a very inferior bullet may have been expended upon the animal.

If the animal is small and harmless, this should be the desired result. If, on the other hand, the animal should be large and danger-ous, there cannot be a greater mistake than the hollow Express projectile.

I have frequently heard persons of great experience dilate with satisfaction upon the good shots made with their little .450 hollow Express exactly behind the shoulder of a tiger or some other animal. I have also heard of their failures, which were to themselves sometimes incomprehensible. A solid Express .577 *never* fails if the direction is accurate towards a vital part. The position of the animal does not signify; if the hunter has a knowledge of comparative anatomy (which he must have, to be a thoroughly successful shot) he can make positively certain of his game at a short distance, as the solid bullet will crash through muscle, bone, and every opposing obstacle to reach the fatal organ. If the animal be a tiger, lion, bear, or leopard, the bullet should have the power to penetrate, but it should not pass completely through. If it should be a wapiti, or sambur stag, the bullet should also remain within, retained in all cases under the skin upon the side opposite to that of entrance. How is this to be managed by the same rifle burning the same charge of powder with a solid bullet?

The penetration must be arranged by varying the material of the bullet. A certain number of cartridges should be loaded with bullets of extreme hardness, intended specially for large thick-skinned animals; other bullets should be composed of softer metal, which would expand upon the resisting muscles but would not pass completely through the skin upon the opposite side. The cartridges would be coloured for distinction.

If the metal is pure lead, the bullet .577, with an initial velocity of 1650 ft per second, will assuredly assume the form of a button mushroom immediately upon impact, and it will increase in diameter as it meets with resistance upon its course until, when expended beneath the elastic hide upon the opposite side, it will have become fully spread like a mature mushroom, instead of the button shape that it had assumed on entrance. I prefer pure lead for tigers, lions, sambur deer, wapiti, and such large animals which are not thick-skinned, as the bullet alters its form and nevertheless remains intact, the striking energy being concentrated within the body.

The difference in the striking energy of a hollow bullet from that of a solid projectile is enormous, owing to the inequality in weight. The hollow bullet wounds mortally, but it does not always kill neatly. I have seen very many instances where the .500 hollow Express with 5 drams of powder has struck an animal well behind the shoulder, or sometimes through the shoulder, and notwithstanding the fatal wound, the beast has galloped off as though untouched, for at least a 100 yds, before it fell suddenly, and died.

This is clumsy shooting. The solid bullet of pure lead would have killed upon the spot, as the bullet would have retained its substance although it altered its form, and the shock would have been more severe. The hollow bullet exhibits a peculiar result in a *post-mortem* examination: the lungs may be hopelessly torn and ragged, the liver and the heart may be also damaged, all by the same projectile, because it has been converted into small shot immediately upon impact. Frequently a minute hole will be observed upon the entrance, and within an inch beneath the skin a large aperture will be seen where an explosion appears to have taken place by the breaking-up of the lead, all of which has splashed into fragments scattering in every direction.

Common sense will suggest that although such a bullet will kill, it is not the sort of weapon to stop a dangerous animal when in full charge. Weak men generally prefer the hollow Express because the rifle is lighter and handier than the more formidable weapon, and the recoil is not so severe, owing to the lightness of the bullet.

My opinion may be expressed in a few words. If you wish the bullet to expand, use soft lead, but keep the metal solid. If you wish for great penetration, use hard solid metal, either $\frac{1}{10}$ tin or $\frac{1}{13}$ quick-silver. Even this will alter its form against the bones of a buffalo, but either of the above will go clean through a wapiti stag, and would kill another beyond it should the rifle be .577 fired with 6 drams of powder.

The same rifle will not drive a soft leaden solid bullet through a male tiger if struck directly through the shoulder; it will be found flattened to a mushroom form beneath the skin upon the other side, having performed its duty effectively, by killing the tiger upon the spot, and retaining intact the metal of which it was composed.

A *post-mortem* inquiry in the latter case would be most satisfactory. If the bullet shall have struck fair upon the shoulder-joint, it will be observed that although it has retained its substance, the momentum has been conveyed to every fragment of crushed bone, which will have been driven forward through the lungs like a charge of buckshot, in addition to the havoc created by the large diameter of an expanded .577 bullet. Both shoulders will have been completely crushed, and the animal must of course be rendered absolutely helpless. This is a *sine qua non* in all shooting. Do not wound, but kill outright; and this you will generally do with a .577 solid bullet of pure lead, or with a Paradox bullet 1¾ oz hard metal and 4½ drams of powder. This very large bullet is sufficiently formidable to require no expansion.

Gunmakers will not advise the use of pure lead for bullets, as it is apt to foul the barrel by its extreme softness, which leaves a coating of the metal upon the surface of the rifling. For military purposes this objection would hold good, but so few shots are fired at game during the day, that no disadvantage could accrue, and the rifle would of course be cleaned every evening.

The accidents which unfortunately so often happen to the hunters of dangerous game may generally be traced to the defect in the rifles employed. If a shooter wishes to amuse himself in Scotland among the harmless red deer, let him try any experiments that may please him; but if he is a man like so many who leave the shores of Great Britain for the wild jungles of the East, or of Africa, let him at once abjure hollow bullets if he seeks dangerous game. Upon this subject I press my opinion, as I feel the immense responsibility of advice should any calamity occur. It is only a few months since the lamented Mr Ingram was killed by an elephant in the Somali country, through using a .450 Express hollow bullet against an animal that should at least have been attacked with a No. 10. I submit the question to any admirer of the hollow Express. "If he is on foot, trusting only to his rifle for protection, would he select a hollow Express, no matter whether .577, .500, or .450; or would he prefer a solid bullet to withstand a dangerous charge?"

India is a vast empire, and various portions, according to the conditions of localities, have peculiar customs for the conduct of wild sports. In dense jungles, where it would be impossible to see the game if on foot, there is no other way of obtaining a shot except by driving. The gunners are in such case placed at suitable intervals upon platforms called mucharns, securely fitted between convenient forks among the branches of a tree, about 10 or 12 ft above the ground. From this post of vantage the gunner can see without being seen, and, thoroughly protected from all danger, he may amuse himself by comparing the success of his shooting with the hollow Express or with the solid bullet at the animals that pass within his range, which means a limit of about 50 yds. I contend that at the short distance named, a tiger should *never* escape from a solid bullet; he often escapes from the hollow bullet for several reasons.

It must be remembered that animals are rarely seen distinctly in a thick jungle, countless twigs and foliage intercept the bullet, and the view, although patent to both open eyes, becomes misty and obscure when you shut one eye and squint along the barrel. You then discover that although you can see the dim shadow of your game, your bullet will have to cut its way through at least twenty twigs before it can reach its goal. A solid bullet may deflect slightly, but it will generally deliver its message direct, unless the opposing objects are more formidable than ordinary small branches. A hollow bullet from an Express rifle will fly into fragments should it strike a twig the size of the little finger. This is quite sufficient to condemn the hollow projectile without any further argument.

WILD BEASTS AND THEIR WAYS
(MACMILLAN 1891)

The Selection of a Rifle

F. VAUGHAN KIRBY

he question as to the most efficient and generally useful rifles for shooting the various kinds of game is a very wide one, and a matter upon which it is difficult to attempt to give entirely unprejudiced advice, seeing that the very fact of one's having formed an opinion implies a certain prejudice in favour of the style of weapon upon the efficiency of which he bases those opinions. Therefore the most that an individual sportsman can do is to give his experience, and leave others to form their own judgment *pro* or *con*. And there should be no question as to the value of the opinion of any practical sportsman: theory is all very well, but it will bring neither lion nor buffalo to bag; nothing but practice and experience in the field can avail anything towards the attainment of success. It is so difficult a matter when one walks into a gunmaker's to avoid being led astray by any amount of plausible theory, though of course if a man *knows what he wants*, he will order and get it without any more ado. There is no doubt that one can always rely upon getting thoroughly good sound weapons from any of the leading gunmakers if he is prepared to pay the price for them; but the efficiency of these in the field is not always to be taken as quite such a matter of course.

The old question of large- *versus* small-bore rifles is still an open one. Every sportsman must have been strongly impressed by the advice and suggestions given by that veteran Nimrod the late Sir Samuel Baker in his last work, "Wild Beasts and their Ways": he has ever stood in the front rank of the advocates of heavy, large-bore rifles; but still even the weight of his authority has not turned the scale in their favour, possibly because men of his build and physical strength are the exception, not the rule. But, on the other hand, neither have the opponents of heavy rifles scored any victory, not even though the introduction of the little .303 rifle as a sporting weapon has come to their assistance. It appeared to me, from the conversations I had when in England in 1893 with some of the leading gunmakers, that the tendency amongst them is to jump at conclusions too quickly, and to prophesy all sorts of wonderful results from this new weapon before it has had a fair trial. Now, without condemning this rifle, I am of opinion that it should be given such fair trial, its failures being recorded as well as its successes, and not be accepted out of hand as the rifle of the future. Not until this is done can any reliable judgment be formed upon the matter.

Amongst the first to bring this rifle before the notice of the sporting public has been my friend and erstwhile comrade in arms, Mr Henry T. Glynn, a keen and skilful sportsman of great experience; and his arguments in its favour have appeared over his name in the colums of the "Field" upon several occasions. He has the courage of his opinion also, for he has lately ordered other similar weapons from England; and, very naturally, his judgment, based upon practical experience of the rifle in question, is worth more than mine, or that of any one else who has never used it, and who, therefore, can but theorise.

But there are certain broad points connected with the question which even a theorist, if he has any knowledge of big-game shooting, can discuss; and as such I must admit I am by no means satisfied with the position taken up by the supporters of the .303.

Let us see, in the first place, what are the advantages claimed for this rifle; and then endeavour to ascertain whether these are real or imaginary. Be it remembered that I do not seek to become argumentative or to display undue prejudice; I merely wish to throw such light upon the question as shall assist – if even in a small degree – in enabling more competent judges than myself to get at the truth.

The advantages claimed are, I believe, four in number – viz., general lightness, handiness, and absence of recoil; absence of smoke; increased accuracy and flat trajectory; and great penetration. Now I think that most sportsmen in big-game countries will agree with me in dismissing the arguments in favour of the first of these as untenable, inasmuch as men who hunt in such countries are not, as a rule, of such slight physique as to be unable to handle a far heavier weapon with comfort, ease, and efficiency throughout a day's sport. A double .303, if a first-class weapon, will be less than 1 lb lighter than a good double .450, and only about 4 lb less than a double .577. As to recoil, – if using the larger bores at target practice, it will be just noticeable; but if fired at game, in the excitement of the chase, nothing less than a Magnum .577 will produce any recoil worth mentioning.

The cartridges are light certainly, and I have heard supporters of the .303 say, "You can put a hundred of these cartridges into your pocket and not feel the weight!" Granted, – but who wants to carry a hundred or even fifty cartridges for a day's sport, unless he be indeed on *slaughter* bent? Speaking for myself, the weight of an ordinary belt of cartridges – containing, say, thirty – troubles me so little that many a time I have worn the belt unthinkingly for hours after returning to camp. When on the march with carriers, one can take a large number of .303 cartridges without any trouble, – an unquestionable advantage, but surely not sufficient of itself to warrant the adoption of the lighter weapon, unless something else can be urged in its favour.

The absence of smoke is, in my opinion, the strongest and only tenable argument yet advanced in favour of this rifle. Too well do I know the annoyance and risk occasioned by the dense cloud of smoke hanging round the muzzle of one's rifle, in the damp air of early morning, or in thick bush or other cover, when upon the other side of the smoke-cloud a wounded lion is crouching – growling for all he is worth – or an old buffalo, exasperated to retaliation, stands at the point of charging! And if they *do* charge under these circumstances, they will most assuredly go straight for the smoke! Nevertheless, this advantage of the absence of smoke is only obtained, be it remembered, by the use of nitro-powders, the tremendous strain of which upon a breech-action is, I think, not denied.

As to the increased accuracy and low trajectory, I cannot for the life of me understand this argument; because, practically speaking, a man armed with any ordinary accurately sighted Express or other rifle can place his bullet exactly where he wishes, supposing him to be a good shot; and if he fails to do this, he knows it is his own fault, not that of the rifle. Take the list of weapons used at any gun-trial and pick out that one which shows the *greatest* deviation in the flight of the projectile, and what does it amount to? Can any sportsman honestly say that he believes the 1½-in or 2-in deviation is going to make any difference to his shot, fired under the ordinary circumstances attendant upon big-game shooting? In such cases – that is, in what I may term rough shooting, where the shot has to be taken, perhaps at an animal running through thick bush or bounding through cover, or when a man is winded after a long run or a stiff climb – he is satisfied if he places his bullet *within a hand's-breath* of the spot he aims at – at least I know I am; and when in exceptional cases he wishes to shoot with as perfect accuracy as possible – as when a dangerous animal is charging, or giving a good standing shot – he has the weapon to do it with, if armed with *any* modern rifle by a good maker. Therefore I think that, while for target and long-range shooting the slightly greater accuracy and flatter trajectory which, owing to the small size of the bore and greater initial velocity of its projectile, the .303 certainly possesses, is an advantage, I do not consider that it is one which will be appreciable under the circumstances which ordinarily obtain in big-game shooting. I have always used Metford rifles of late, and have found that in thick bush country, where most big-game is sought for, their point-blank range of 160 yds is ample for all requirements, and I never on any occasion require to shift my sights.

The next claim made for this rifle, that of penetration, is a good one, but it must not be taken out of hand as proving superiority. It is unnecessary to remind sportsmen that too much penetration in the case of soft-skinned dangerous game is almost as bad as too little. The bullet should have just sufficient penetration to pass through an animal, when fired from any angle, until it reaches the skin on the other side, *where it should remain.* If it goes clear *through,* half of its energy and striking force is wasted, instead of being expended upon the beast, as is necessary if the greatest possible shock to the system, the heaviest knock-down blow, is to be given.

For this kind of shooting – *i.e.,* soft-skinned dangerous animals – various forms of the Tweedie and Jeffries bullets are used with good results; indeed, when the size of the bore is taken into consideration, they certainly are most destructive weapons, the wound produced being incredibly severe, owing to the enormous velocity attained by the projectile.

But so also are good rifles of the larger bores; they make wounds as deadly as, not to say more so than, the .303, because, naturally enough, the heavier bullets, if possessing sufficient penetration, will produce a greater shock to the system of the animal struck than the smaller and lighter ones can do.

Then, as to the biggest game – elephants, rhinoceros, and buffalo; it is *only when picked shots* are obtained that these rifles are of any use on such animals, and in such cases other hard-driving rifles are certainly equally as efficient. At any rate, I can testify to the capabilities of two – the Gibbs' Metford, Nos 1 and 2, No. 1 firing a long 75/540 cartridge, and No. 2 a 90/570. The latter rifle is the most destructive and efficient weapon I have ever seen in my life; and Mr Selous has very clearly demonstrated what can be done with these Metford rifles upon elephants and other big game. With a Gibbs' Metford 90/570 I have obtained most surprising results, not, however, by my good shooting, for, as a matter of fact, I am an indifferent shot – the good qualities are in the rifle. With it I have killed a large bull elephant with a single shot, and several rhino with one bullet: on one occasion I dropped a big rhino bull in his tracks *with both shoulders smashed.* With *one* bullet I killed an eland bull and wounded another so severely that he only ran 150 yds and dropped dead; and on each of three occasions when hunting in Nyasaland I secured two Lichtenstein hartebeeste with *one* bullet. Another day, whilst hunting in the Elephant Marsh, I shot eight buffalo – seven big bulls and a cow – in eleven consecutive shots, two of which were clean misses. But, as I say, these were more or less picked shots; and if these animals had been hit anywhere except in a vital spot, they would have gone away practically unharmed, whether the rifle used had been a .303, .405, .500, or .577. My friend Mr H. A. Hillier, judicial consular officer at Tshiromo, British Central Africa, a fine shot and keen sportsman, on one occasion put three bullets from a .303 into a rhino bull and failed to bag him. If he had been armed with a 10-bore and 8 drams, the rhino would have been his at the first shot. The .303 would have a slight advantage, supposing that it could drive a bullet into the vitals of an elephant, rhinoceros, or buffalo, after entering at the buttock, the animal standing tail-on, or three-quarters away; but I do not know if it *will* do this: in any other position, another rifle will kill a picked shot equally well.

And now to sum up. The .303 is a handy and, within limits, efficient weapon, the cartridges which are used with it being so light and small that a far greater number of them can be carried than of those of larger bore rifles in an equal space. It has no recoil and practically no smoke, is absolutely accurate, possesses enormous penetration, a very flat trajectory, and is capable of producing very deadly wounds, notwithstanding the projectile is so small, owing to the high rate of speed at which it is driven.

In the matter of handiness and absence of recoil, I have endeavoured to show that such cannot be fairly claimed as advantages proving superiority, inasmuch as any man of ordinary strength and stature can use a heavier weapon with perfect ease; and that the recoil of such heavier weapons is not felt when shooting at game any more than that of the .303. In that the nitro-powder used in the cartridges produces little if any smoke, this rifle can claim an important advantage; but the use of this powder is in itself a disadvantage, as it exercises too great a strain upon the chamber and breech-action of a rifle.

The rifle is very accurate, more so – but only in a slight degree – than a .450 or a .500 bore; in fact, the mean deviation of its projectiles is so little less than that of the projectiles of the larger bore as to be unappreciable when the weapons are used under the usual circumstances of big-game shooting.

Its penetration is very great, but it is admitted that this is a disadvantage when used upon thin-skinned animals; therefore bullets are now made for it which give just the penetration required – that is, such as any well-made .450 or .500 bore gives: but the bullets used in the latter rifles being heavier, will, *cœteris paribus*, give a greater shock to the system of the animal struck than the smaller bullets of the former. With the larger kinds of big game it possesses no advantage over .450- or .500-bore rifles: it will kill *picked shots*, so will they; but any one who is accustomed to big-game shooting in dense bush-country will know how much or how little value to attach to that, picked shots being unquestionably the exception, not the rule.

The fact is that from the first the .303 rifle has been greatly overrated. If its supporters would be satisfied to claim for the weapon great destructive powers upon thin-skinned beasts (I would here include the easily-killed giraffe, for although its hide is thick, any ordinary bullet quickly finds its vitals), then those who, like myself, prefer something heavier, would very willingly concede so much, even though we do not admit its superiority. But they would have us believe that it is efficient upon the biggest game, and that, armed with such a weapon, one does not require anything larger for elephant, rhinoceros, or buffalo. My friend Mr Glynn, an ardent advocate of the .303, in speaking to me lately, summed up the matter thus: "The .303 is a good weapon, and I shall stick to it. For koodoo and suchlike, and even for buffalo, I have found it perfect, *but for ponderous game one must have something heavier.*" This fully bears out the remarks made by Mr Coryndon in a letter to the "Field", wherein, while admitting the destructive powers of the .303 on *waterbuck* and other antelopes, he strongly advises something heavier for the largest game.

Mr Glynn, it will be seen, included buffalo amongst the game that could be easily killed with the .303; but it is perhaps as well to remark that in the district where he was lately shooting buffalo – near the Pungwe river, on the south-east coast of Africa – buffalo were very numerous, and comparatively tame and easy of approach. I also found this to be the case in British Central Africa, so much so that picked shots were the *rule*, and any good driving rifle would have performed equally well, at any rate in my case.

A very distinct disadvantage of these small-bore rifles is that when any but the smaller antelopes are wounded by them, there is no blood-spoor upon which the sportsman can follow up his game and secure it. Any one who knows what sport is in thick bush-country will recognise how heavily handicapped one would be in such a case.

Mr Hillier, to whom I have made previous reference, writing me lately from Tshiromo, British Central Africa, says: "I wounded a big bull koodoo with my .303, but did not get him, though I am sure he was badly hit. I followed the spoor for some miles, but had to give in." And again: "I am not quite satisfied with .303; I am sure I do not get anything like all the game I hit with it." *Verbum sap.!*

Hitherto my remarks have been confined to the .303-bore rifle *versus* .450 and .500 bores, and I think I have said enough to prove that I for one am not an advocate for the use of these small-bores against the biggest game. These are to be bagged in either of two ways – by shooting the animal dead upon the spot, or by giving it such a paralysing shock that it shall be disabled and easily run into. Now in order to enable the sportsman to bag his animal on the spot, it is a *sine quâ non* that he shall obtain a picked shot, in which case he could use a small rifle (.303, .450, or .500) with as much success as he could one of larger bore – 8 or 10. (When speaking of "picked shots", I mean such as a sportsman would obtain after stalking his game to within 50 yds, or even 100 yds, if he was using a smaller, and therefore more accurate, weapon.) But as the bigger bore will give a crushing blow and a paralysing shock to a beast, no matter where he gets the bullet, while the small-bore would have no effect whatever in such a case, the advantages undoubtedly all lie with the former.

Now let us glance again for a while at another class of animals – thin-skinned but dangerous game, such as lions and leopards. I have shot these with .450- and .500-bore rifles, the bullet passing through lungs or heart, and yet they have charged. I have also shot them with heavy 10- and 12-bores: sometimes they have charged, but more frequently the heavy shock to the system has knocked all the charge out of them, even though they have not died at once.

Both lions and leopards are animals that die quickly when shot through the vitals, but even in the few moments of life left to them they can do a vast amount of damage. With such animals the great desideratum is not penetration alone, but accurate shooting, combined with due penetration *and* effective killing-power (the terms are not synonymous), which is obtained by giving a heavy shock to the system.

It must not be thought that I am advocating the use of big-bore rifles for lion- or leopard-shooting, – on the contrary, they are far too clumsy and wanting in the necessary accuracy; but I wish to show that I consider that rifle most suitable which has the most effective killing-power, combined with accuracy. The heavier the projectile used in combination with a fair powder-charge (the combination will be formed with a view to great accuracy), the greater will be the shock which the animal receives; and the greater the shock, the quicker he will succumb, and the less likely he is to do damage.

I have had occasion to mention Express rifles somewhat frequently, but have no wish to be understood as advocating their use – that is, in the exaggerated form in which they frequently appear nowadays, and wherein everything, even effective killing-power, is sacrificed to "low trajectory", for reasons which I will explain. There is no question but that this class of rifles has become very popular of late years; nor can it be wondered at, considering their very low trajectory, and their efficiency against small, harmless, thin-skinned game. It is not surprising, therefore, that the late Sir Samuel Baker's severe strictures upon this class of weapon called for much comment and some criticism. And yet there is no doubt that fine old sportsman knew full well what he was writing about when he condemned the Express rifle of the present day – a weapon with an abnormally heavy powder-charge, and a bullet so ridiculously light that, as a well-known correspondent to "Land and Water" has said, "It will blow to shreds upon striking a hare."

I should think that very few of those who advocate using such weapons for, say, tiger-shooting, have ever had to stop a tiger's charge on foot – unless, indeed, a tiger is easier killed than a lion or leopard; and as for some of the larger African antelopes, they laugh such toys to scorn. Instances have been multiplied to show that under some circumstances (usually those in which there is more than ever need for efficiency, such as when the sportsman is charged by a lion or tiger) this bullet is utterly untrustworthy, and Sir Samuel Baker mentions more than one case in point. But because the principle happens to be carried *ad absurdum*, it is not to declare it in itself faulty.

Study, above all things, to obtain effective killing-power, and combine it with the greatest accuracy that can be obtained; and do not reverse these qualities in order of merit. Have, in fact, a *modified form* of Express (that is, a weapon in which a fairly large powder-charge – but less than the usual maximum Express charge – is used in combination with a heavy, slightly hollowed, conical projectile: such a weapon is the Gibbs' Metford), and the weapon will at once commend itself to all practical sportsmen.

I believe in the hollow bullet within reason; but let the hollow be small, leaving substantial walls on either side, and shallow, so that if the point breaks up a heavy butt shall remain. Such a bullet will retain its component parts intact if it does not meet with too much bone-resistance, and the very smallest hollow is sufficient to cause it to "mushroom" out; while if the point should get smashed up by such contact, the heavy butt remains to travel on upon its destructive course.

A .461 Metford is perhaps as perfect a weapon for lion-shooting as one can desire. A bullet from this rifle, well placed, at 40 yds will stop almost any lion from attempting to charge; or if it does make the attempt, it will assuredly fall dead in the act. Of course if a lion has already started and is at close quarters, he is very difficult to stop, and will do an infinity of harm even after receiving a mortal wound.

I believe that a .450 rifle can be made equally as effective as a .577;

for the difference in the bore is not very great after all, and a .450 can be made to carry a far heavier bullet in comparison than a .577, as the latter becomes too clumsy and has too much recoil if anything more than the usual 5½ or 6 drams and the 620-grain bullet be used.

For years I have used Gibbs' Metford rifles of .461 bore, and for all thin-skinned game, lions, and leopards, have never seen them beaten, if equalled. The Express charge for those rifles is 90 grains and a 360-grain hollow bullet. This is perfect for lions, leopards, and antelopes; and last year I shot four hippos with a similar charge. For so comparatively small a bullet it performs most wonderfully. A charge of 75 grains and 540-grain solid bullet can be used with the same rifle for long ranges, and is all that can be desired for hippos, buffalo and giraffe. The bullet is of course hardened.

I have referred elsewhere to the splendid performances of another .461 Metford which Mr Gibbs built for me, carrying a charge of 90 grains and solid or hollow bullets of 570 grains; and I think it will be admitted that nothing better could be desired. Held straight, it will account for anything less than an elephant, and even for them on occasions, as I have shown, though these animals can only be killed with a small-bore rifle under special circumstances. Mr Gibbs has always given the greatest satisfaction with the weapons he has built for me; but I wish it to be clearly understood that in making particular mention of his name, I do not in any way suggest superiority over other first-class makers. That his weapons are second to none both in price and efficiency cannot be gainsaid, but that is not to say that those turned out by our other leading gunmakers are not as costly and as good — in fact, where these qualities obtain in all, it would be invidious to draw comparisons, because, especially where one finds himself suited with a certain make of rifle, naturally he will adhere to it, and his experience after that with those of other makers will be small.

Although believing that a .450 is the very smallest bore that a man should take in hand for use upon game of any size, I do not think that rifles of very slightly larger bores possess any real advantage over the .450, always supposing that the charge and projectile used in the latter is carefully regulated.

My experience does not bear out the fact that a .577 will stop a charging lion better than a .450. If hit in the head, heart, or lungs, or if neck, fore-shoulders, back, or hind-legs be broken, any of these shots either kills the most dangerous of the carnivoræ outright, or places them entirely in one's power; and a .450 will do this as effectually as a .577. Hit anywhere else, neither .450, .500, nor .577 will stop them.

As regards breech-actions, I have found Field's patent the best for all-round hard work for single rifles; and it has the further advantage of being extremely simple in its mechanism. I have tried Martini, Swinburn, Westley-Richards' falling-block, and the Deeley-Edge, but like none of them so well as Field's sliding-block.

For heavy big-bore double rifles I prefer the under-lever double-grip action. This is all merely a matter of taste to a great extent: a man accustomed to a certain action feels awkward with any other. But for dangerous game double rifles should always be carried, not so much for the sake of the extra chance it gives one – for single breech-actions are now so rapidly manipulated that the difference is but slight – as for the greater safety ensured in case of a charge or a miss-fire.

In choosing a weapon, the sportsman will further do well to consider whether he is likely to hunt in "fly-country" or not, as in the former case horses cannot be used. The bush here is usually of a denser character, and the sportsman will be intent upon the larger game – rhinoceros or buffalo – and would necessarily have a large-bore rifle with him, carried by a boy, though retaining his lighter weapon as well. If hunting on horseback out of "fly", a fairly light rifle is a *sine quâ non*, as a heavy weapon thus carried drags a man to pieces in no time; and there is always this advantage on horseback, that even if the first shot be badly placed, the sportsman can quickly come up with his game and deliver another.

For big-game shooting on foot in dense bush the larger the bore the better, I believe; small bores in such cases give great disappointment. So that no matter how much reliance a man may place in his hand-hitting small-bores, if big-game be sought a large-bore rifle should form part of his battery.

One occasionally hears of repeating-arms being suggested as useful additions to a battery; but let the intending sportsman take the advice of *one who has used them*, and let them severely alone. They are good enough for what they were intended – Indian border warfare – but as weapons to be used upon dangerous game, they are useless toys, never in balance, and usually possessing an abnormally high trajectory. One may well be forgiven, also, for considering them unsportsmanlike. Pumping lead into an animal from a hand-mitrailleuse is scarcely in accordance with one's ideas of fair sport.

There is one point which suggests itself as worthy of passing remark. The expression very often crops up, "an efficient all-round rifle", and it seems to me that the description of a fatally misleading one. In common with a good many others that I know of, I have had a pretty severe attack of "all-round-rifle" fever, and experience in the field was the doctor that cured me: he is a splendid practitioner, and the only really qualified one, – theory is a fraudulent quack. I hold strongly to the opinion that such a rifle cannot exist; therefore, to base one's arguments on that which is non-existent is obviously erroneous. The term "all-round rifle" for use in a big-game country, I take to mean a weapon which can be used indiscriminately with efficiency on all game that may show itself, and thus enable a man who can only afford limited battery, or who has perhaps no means at his disposal of carrying more than one weapon, to do, or attempt to do, execution amongst thick-skinned animals, the larger carnivoræ, and antelopes alike, – a rifle, in fact, which shall be as efficient amongst springbuck, blesbuck, oribi, and rhébuck of the hill-country, as amongst the sable, roan, and other large antelopes of the bush-veldt; as effective upon the tough large-boned rhinoceros, buffalo, and giraffe as upon the thin-skinned but more dangerous carnivoræ. Surely, to any one who knows what big-game shooting is, such an idea cannot commend itself. That the sportsman in all lands should have a handy rifle to be his constant companion I quite admit, but entirely deny that he can use it as an all-round weapon. I am aware that I have drawn attention to the efficiency of a .461 Metford when used upon rhino, buffalo, &c., but it was only in order to show what a powerful weapon such can be made, not as advising the constant use of such on the biggest game.

For preserving animal trophies in the hunting-veldt, a very simple outfit of tools and preservatives is required. With a good pocket-knife carrying one stout 4-inch blade and one or two smaller ones, the largest and the smallest animals can be operated upon efficiently. A good Turkey-stone, and three pairs of stoutly made scissors – large, medium, and small – are very necessary, and will come into use as frequently as the knife.

If it is desired to save the head trophies alone of the Felidæ, jackals, hyænas, and hunting-dogs, the skin of the head must not be cut at all, save to sever the neck from the rest of the carcass. By careful manipulation the skin can then be pulled clean over the head towards the nose, severing the ears at their bases. All details of this kind can readily be learned by a perusal of Montagu Browne's excellent work, "Practical Taxidermy", – the very best book of its kind ever written for amateurs, as it seeks to instruct and simplify, not to bewilder the tyro, as most others do. Be careful always to skin the ears to their tips. This can best be done by pushing the handle of a scalpel, or any flat bone or horn instrument, up towards the tips, and carefully removing all fleshy matter around the base. Cut away as much of the cartilaginous matter around the nostrils as possible, and the flesh between the mucous membrane and outer skin of the lips. Always retain the mucous membrane of the eyes. The greatest care must be exercised over both ears and eyes, and even then a slip will occur sometimes. Let your object be to remove as far as possible all fleshy matter from the head-skin, but remember that it is better to cut too little than too much. When the head-skin is fleshed and cleaned it must be thoroughly rubbed on both sides with a mixture of burnt alum and saltpetre, of which a good supply should always be taken. The proportion of each to the other is 1 lb of burnt alum to ¼ lb of saltpetre; mix it into a thick paste with water, and put it on freely with a large brush. It is always well to paint the eyes, nose, lips, and inside of ears with this preservative, mixed with a few drops of carbolic acid, before starting to skin the head, and as it counteracts all tendency in the hair to slip. There are any number of preservative preparations before the public, but I would strongly advise any one not to waste money upon them. They may be good, but better they cannot be than the simple preparation I have mentioned, and the knowledge of which I also owe to that useful book. Whether the head be that of the antelope, of the Felidæ, buffalo, or giraffe, it is equally effective, and is as cheap as effective. Hang the head-skin up to dry in an airy spot, with the fur inside. But in tropical and sub-tropical districts I strongly recommend that they be carefully turned back to their natural position, so that the fur or hair is outside. This should be done just as they commence to get dry, but before getting too hard. It enables the collector to give them the necessary turpentine bath occasionally – an *absolute necessity* if the skins are to be preserved from the ravages of insects. Horned heads should be severed in like manner from the body, always *leaving plenty of neck*. The most common mistake made, and perhaps the most serious one, is that of cutting off the neck too short. If the skin can be taken off just before the shoulders, so much the better – the underpart of the throat especially requiring to be long. With horned heads the back of the neck must be skinned up – if there is any mane, run the knife along close to it – till between and a little behind the bases of the horns: make branch cuts towards these, and proceed exactly as described in the book above referred to. Zebra and giraffe must also be cut up the back of the skull, and not underneath jaw.

I have never yet succeeded in successfully skinning the "horns" of giraffe: it is a most difficult task. I have always skinned up to the bases as far as possible, and then sawn the horns from the skull. A hole can be bored with a gimlet down each horn from the top, and carbolic acid dropped in. The whole must be thoroughly smeared inside and out with the alum and saltpetre preservative. If one has stowage room, it is better not to saw the skulls of horned heads down the centre, as it tends to seriously weaken them, but where space is limited it must be done. The wart-hog or *vlak-vark* is one of the most difficult animals to operate upon, and I have never yet done one successfully without cutting it under the throat to about the commencement of the chin: this greatly assists in getting the skin clear of the tusks.

Boil all skulls carefully (recollect that *care* must be exercised in all matters pertaining to the preservation of trophies – care, patience, and watchfulness), and as soon as the lower jaw will come away, take it out and scrape it: if boiled too long it is damaged. I have always found a large riveted galvanised iron bucket useful – nay, invaluable – for cleaning heads. When the skulls are scraped clean, and the brain-matter removed, if a horned head, the horns must be pulled off from their bony cores (good employment for a lazy native), washed inside with hot water, and the core cleaned and painted with carbolic solution, then dried. The cores can be sawn off so as to leave 4 to 5 ins of the butt upon which to replace the horns. This can be done when all is dry and free from smell. The horns of wildebeeste and water-buck are very hard to get off their cores, but one can always set some of the idlers about a camp to do that.

Wrap carefully in *dry* grass when packing, and never place skulls in the same part of the waggon – or even in the same waggon, if it can be avoided – as the head-skins.

Constantly overhaul for beetles – *Dermestes lardarius* is now a "by-word and a reproach" – and soak freely with turpentine, of which several gallons should be carried.

Ticket all specimens with a number, having reference to a similar number in the "note-book", wherein dimensions and other remarks will be accurately noted.

If trophies are to be stored for any length of time, hang in as light a place as possible, as if put away into dark corners they will inevitably be found out by the beetles sooner or later.

Six-inch "French nails" are very handy for pegging out skins that are required for mounting; they do not tear so much as pegs.

IN HAUNTS OF WILD GAME
(Blackwood 1896)

Rifles and Camp Management

G. P. SANDERSON

I propose to offer a few remarks upon rifles, and on the medical portion of camp-management. I can look back to having lost so many animals when a beginner – animals toiled after without grudge, and the loss of which, through the ineffectiveness of my rifles for the work in hand, cost me pangs at the time which only the young sportsman can understand; and I have suffered so much from the malarial fevers that are the most dreaded enemy the sportsman has to contend against in campaigns into the localities where large game is to be found, – that I hope my experiences may save some from similar disappointments of the chase, and from the shiverings of ague and burnings of fever that I have endured, and which may be averted with knowledge and care.

There is perhaps no subject upon which more frequent discussions arise amongst sportsmen than that of the best rifles for game. The matter really admits of no great latitude of opinion, nor is it men who have had much experience that differ. The conflicting views are held by those who speak more from theory or a limited experience than extensive practical knowledge. There are two well-known sportsmen, amongst others, whom every one will admit to be thoroughly qualified to speak on the subject, – namely, the late Captain James Forsyth, Bengal Staff Corps, author of the *Sporting Rifle and its Projectiles* (which I strongly recommend to any young sportsman who has not read it); and Sir Samuel Baker, whose experience with large game is unrivalled. Both advocate the use of the heaviest rifle the sportsman can manage upon all sorts of game. Yet it is not unusual to hear men express a decided opinion to the contrary, generally conveyed in the formula, "A 12-bore is big enough for anything". Sir Samuel Baker says that such should rather say, "I cannot carry a heavy gun", or, "I cannot shoot with one", than speak against them on principle.

All the world over animals are divisible into but two classes considered as objects for the rifle, and for each class a distinct rifle is required. The first consists of such ponderous beasts as the elephant, rhinoceros, buffalo, and bison, whose hides are tough and whose bones are massive. The second comprises tigers, bears, and all descriptions of deer and smaller animals; these may be termed the soft-bodied class. For the former a ball of immense smashing power is necessary, otherwise it may be arrested by powerful bones and muscles before it can do sufficient damage; for the second class, whose bodies do not offer a quarter the resistance of those of the larger quadrupeds, a different kind of effect – that of the express or explosive bullet – is the most advantageous, because it can be produced by a rifle of a more manageable description than one required to effect as great results with a solid bullet.

I have generally found men who do not use or understand heavy-game rifles make one or other of the following remarks on examining them: "What a weight! who could carry that?" or, "It must kick fearfully!" It will be understood that, as regards the first objection, such pieces are only taken in hand by the sportsman when actually firing at game, and are at other times carried by his attendants. I may also say that the weight seems very much less under the exciting circumstances in which such pieces are generally used than when they are handled in cold blood. As regards the kicking, their weight being proportionate to the charge of powder used, they recoil little more than an ordinary 12-bore.

It is sometimes argued that hundreds of large animals have been bagged with 12 or 14 bore rifles, or even smaller weapons. True: but how many more have escaped or have been consigned to die lingering deaths, that would have been secured with heavier metal? A 14 or 16 bore, with 4 drams of powder, is sufficient to kill even an elephant if a fair shot can be had at his brain. But suppose the elephant to be rushing through a tangled break or long grass, when only a hurried and indistinct shot can be had at him, the smaller gun would be useless unless its ball reached his brain, whilst the heavy projectile would floor or stun, even if it did not kill him. A rifle for heavy game should be capable of meeting these contingencies – not be adapted only for picked shots and bright moments.

A few years ago 12-bore rifles (1½-oz. ball) were more generally used perhaps than any others for general shooting, but the introduction of the express has led to their very general supersession for sport with the lighter class of game. I think all experienced sportsmen are agreed that 12-bores are too insignificant for use upon the heavy class, and that they form a half-and-half weapon, neither one thing nor the other – wanting the accuracy, handiness, and killing power of the express, and the smashing effect of a large bore – and are weapons which we may well dispense with in the present day. Some sportsmen – not very keen ones – like a 12-bore on the ground that it gives them, within the compass of one weapon, a better chance with both classes of game than a large-bore or an express; that is, they seek to adapt one piece to widely different uses. As well might a man hope to find combined in the same horse the speed of a Derby winner and the power of a Suffolk Punch! The only description of shooting for which a 12-bore is still useful is at beasts of the lighter class which may happen to be seen but indistinctly through masses of twigs or other obstructions. The express bullet is not always to be depended upon for covert-shooting. Its conical form leads to its being easily deflected from its course. I have frequently found no further traces of an express bullet after a shot fired through thick cover, where a spherical ball would certainly have reached its mark. But shooting through thick places, even in an Indian jungle, is decidedly exceptional.

Sir Samuel Baker recommends the use of a four-oz. (No. 4) ball for very heavy game. That even this ball, projected by 12 drams of powder, will frequently fail to floor an elephant, or to put a bison or buffalo *hors de combat* at once, I have proved; yet men who have never used them will argue against such heavy weapons as unnecessary.

I at first killed several elephants with a No. 12 spherical-ball rifle, with hard bullets and 6 drams of powder, but I found it insufficient for many occasions. I then had a single-barrelled C.F. No. 4-bore rifle, weighing 16½ lbs, and firing 10 drams, made to order by Lang & Sons, Cockspur Street. A cartridge of this single-barrel, however, missed fire on one occasion and nearly brought me to grief, so I gave it up and had a No. 4 double smooth-bore, C.F., weighing 19½ lbs, built by W. W. Greener. This I have used ever since. I ordinarily fire 12 drams of powder with it. This is as far as man can go with powder and lead, if I except Sir Samuel Baker's half-pound shell-rifle, the "Baby"; and though the above gun has failed me once, it usually effectually settles any difference with an elephant.

I have another favourite weapon, a No. 8 double rifle, firing 12 drams, and weighing 17 lbs, also by W. W. Greener. As may be imagined it has enormous penetration, and is very accurate. I have stopped and killed charging elephants with it, but I prefer the 4-bore for certain occasions in elephant-shooting.

Heavy-game rifles are, of course, only taken in hand when the game is met; the sportsman could not carry them far himself. Any man of medium strength will find himself capable of handling a 17 to 20-lb rifle, and of firing 12 drams with spherical ball, under the excitement of elephant-shooting. As regards recoil, it is not serious with such weighty guns. A friend of mine, the well-known "Smooth-bore" of Madras, once fired at a tusker with my No. 8 double rifle and 12 drams. I usually keep the left barrel of heavy pieces on half-cock, as the jar to the left lock in firing the right barrel is very great. "Smooth-bore" did not think of this, and we afterwards found that the left barrel had also had its fling at the tusker. My friend had fired 24 drams and a pair of 2-oz. bullets almost simultaneously, but said he did not feel any severe recoil!

All rifles for elephants and heavy game should be double-barrelled, as they have to be made as heavy if single to withstand the recoil, and the danger of a miss-fire is a fatal objection to single-barrelled weapons. It is evidently useless to have a light large-bore, as the recoil of such a weapon precludes the use of a charge of powder proportionate to the weight of the ball. A recent writer on Indian sport speaks of "a powerful 6-bore (2⅔ oz.) rifle, burning 4 drams". About three times this charge would be more nearly what such a rifle would require. A big ball before a light charge of powder is as useless as a heavy sword in the hands of a weak man.

Were I asked my opinion as to a battery to be taken out to India I should recommend a .450 express[1] as the sportsman's own weapons – the one to be always in his hands, whether tiger-shooting in the jungle or antelope-stalking in the plains; and a heavy rifle of N. 8 gauge, to burn up to 12 drams of powder, and weighing between 16 and 17 lbs, for anything larger than tigers. Of course if the sportsman can afford a pair of the latter weapons so much the better. If he intend to shoot elephants – and the day may come when elephant-shooting will be allowed again in India – he should have a still larger double rifle or smooth-bore. I should recommend a No. 4. I have, for my own part, become so thoroughly impressed, after giving them a fair trial, of the indispensability of heavy rifles for large game that I disposed of a pair of pet 12-bores I had, and with which I had killed many big beasts, in favour of a double 4, a double 8, and a double express. Without something of the cannon kind, game of the ponderous class cannot be brought to fighting quarters with even a moderate degree of safety or effect. The sportsman will have to follow the ignominious plan of popping at them from safe places, or, however boldly he may encounter them, he will find small weapons entail constant disappointment. With really heavy metal he feels

---

[1] Messrs Lang & Sons, 22 Cockspur Street, are now building for me a .450 express, to burn 5½ standard drams. The advantages which will be secured by this unprecedentedly large charge will be apparent to those who understand that most admirable weapon the express. About 4½ drams is the largest charge that has been used hitherto in the .450. Powder-measures supplied by various gunmakers differ considerably, and often bear about the same proportion to the standard measures as the reputed quart does to the imperial. It is advisable, therefore, to have a guarantee from gunmakers to the actual amount of powder which their cartridges are capable of holding.

that confidence and power to overcome the hugest beasts which constitute the chief elements of pleasure in following and facing them.

I am decidedly opposed to the use upon buffalo, bison, and such animals, of the express rifle of either .500 or .450 bore (equivalent to 38 and 50 spherical gauge). The express is essentially a rifle for soft-bodied animals, and is not adapted for use on those with thick hides and massive bones. Though bison have not unfrequently been killed with the express, a return of the beasts wounded and lost for each one bagged would, as far as the experience of my friends and myself goes, be a terrible document. Sir Samuel Baker says: "A hollow bullet fired from an express rifle will double up a deer; but it will be certain to expand upon the hard skin of elephants, rhinoceros, hippopotami, buffalo, &c., in which case it will lose all power of penetration. When a hollow bullet strikes a large bone, it absolutely disappears into minute particles of lead, and of course it becomes worthless."

Two sportsmen, Captains E. and P., perhaps the best shots in Southern India, if the Bangalore rifle-meeting performances are a test, who have shot in the Billiga-rungun hills with me, have, after ample experience, denounced the use of the express on bison. On one occasion P. fired six times at a bull with a .500 express and hollow bullets: the sixth shot, which was in the head, killed it; but the others, which were all accurately placed behind the shoulder, beyond sickening the beast failed through want of penetration. E. fired eleven shots amongst bison with both solid and hollow hardened bullets, with unsatisfactory results: one bull that was dropped, and again floored whilst struggling on to his legs, and left for dead whilst E. pursued the herd, got up, and was never seen again. If a *solid* hardened bullet be used with an express, the principle of the weapon, and the cause of its immense efficiency on soft-bodied animals, are lost, and the rifle becomes merely a hard-hitting small-bore. No one will dispute the sporting truism that "a good big 'un is better than a good little 'un"; and both theory and practice sufficiently show that a hard-hitting large-bore, before which the largest bones are as those of chickens, is the proper weapon for heavy game.

My experience of shells has been too limited to allow of my saying much on the subject. What I have seen of them has led me to discard them myself as unnecessary, but I do not wish to condemn them. I have found Forsyth's swedged shells fairly effective in a 12-bore rifle; but Mr W. W. Greener advised me against having them for an 8-bore he was making for me, on the ground of their not possessing sufficient stability for a large-bore and heavy charge. He recommended a steel-core bottle-shell in preference. I tried three Forsyth's shells, which I made and loaded carefully myself, with the above rifle (No. 8) and 6 drams of powder, at a target 40 yds distant. Two of these flew into two pieces each; these pieces struck three feet apart, and effectually frightened me from trying any more experiments. I think that with the express – which acts like an explosive bullet – for the lighter class of game, and with heavy solid spherical bullets (the only reliable bone-smashers) for the heavier class, sportsmen will find themselves able to do without shell-rifles of a calibre between the two.

Supposing the young sportsman to have provided himself with an efficient battery, I will now proceed to make a suggestion or two for his camp-management.

It will be unnecessary for me to enter into details about equipage. Excellent hints on the subject of tents and kit may be found in many books on Indian sport, and in others devoted entirely to the subject. The great principle to be borne in mind in making arrangements for jungle-life is, that the sportsman should make himself and followers as comfortable as possible. Any amount of hard work may be done by all during the day if they have dry clothes and a comfortable dinner and bed at the end of it. Roughing it when there is no necessity – and there seldom is nowadays in India – is a mistake which only the inexperienced fall into. There is rarely any reason why a sportsman should sleep without sheets, drink out of a tin pot, or dine off a box, though these are merely discomforts. In matters actually affecting the health of the party in jungle localities, it is suicidal not to know what are the precautions to be observed, or to neglect them.

Malarial fever is the great obstacle with which the sportsman in Indian jungles has to contend; but, though it is a dread reality, it is at the same time made more of a bugbear to the inexperienced than it need be. Miasmatic air, from its heaviness, lies and travels close to the ground, and it is probably not active during the day when the jungles are warmed by the sun. Cold and dampness are its great auxiliaries. It appears to be taken into the system by inhalation, and it is supposed the poison also exists in water contaminated by decaying vegetable matter. As evening closes in there is a raw feeling in the air in the jungles which the sportsman must perceive is inimical to health. Some jungle-tribes build their houses on platforms ten feet high, knowing by experience the advantage to health in being thus elevated. But as a moving camp cannot take this precaution, the miasma about the sleepers must be destroyed or dissipated. This is to be done by keeping up fires to windward. The pestilential exhalations are thus carried up in the current of lighter air, or are consumed. Small tents of thick material should be used for master and servants, as they are warmer than large ones. At night the jungle-people in each camp, or some of the sportsman's own men, should keep up a fire as close as possible to the tents, and so placed that the warm air from it may blow over them. Whilst within its influence it is impossible that malaria can touch the sleepers. Let the sportsman but go out of the circle of the fires during the night, and he will feel how cold and raw the air is compared to that within their genial influence.

Every one must sleep well off the ground. The sportsman's cot should be at least three feet high – raised by forked uprights if necessary – and he should sleep within mosquito-curtains.[1] For his servants, if nothing else is available the tent-sacks should be stuffed with straw or dry grass; these will raise the men above the dampness of the ground. Servants are excessively careless, and unless the sportsman see after them himself they will take no precautions on their own account. All rank vegetation close at hand should be cleared away, by burning if possible, and the camp should be situated on as high and dry ground as can be found, but must not be exposed to high winds.

The sportsman should invariably change his clothes and boots if wet from rain or perspiration the moment he comes in; not go out earlier, nor remain out later in the evening, than necessary; and have his meals as regularly as possible. It is a good plan to take something, if only a few biscuits, with one, as in the heat of the chase one may lose the men who carry the luncheon-basket. Temperance in the use of liquor is of course absolutely necessary. Everything that tends to debilitate the system renders it liable to the effects of malaria. The sportsman whilst undergoing unusual exposure and hard work can ill afford to be careless in any respect. One frequently feels so well with the pleasant exercise and excitement of a jungle-trip that there is a tendency to excess or heedlessness.

I always have the water for my own and servants' cooking and drinking boiled and cooled before using. I have been almost exclusively a water-drinker for years, and believe that no one need be afraid of any water if this precaution – or better still, distillation – be adopted. A small still is easily carried about, and the water of any puddle can then be used. The plan of putting brandy into water to kill the deleterious matter is admitted to be perfectly useless. If out early or late, a cheroot is an excellent precaution against breathing the miasma which is prevalent at those hours, or a torch of dried bamboos carried in the hand will effectually dispel the cold air. Exposure to dew must be particularly avoided.

Some sportsmen take two or three grains of quinine daily whilst in

---

[1] In some parts of India the nights are so sultry, even in the forests, that this would hardly be possible. It is doubtful, however, if miasma is abroad in such a temperature.

feverish localities. It may do good and can do no harm, but it can be of little avail without every precaution in other respects. I was amused on one occasion by two friends who came to my camp for bison-shooting. They were imbued with a wholesome dread of fever, and had brought with them a large bottle of medicine, in the averting powers of which they placed much reliance, and with which they frequently refreshed themselves. They went to the top of the Billiga-rungun hills, and in the heat of the chase after bison stayed out in the jungle two nights, sleeping in improvised shelters hardly sufficient to keep off the dew, without a fire, and on the ground! I had been unable to accompany them; but when they returned and told me of their doings, and of the constancy with which they had applied themselves to their medicine, I assured them that all the quinine mixture in the world would not counteract exposure such as they had undergone. They returned to their station in a great fright, and had hardly got there before they had such severe fever as almost sent them both to England. It is thus that fever often comes to be made the spectre it is to the inexperienced. One gets it through reckless carelessness, and speaks of the deadliness of the jungles he visited, whilst he might have lived in them in safety for a month with proper care. I presume malarial fevers are similar in most parts of India, and that the following observations, though made particularly with regard to Mysore, will apply equally elsewhere:—

Fever in Mysore is of two kinds: that prevailing at certain seasons in open country, where there are no jungles within many miles, and which seems due entirely to the sudden variations of temperature attendant on the changes of season; and the more noxious kind, similar, but more severe, in its symptoms, contracted in jungle localities, and apparently the result of miasma or poison arising from decaying vegetable matter. These fevers are very seldom fatal to Europeans, except the latter in aggravated cases; but they are most difficult to shake off, recurring at varying stated periods, often for many years. They debilitate the system, and may bring into prominence any other weak point the patient has.

Amongst natives, on the other hand, malarial fevers are exceedingly fatal. Far more succumb to them every year than to cholera and small-pox put together. As fever, however, is insidious in its working, and is not infectious, it causes little alarm, and comparatively little is heard of it. It appears to be owing to the greater natural strength of the European constitution that Englishmen withstand, or throw it off, where natives succumb. Nursing in the stages where the patient is inclined, through prostration, to do nothing but die quietly, also puts to right those who, if left as the native frequently is without suitable nourishment and attention, would fare little better than he does.

Fever is most prevalent about the commencement and end of the rainy season. The alternations in temperature are then considerable, and the winds in the open country are chilly. In the jungles, the decaying vegetation is stirred up by light rains which are insufficient to wash it away. The jungles are most healthy during the hot weather, when the undergrowth has been burnt. This burning is the grand destroyer of all malaria, and the spotsman may tramp the then begrimed forests in perfect safety.

Fever generally shows itself in a week or ten days after the person has been subjected to the influence that has caused it. It begins with lassitude, headache, loss of appetite, and pains in the limbs. Severe shivering fits follow, generally accompanied by vomiting. After a few hours of this, more or less, a hot fit, equally intense, commences, at the end of which the patient probably perspires freely (if steps have been taken to induce this great desideratum in fever treatment). The attack is then over for the time. It may recur the next, second, or third day. I have had perhaps as much experience of fever as any one, before I understood how to avoid it, and may briefly illustrate its course in my own case. Ten years ago I had my first attack. I was prostrated, with intervals of delirium, for a week, and had to take two months' leave of absence for change of air. For about three years fits occurred at gradually lengthening intervals, and of decreasing severity. They were induced by much exposure to the sun or night air, over-fatigue, or irregularity of any kind. I subsequently contracted fresh attacks, but these did not take such hold upon me as the first. One may become to some extent acclimatised to fever, as one never can to exposure to the sun.

Though I think I might almost set up as a medical practitioner if I only had fever cases to deal with, as my experience in treating myself and followers has been of an extensive character, I will not lengthen my remarks by going into that subject. Should a sportsman unfortunately contract fever, he will find admirable directions, in small compass, for self-treatment, in the medical portion of a small work entitled *The European in India*.

I may add one suggestion which, if I remember rightly, is not contained in the book referred to, that the vapour-bath, made with a vessel of boiling water placed under a chair, upon which the patient sits, the whole being enveloped in a thick blanket, will be found a valuable addition to the other treatment, and soon steams the chills of fever out of the sufferer's bones.

A word for Indian servants, than whom there probably are not better in the world for camp-life. How delighted one's "boys" are when "going shooting" is the word! They are cheerful and willing under great discomforts, and with few appliances make their master as comfortable in the jungles as in headquarters. The manner in which a good camp-servant will serve up dinner, from soup to pudding, is astonishing. His cooking-range is but a shallow trench in the ground, in which is the fire, and over which the earthen pots simmer, the whole sheltered perhaps from a howling storm by a tree or a few mats. The sportsman soon finds that, if only from motives of convenience, it is necessary to look to his servants' welfare. Englishmen in India are, as a rule, very kind to their servants, who become warmly attached to good masters' interests; but for want of forethought young sportsmen's followers are sometimes subjected to discomforts which do not arise from want of humanity, but of knowledge. For my own part, having resided so much amongst natives – often not seeing a European for months together – I feel that sport would not yield me one-half the pleasure it does if my people did not enjoy it with me, and feel interested in their master's success. It would be unpleasant to think that they disliked my trips into the jungles, and probably with reason, if they were to be exposed to danger of fever. A rig-out of warm clothes and a blanket at intervals, with a small travelling allowance to compensate for the extra expense they are put to for their food, keep servants healthy and contented. If the marches are long, the sportsman's means of transport – usually carts in Southern India – should be increased for the servants' convenience. Long foot-marches on cold nights or hot days soon knock up domestics accustomed to life in comfortable quarters.

THIRTEEN YEARS AMONG THE WILD BEASTS OF INDIA

(W. H. ALLEN 1879)

My Ideal Rifle

JAMES SUTHERLAND

erhaps, when discussing big game and big game hunting, a few remarks on rifles will not be out of place, but as the subject is naturally one open to endless discussion, I shall express a personal opinion rather than dogmatise. During my hunting career, I have used all kinds of rifles from the 4 bore, black powder, elephant rifle downwards, but as the black powder rifle is a thing of the past, I shall confine my attention to modern high-velocity, smokeless powder rifles, which are infinitely superior to their predecessors on account of their greater range, velocity, power and lightness.

In the first place, the man behind the rifle is so obviously of primary importance that the fact may be dismissed without further comment, while the great consideration in all hunting is to kill and not merely to wound the game fired at. With regard to the weapon, practically any modern rifle will kill game if the bullet penetrates a vital part such as the brain, heart or vertebræ, but under ordinary conditions, such as dense cover with sharp contrasts of light and shade, these shots are difficult, and what is requisite is a rifle with a flat trajectory, which will, should a vital spot be missed, deliver a smashing, disabling blow.

With a .303, I have killed all kinds of game from elephants downwards, but it must be remembered that the hunter who uses a weapon of such calibre against large and dangerous game at close quarters in bush country, runs considerable risk of losing his life, for the bullet has neither the requisite weight nor velocity always to prove thoroughly effectual. And with regard to their use against smaller game, though such light bullets have great penetration, they do not administer a sufficiently paralysing blow to prevent a wounded animal from bolting and thereby obliging the hunter to pursue his quarry for miles, with a chance of losing it altogether and leaving it to die a lingering death in the bush. My experience has, therefore, taught me to consider the .303 a thoroughly unsuitable and unsportsmanlike weapon, the use of which should most emphatically be discontinued. For all kinds of game, save rhinoceroses and elephants, my ideal rifle is one that fires a bullet, lead-nosed or copper-capped, weighing between 350 and 400 grains, and leaving the muzzle with a velocity of 2,300 ft or more per second; for the simple reason that such a bullet expands, tears a large hole and spends all its energy in the animal without slipping though.

Against small game, I have for some years used a .318 rifle and find it, especially in conjunction with Westley Richards patent copper-capped bullets, immeasurably superior to either the .256 or .303, and one which has on account of its high velocity and ideal form of expanding bullet, all the advantages of long range and flat trajectory associated with the small bore, and a large amount of the shock-giving qualities obtained with a larger bore rifle, without the recoil inseparable from that weapon.

The elephant and rhinoceros, being in a class by themselves, require a rifle firing a much heavier bullet. After experimenting with and using all kinds of rifles, I find the most effective to be the double .577 with a 750 grains bullet and a charge in axite powder equivalent to a hundred grains of cordite. The heavier double-barrelled .600 bore rifle, with a bullet weighing 900 grains, lacks the penetration of the .577, while its weight (16 lbs against 13 lbs of the latter) renders it a much more awkward weapon to handle. I think the superiority of the .577 over the .450 and .500 rifles, will be evident when I state that I have lost elephants with these last two rifles, while I have bagged others with identically the same shots from a .577.

When using double-barrelled rifles against big and dangerous game, it is of supreme importance to have a thoroughly reliable ejecting mechanism, and I find that a single trigger is a vast improvement on the old double-trigger, for, apart from eliminating the risk of a bruised finger, the single trigger is infinitely quicker, enabling a double shot to be placed almost simultaneously, if necessary. I have used the single trigger for some years and would on no account go back to the double. Another factor to be considered with regard to a rifle for big game is the length of the barrels. It is my opinion that they should be as short as possible, certainly not longer than twenty-six inches; for a rifle with barrels exceeding this length is extremely awkward to manipulate in bush country. The double-barrelled .577 which I have used for several years and found admirable in every detail was built for me by Westley Richards & Co., of Bond Street. The construction of the locks is excellent and simple to a degree, so that should anything go wrong with the mechanism in the bush, where you cannot take a taxi to your gunmaker, there is no difficulty in instantly detaching a lock by hand and replacing it with a duplicate. The single trigger and ejector attached to this rifle have on no occasion failed to act.

In open country, against elephants and rhinoceros, where the quarry is difficult to approach and long shots are often required, I find that I can do all that is requisite with a small bore rifle, such as the .318, using, of course, solid nickel-covered bullets, for, owing to the easy manipulation afforded by such a weapon, a more deliberate aim can be taken than with a heavy rifle.

I have dwelt at some length on this subject of rifles, for I feel that the matter is one of importance, from the point of view not only of the hunter, but of the game. The point of view on which I insist is one of common humanity, and the young hunter should think deeply over the subject of weapons before going out against game with any small bore magazine rifle. For, as I have already said, the penetration of these rifles is great and the bullet so small, that an animal hit in any but a vital spot may escape to die in agony in the bush, while the sportsman, finding that he has not bagged his quarry, often indiscriminately empties his magazines into other animals of the herd, trusting to drop one or more out of the number. There is no censure strong enough for this reckless cruelty, and I feel that much of it would assuredly be avoided, if the hunter would only give the foregoing notes his careful consideration.

THE ADVENTURES OF AN ELEPHANT HUNTER
(Macmillan 1912)

List of the Names of Most of the Leading Gunmakers and Prices Charged for their Best Rifles.
THE SPORTING RIFLE AND ITS PROJECTILES by Lt. James Forsyth (Smith, Elder 1867)

| Name of firm | Double Barrelled | | Single Barrelled | | Gun Case |
	MUZZLE	BREECH	MUZZLE	BREECH	
J. PURDEY 314½ Oxford Street, London	£78	—	£36	—	Without case
C. W. LANCASTER 151 New Bond Street London	£73/10	£84	£36/15	—	With case
J. D. DOUGALL 59 St James's Street London	£60	£65	£40	£45	With case
MANCHESTER ORDINANCE AND RIFLE COMPANY 44 Charlton Street Manchester	£68/5		£40/8		With case
ALEXANDER HENRY 12 South Street St Andrews	£63	£63	£30	£30	With case
GEORGE H. DAW 57 Threadneedle Street London	£63	£63	£30	£40	With case
WESTLEY RICHARDS Birmingham	£52	£65	£30/5/6		With case

WILKINSON & SON 77 Pall Mall London	£52/10	£57/10	£30	£34/10	Without case
JOHN BLISSETT 333 High Holborn London	£52/10	£57/10	£36/10	£47/5	With case
WILLIAM R. PAPE Newcastle-upon-Tyne	£45	£45	£24	£28	With case
S. and C. SMITH 64 Princes Street London	£44/2	£48/6	£27/6	£23/2	Without case
WM. & JNO. RIGBY Dublin	£42	£47/5	£21	£26/5	Without case
REILLY & CO. 502 New Oxford Street London	£42	£47/5	£21	£26/5	With case
WILLIAM GREENER* Rifle Hill Works Birmingham	£35	£35	£15	£15	With case

* Not W. W. Greener also of Birmingham, who Forsyth states was also selling rifles at much the same prices as William Greener.